The
Happiness
Bible

D0115661

The
Happiness
Bible

The Definitive Guide to Sustainable Well-being

Cheryl Rickman

FIREFLY BOOKS

A FIREFLY BOOK

Published by Firefly Books Ltd. 2019

First printing

Publisher Cataloging-in-Publication Data (U.S.)

Library of Congress Control Number: 2018947686

Library and Archives Canada Cataloguing in Publication

Rickman, Cheryl D., author
        The happiness bible : the definitive guide to sustainable well-being / Cheryl Rickman.
Includes bibliographical references and index.
ISBN 978-0-228-10120-8 (softcover)
        1. Happiness. 2. Self-actualization (Psychology). 3. Conduct of life. I. Title.
BF575.H27R53 2019   158.1   C2018-903582-X

Published in the United States by
Firefly Books (U.S.) Inc.
P.O. Box 1338, Ellicott Station
Buffalo, New York 14205

Published in Canada by
Firefly Books Ltd.
50 Staples Avenue, Unit 1
Richmond Hill, Ontario L4B 0A7

Printed in China

First published by Godsfield Press, a division of Octopus Publishing Group Ltd, Carmelite House, 50 Victoria Embankment, London EC4Y 0DZ

Commissioning Editor: Leanne Bryan; Art Director: Yasia Williams-Leedham
Assistant Editor: Nell Warner; **Design:** Grade Design; **Picture Research Manager:** Giulia Hetherington; **Picture Library Manager:** Jennifer Veall; **Production Controller:** Dasha Miller

Contents

A HISTORY
OF HAPPINESS
and why it matters

"Happiness is the meaning and the
purpose of life, the whole aim and
the end of human existence."

ARISTOTLE, GREEK PHILOSOPHER

The state of blissful being

Happiness matters because, frankly, life is too short not to consider how best to live it. And, just as life is short, so it can also be difficult. Happiness can make life feel less difficult, and therefore we crave it. Yet there is more to happiness than its life-enhancing qualities, as we shall find out over the following pages.

"Happiness has long been presented as 'the meaning and the purpose of life'."

This state of blissful being is universally desired, and has been so for many millennia. Ever since Socrates sowed the seed of a desire for happiness in the 4th century BCE, in Plato's text *The Euthydemus* (see page 12), and the Chinese philosopher Zhuangzi wrote *The Tao of Perfect Happiness* the next century, defining it as our "ultimate human goal", happiness has long been presented as "the meaning and the purpose of life".

Given the critical role of happiness as the ultimate objective of our existence, it's no surprise that so much time has been devoted to its attainment across the globe over the past few thousand years. From the Buddha in Nepal to the Greek philosophers Socrates, Epicurus and Aristotle; from the eudaemonic notion of living well (see page 11), to the hedonic notion of frequent positive experiences (see page 83), the quest for happiness has long been favoured and pursued.

In the Enlightenment era the British philosopher John Locke coined the phrase "the pursuit of happiness", which the American Founding Father Thomas Jefferson incorporated into the 1776 American Declaration of Independence. Today, *World Happiness Report* surveys, and the 21st-century growth of the field of positive psychology (see Chapter Four), demonstrate the continued interest in not just a fleeting feeling of pleasure, but the more enduring state of human flourishing.

Above: Across the world, we all smile in the same
language. As human beings, we are united in our
quest for happiness.

What is happiness?

Happiness has many definitions. On one level, it is about expectation and reaction. So rather than being about what the world gives you, happiness is what you *think* about what the world gives you; how you see and respond to life events, and your expectations concerning what life *should* be like. So if life meets your expectations, you're happy. If it doesn't, then you're not.

This is one simplistic way of viewing happiness: as a response to life – to what you have and to what life gives you – and your expectations concerning it. Yet scientific studies of identical and fraternal twins suggest that our reaction to life circumstances dictates only 10 per cent of our happiness levels.

Now, back to our question about what happiness is.

Scientist turned Buddhist monk Matthieu Ricard describes happiness as being "a deep sense of flourishing, not a mere pleasurable feeling or fleeting emotion but an optimal state of being".[2] Meanwhile, Sonja Lyubomirsky, the author of *The How of Happiness*, defines it as "the experience of joy, contentment, or positive wellbeing, combined with a sense that one's life is good, meaningful, and worthwhile".[3]

Flourishing fact

A study undertaken by researcher Sonja Lyubomirsky suggests that 50 per cent of our happiness is predetermined genetically, with only 10 per cent of our happiness determined by our life. It discovered that we are born with a certain "happiness set-point" (see Chapter Four), to which we return "even after major setbacks and triumphs".[1] Thankfully, the other 40 per cent of our happiness lies within our control; it is down to us and our own thoughts and actions. It is this percentage that we can directly affect through our own intentional efforts, and we shall explore those in detail later on in this book.

The three dimensions of happiness

The word "combined" is important here. For it is the combination of three main components of happiness that psychologists deem as being essential to a happy and well-balanced life:

1. Hedonic (or affective) happiness comes from our everyday mood and the passing pleasures that we experience.

Above: Scientist turned monk, Matthieu Ricard, was dubbed the "happiest person in the world" after scoring significantly higher than hundreds of volunteers in a happiness study.

2. Eudaemonic happiness is generated by the sense of purpose and meaning that comes from serving others and contributing to the world. Aristotle was the originator of the concept of eudaemonia, which derives from the Greek words *eu* ("good") and *daimōn* ("spirit").

3. Cognitive happiness is based on how we feel about our lives overall; our sense of life-satisfaction and our own answer to the question: Am I living a good life?

All three dimensions of happiness are important, with some contributing greater long-term benefits than others, as we'll explore in the next chapter.

Distinguishing between being happy *right now* and being happy *overall* is the key to happiness research. It is the latter component, cognitive happiness – that is, how we feel when we step back, consider and evaluate our lives, and how this measures up to our expectations about what a good life should be – that experts use to measure happiness. However, that assessment depends on how high you set the bar, which we'll explore further in Chapter Two.

Each of these dimensions connects and overlaps. We might feel plenty of positive emotions on a daily basis, in which case we'd probably report a good level of overall life-satisfaction, and therefore a high level of cognitive happiness. Yet we can have utterly negative days and still feel as if life is generally good and satisfactory.[4] And there are many contributors to each of these dimensions of happiness.

What causes happiness?

What causes happiness is subjective. Happiness – like success – looks different to different people, depending on what life conditions are deemed satisfactory and what experiences make people feel happy.

On one side of the world, happiness may come from quenching thirst with fresh water, or from the cessation of violence. On the other side, it may come from sipping coffee on a Sunday morning with loved ones. And given that happiness is a historical and social construct, our personal definition of it will depend on when and where we were born.

In general, contributing factors to happiness include the freedom of choice to make life decisions, good-quality social relationships, trust, equality, virtue and vitality. Engagement, achievement and a sense of purpose are also factors. However, the hallmarks of happiness, as defined by ancient and current thinkers alike, remain remarkably similar.

Happiness throughout history

Although the Old English and Old Norse root of the word "happiness" is derived from the Icelandic word *hap*, which means "luck" or "chance", philosophers have long believed that happiness could be achieved with effort through our own choices and behaviour. Why leave something so important to mere chance and fortune?

Timeline of happiness

- **c.563–483 BCE:** The **Buddha** saw happiness as the freedom from "the cycle of craving" to achieve peace of mind or equanimity. This mental state takes practice.

- **c.427–348 BCE: Plato** focused on eudaemonia (a flourishing life) and the idea that we ought to learn to fulfil our true nature by virtuous reason and balance, so that we would not be led to extremes, but would tread the middle path.

- **c.384 BCE:** In Plato's *The Euthydemus*, a Socratic dialogue, which was the first piece of Western philosophy to discuss happiness, **Socrates** sowed the seed of a

Right: Socrates believed introspection was vital to finding happiness.

Right: Happiness is subjective. For some, a hot cup of coffee on a Sunday morning will spark the feeling.

desire for happiness, and the notion that happiness is dependent on, and achievable with, effort. He was an advocate of self-knowledge, self-questioning and the consequential "considered life" as the route to happiness, although true happiness would only come from a virtuous elevation of the higher self.

• **c.384–322 BCE: Aristotle** (Plato's student) introduced the world to the idea of a

science of happiness. He developed the link between happiness and character, encouraging us to contemplate and cultivate our inner virtues.

• **c.370–287 BCE: Zhuangzi** was an advocate of "going with the flow" via the practice of *wuwei*. Noticing simple pleasures, living in the moment, accepting what is and using Taoist breathing techniques formed a key part of this tranquil notion of happiness.

Throughout history there are many other commonalities. The mindful practice of being present and living in the moment has long been considered a key factor in optimizing happiness, along with self-awareness, character development and the importance of balance in life.

Work in progress

Some happiness thought-leaders focused on the mind, some rejoiced in nature, while others emphasized the importance of human relationships. Yet throughout history all commentators have shared the common view that our lives are a work in progress. Indeed, we're still learning. For despite happiness being the most desired state for many millennia, we have yet to master it.

According to research, today – in spite of having more freedom, a better work–life balance and more material gains than ever before (many of us can now instantly shop without leaving our houses, have our groceries delivered and afford more holidays) – entire nations are generally no happier and, in some cases, less happy than they were 50 years ago.

We know that having more materially does not equate to experiencing greater happiness, due to "the hedonic treadmill" (see Chapter Two). In fact the statistics revealing our modern-day lower levels of contentment merely demonstrate what the Buddha and Aristotle already knew centuries ago: that mastering the ability to sustain happiness is not an easy endeavour. It takes effort.

Opposite: The mindful acts of cherishing the moment and relishing nature have long been considered ways to maximize happiness.

Timeline of happiness

- **c.341–270 BCE: Epicurus** believed that *hedone* (that is pleasure, inner tranquillity of the mind, good friendships and the avoidance of pain) was the most vital determinant of happiness. He advocated contemplation and reminiscence to avoid pain – for example, focusing on joyful memories in order to counter sad present moments.

- **c.301 BCE:** The ancient **Stoics** were also advocates of a virtuous life, and focused on the idea that we could achieve happiness via objectivity and rational thought.

Right: English philosopher John Locke suggested the notion that health, liberty and property were important in the pursuit of happiness.

- **1632–1704: John Locke**, a philosopher of the English Enlightenment, focused on the pursuit of happiness as being critical for individuals and governments alike; this followed Italy's 18th-century concept of *pubblica felicità*, or "public happiness". Locke's "pursuit of happiness" was about moving away from the instant gratification of false pleasures toward more long-lasting, true pleasures.

- **1785–1873: John Stuart Mill** and **Jeremy Bentham** coined the doctrine of "utilitarianism", whereby the greatest happiness of the greatest number became the route to true happiness.

- **1943 to the current day: Abraham Maslow** gave us the term "positive psychology", which was further developed in the 1990s by **Professor Martin Seligman** and others, as a study of cultivating what is right with us, rather than the more traditional focus of psychology on fixing what is wrong.

An elusive condition

Happiness does not just happen. Pleasure does, fortune can, but happiness is an altogether more elusive state of inner contentment; something that needs attending to. As such, happiness is a skill as much as a state. It takes effort, even practice.

Both modern research and ancient thinking on the topic of happiness concur that true happiness is dependent on far more than the simple pursuit of pleasure and the satisfaction of external desires, which provide only fleeting temporary joy. As Anthony Seldon says in his book *Beyond Happiness*, "Pleasure is a state of having. Happiness is a state of being."

The bearded pioneers of happiness throughout history, whom we have discussed above, agree. They were advocates of peace of mind over pleasure, of virtue over hedonism, of internal contentment over external craving and of eventual knowledge

——————————————

"Happiness is an experience, a sense, a feeling, an emotion, a state-of-mind, a state-of-being"

——————————————

Below: Happiness is a journey. It's a way of being and seeing the world as we journey from one moment to the next, experiencing, feeling and sensing happiness.

Above: Happiness rises and falls, comes and goes. We can, with some effort, increase the upward spirals and decrease the downward ones on our journey through life.

over instant gratification – of happiness as a journey. And while the contributory factors to that happy experience may be varied and may depend on the individual, the definition of happiness as a positive state-of-being and the peaceful contentment of loving the world just as it is right now, is the definition we'll use in this book. For happiness is more than a response to what life gives you. Happiness is an experience, a sense, a feeling, an emotion, a state-of-mind, a state-of-being, a sense of life-satisfaction and a lens through which we see the world.

Happiness as a journey

Rather than being a fleeting moment, happiness is a collective experience of those moments; a signal of a life well lived in an optimal state. And while this state is not permanent and can rise and fall, come and go, it is possible to increase and sustain our "set-point" over the long term, to create a long-lasting, higher level of happiness.

Indeed, with some effort we can increase the upward spirals and decrease the downward ones on our journey through life (see Chapters Four and Five), remembering as we go that happiness is as much about tolerance and acceptance as it is about serenity and fulfilment. It is about knowing that we can intentionally cultivate our inner resources to enable us to cope with life, raise and sustain our "set-point" and feel content, whatever our circumstances may be.

So this book will explore happiness as a journey: what it is, what it isn't, and why – as a top-ranked human endeavour – happiness matters to us at least as much as our health does.

Why happiness matters

Why does happiness matter so much? Today it is widely accepted that happiness *enables* us, on a personal, societal and economic level. Happy people tend to be healthier, more productive and better able to think with clarity.

According to the *World Happiness Report* of 2012, a greater level of happiness predicts better future physical health. Indeed, those with higher positive affectivity recover faster from colds and are less likely to catch them in the first place[5]. Positive affectivity describes how much people tend to experience positive emotions and sensations and, consequently, how they interact with others and react to circumstances. Those with high positive affectivity tend to be enthusiastic, energetic and resilient. Those with low positive affectivity tend to be lethargic and anxious. Those with higher positive affectivity also have better cardiovascular, anti-inflammatory and neuroendocrine activity, with lower mortality rates, according to five-year clinical studies carried out by University College London.

Happy people also recover better from adversity. Scientists have discovered that we can store positive emotion in a reserve and tap into it when the going gets tough.[6] So the more we can cultivate positive emotions, the deeper our positivity reserves will be, and the better we become at bouncing back from adversity. As such, we are like solar panels: storing sunshine so that we can shine sooner after the rain

falls than we otherwise might, without that positive energy. The more positive emotions we experience throughout our lives, the more our resilience is bolstered. Ultimately we function better, the happier we are.

People who flourish in their daily lives often outperform their unhappy counterparts, as discovered by economists from the University of Warwick[7] and by an Italian study of software developers.[8]

In a University of Warwick lab test of 276 people with similar backgrounds and life circumstances, those who had a happy mood induced by watching comedy clips answered more maths questions in a productivity task correctly. This and subsequent studies found that ability was not enhanced by happiness but effort was, which made participants more productive. In a peer-reviewed Faculty of Computer Science study at the Free University of Bozen-Bolzano, Italy, 42 students had their affective states measured and were then asked to perform a caption-writing creativity task and an analytical problem-solving task. The results showed that positive affective states of software developers indicated higher analytical problem-solving skills.

Above: Happiness is contagious. The happier those around us are, the happier we are likely to be. So the happiness of other people can lift us up.

The better we feel, the more likely we are to be kind, helpful and creative; and the more generous, light-hearted and effective we are. Conversely, when we feel low, we are more likely to lose interest, lose our temper and lose our ability to solve problems.

Scientists have discovered, as a result of Barbara Fredrickson's "broaden and build" theory of positive emotion (see Chapter Eight), that we are definitely able to think better, with greater clarity and accuracy, when we are happy, because we are more open to solutions. Conversely, when we are angry or anxious, our minds close down, making solutions less obvious.

Yes.

If you want to get more done,
get happy.

If you want to be healthier,
get happy.

If you want to be the best
friend/parent/citizen you can be,
get happy.

If you want to be more resilient
and able to bounce back when
the going gets tough,
get happy.

Emotional contagion

Happiness matters because happiness *enables*; it adds fuel to the fire of living a better life. This means that the happier we are, the happier we become. So happiness is a driver, just as much as it is a result. Notably, happiness is good for the individual, the economy and society alike.

Happiness is contagious, too (experiments carried out by researchers at the University of California at San Diego have revealed that we can "catch" emotional states from each other, and even from strangers and online).[9] This is known as "emotional contagion". It's no wonder that governments across the globe are taking notice and are elevating happiness as a nationwide goal, in some cases, such as in Bhutan (see Chapter Three), even measuring it alongside Gross Domestic Product (GDP).

In being happy ourselves, we can bolster other people's levels of happiness, too. Given this emotional contagion, perhaps it's our duty to seek personal happiness. For in doing so, we can all better tolerate

the daily frustrations of life and become more loving, forgiving and creative.

With all of these incredible benefits, it's no wonder that the state of happiness is so desired.

However, there is a paradox to positivity. Without a firm understanding of where the fleeting feelings of happiness sit within a truly meaningful and joyful existence,

Above: Happiness is good for our health, our relationships, our productivity and our resilience. No wonder it's so desired.

a desire for happiness for happiness's sake can lead to desperation and disappointment, causing the pursuit of it to backfire. That is, unless we attend to our happiness in a balanced way, fully equipped with knowledge about its pursuit.

THE PARADOX
OF POSITIVITY

"The essence of being human is that
one does not seek perfection."

GEORGE ORWELL, ENGLISH WRITER

Happiness as a false reality

We're always being told, "Don't worry, be happy" and "Put a brave face on it". Today, though, more than ever before – being bombarded 24/7, as we are, with images of perceived perfection – the social pressure to feel happy (and not to feel sad) is at an all-time high.

Filtered Instagram imagery and edited social media lifestyles show other people's lives in the best possible light. It's difficult to measure up to all those expectations of a false reality, and yet we try. However, this neurosis to measure up can make us feel down. With a high level of desire comes a desperation to attain – and sustain – what we're striving for; followed by feelings of deficiency if we can't. In fact, some studies show that placing a premium on happiness may even contribute to higher rates of depression, as people struggle to respond well to negative emotional experiences.[1]

If happiness is our ultimate goal and we're not 100 per cent happy all of the time, then we can find ourselves in a perpetual loop of life failing to live up to our unreasonably high expectations, which in turn creates unhappiness, which feeds the loop of disappointment – and so it goes on.

Yet we can't expect ourselves to be happy all the time. Happiness is not our default state, and considering it to be so puts an incredibly unfair onus on us. Such pressure to be beaming constantly only leads to guilt

Flourishing fact
Researchers of depression and anxiety from the University of Melbourne assessed and measured the depressive symptoms – and the social expectations not to feel negative emotions – of 112 people with high depression scores over a 30-day period. The more social pressure not to feel sad or anxious that participants felt, the more likely an increase in their depressive symptoms was.[2]

when we're not feeling happy. As such, our perpetual pursuit of happiness can be a somewhat self-defeating one.

Opposite: The rise in social media has increased the pressure we're under to broadcast our continual happiness, but that's not sustainable. Filtered edited images present a false reality.

"Don't let the perfect be
the enemy of the good."

VOLTAIRE, FRENCH ENLIGHTENMENT
WRITER AND HISTORIAN

Unpicking the pressure

Certainly, desperately seeking happiness
can backfire and generate the opposite
effect, making us feel miserable. These are
the paradoxical effects of pursuing only
positive emotions and trying to eradicate
the negative ones, and they represent a
critical consideration for any book on the
subject of happiness to explore.

To achieve a sustainable level of happiness
it's not simply a case of removing pain and
increasing pleasure – that's not how it
works. We need to unpick this pressure,
so that seekers of happiness can pursue
balance and realistic optimism, rather than
perfection and perpetual joy. Focusing on
positivity and forbidding negativity is just
as counter-productive to our happiness as
focusing on perfection and ignoring reality.

Aspirationally, then, 100 per cent
happiness is an unrealistic expectation,
because we are human beings capable
of feeling a whole range of emotions.
Furthermore, we have to deal with a whole
gamut of circumstances that are beyond
our control. So there is nothing wrong with
us if we don't experience happiness most
of the time.

Perfection – like constant happiness –
is an expectation too far. And by removing
our ridiculously high expectations, we can
remove the pressure and become more
likely to gain a decent amount of happiness.

Opposite: Keeping it real. Removing expectations
of perfection and embracing raw feelings across
the broad spectrum of emotion helps us find balance.

Why unhappiness matters, too

Not being happy is an authentic part of what it is to be human. As we'll discover in this book, having self-compassion and giving ourselves "permission to be human", when we fail or frown, are just as necessary to our happiness journey as positive thinking or pleasurable stimuli.

Unhappiness matters. For happiness isn't about being constantly joyful or denying negative feelings; rather, true happiness is about cherishing the good and coping with the bad. Both happiness and sadness enable us to bounce back more successfully. As the neuroscientist Rick Hanson, who believes in realistic rather than positive thinking, says: "It's important to see the whole mosaic of reality. The good tiles in the mosaic are the basis for growing resources inside myself to help deal with the bad tiles."[3]

As scientific studies show, positive emotions are useful because they grow our capacity for coping. Barbara Fredrickson has discovered in her research on positivity (see Chapter Eight) that positive emotions act as building blocks, which broaden our minds to enable more effective behaviour when responding to trauma and stress.[4]

Equally, experiencing hardship and the consequent negative emotions can strengthen us and give us more confidence

Opposite: Enduring setbacks is empowering. Feeling the whole spectrum of human emotion, including unhappiness, is an important process, for true happiness is about cherishing the good and coping with the bad.

Flourishing fact

Martin Seligman and Chris Peterson made an interesting discovery when they added a questionnaire to their Authentic Happiness website, listing 15 of the worst possible adversities that can happen in a lifetime; 1,700 people completed the questionnaire in the month that followed, while also taking the wellbeing tests. The psychologists discovered that those who had experienced one of the adversities showed more acute mental strength and greater wellbeing than those who had not. Even more surprisingly, those who had experienced three adversities were mentally stronger than those who had endured two, who in turn were stronger than those who had been through one. So even when the worst-case scenario does happen, we often find that we are stronger than we thought, and our subsequent belief in ourselves rises.

"If you want to live a good, happy life, don't chase happiness to the exclusion of other emotions and states. Live fiercely, across the full spectrum of experiences."[5]

JONATHAN FIELDS, AMERICAN WRITER

in our abilities to manage, as the science of post-traumatic growth reveals. Indeed, Friedrich Nietzsche's suggestion that "what does not kill me makes me stronger" appears to be an accurate one.

The power of adversity

Part of accepting and allowing negative emotions to flow is the knowledge that negative emotions are as useful as they are brutal. Like flowers, we need rain as much as sunshine in order to flourish. We are the sum of all that we have endured and experienced. Adversity, mistakes, regrets and tragedy – difficult as they are – can all teach us something useful and we need them in our lives, not only to show us what we are capable of coping with, but to provide sufficient contrast so that we can appreciate the good times. If we expect only sunshine, we're less equipped to cope when the rain pours down on us – as it will, and does, often.

Such contrast enables us to better view our lives through a lens of gratitude. For if

we've seen our lives when things aren't going well, then we're better able to notice and appreciate when things are. Therefore just as mistakes and failure are useful learning tools, so are negative emotions. They provide us with contrast, authenticity and opportunities for increased self-awareness and self-compassion.

The more we permit ourselves to lean into, feel and accept the whole spectrum of human emotion, and choose rationally how best to respond to events that are beyond our control, the happier we enable ourselves to be. When we accept happiness as just one part of the puzzle of human flourishing (where joy, awe and gratitude sit alongside sadness, fear and anger), our mental state improves.

So in our quest for happiness, we must give unhappiness a seat at the table.

Opposite: Just as flowers need sunlight and rain in order to flourish, we also grow from contrasting positive and negative experiences and emotions.

"It's important to accept the
full spectrum of emotions that
we are capable of feeling,
rather than deny them."

Weathering the storm

A life well lived is rich with diversity and wonder – a full and fascinating experience, in which the entire spectrum of emotions is frequently felt. That's a wonderful life. Notably, happiness doesn't come from sailing through life with no problems; it comes from weathering the storm and rising from the depths, solving problems and overcoming obstacles. That's engaging in real life, and that's where our strength and sense of accomplishment come from. And, as we'll see, accomplishment is one of the core pillars of wellbeing (see Chapter Four).

Striving for a perfect life, where we push negative emotions to one side, is like trying to push a beach ball below the water and expecting it to stay down. It won't; it will resurface, just as forbidden negative emotions do. So it's important to accept the full spectrum of emotions that we are capable of feeling, rather than deny them.

Opposite: Life is stormy. We need waves to crash down on us occasionally, so we may appreciate the calmer seas. Learning to navigate through storms brings happiness.

Our negativity bias

One critical reason for this acceptance is because we have an inbuilt negativity bias. Our brain is wired to place emphasis on the negative. A 1980 study by S T Fiske revealed, even when given one piece of positive information and one piece of negative information about a stranger, participants were more likely to judge someone as negative than as neutral[6]. Studies conducted by the American social neuroscientist John Cacioppo, Ph.D in the mid-1990s have shown that the brain reacts more strongly to negative stimuli, with greater electrical activity in the brain's cerebral cortex, than it does to more positive stimuli. It's a trait that we need to work with, rather than fight against.

This negativity bias means that humans are more likely to focus on the negative, and we need five instances of positivity to counter this natural tendency. Thousands of years ago our negativity bias served us well, as fear, anger and doubt protected us from danger, so that we might survive. Nowadays we need it less, but it's still part of our make-up.

Negativity (feeling sad, lonely, envious and disappointed) is a part of what it means to be human. Expecting to eliminate it is setting us up for disappointment. So what *can* we do with our tendency toward the negative?

How to counter negativity

1. Accept that negativity is part of being human: Realize that feelings such as sadness, fear and anger provide important signals about what to do next; as such, they should be acknowledged and expressed.

2. Manage our expectations: Be aware of the social pressure around not feeling sad, and understand that trying to feel good all the time can get in the way of happiness. Acknowledging this enables us to choose how best to react to this pressure and focus on what is realistically achievable.

Flourishing fact

Proof that emotional diversity is linked to our happiness comes from the authors of *Emodiversity and the Emotional Ecosystem*, Jordi Quoidbach and June Gruber. In studies of 37,000 people, using the biodiversity of natural ecosystems as a model, they discovered that "a wide variety of emotions might be a sign of a self-aware and authentic life; such emotional self-awareness and authenticity have been repeatedly linked to health and wellbeing".[7]

Left: When we free ourselves from social pressures around not feeling sad, it can be a huge relief, like a ball bursting out of the water.

3. Remember that we're all in this together: Everyone else is just trying to present themselves in the best possible light, too.

4. Keep things real: While happiness is contagious, unhappiness also resonates and has the power to connect us, so it's worth getting comfortable with sharing our grittier truth – as well as our happiest achievements – from time to time.

5. Work on building our resources and positivity levels: In this way we can minimize, rather than avoid or get rid of, negative emotions. Strive to learn from negative states rather than eliminate them. Doing so bolsters our resilience, as does learning how to maximize positivity.

Happiness is a balancing act

This duality between positive highs and negative lows is part of human nature – the natural way to be. The best we can do is appreciate the good, and learn how to deal with the bad. In doing so we can find balance, which is what sustainable happiness is all about, and has been ever since the days of Buddha and Aristotle.

Indeed, the notion of acceptance and balance of the whole emotional repertoire – of "rolling with it" – has been around since early philosophers began waxing lyrical about happiness. As the Greek Stoic philosopher Epictetus wisely said: "Do not seek to have events happen as you want them to, but instead want them to happen as they do happen, and your life will go well."

This tranquil acceptance of life, and consequential contentment, is the true (and, crucially, achievable) happiness that we shall explore in this book: a mixture of gratitude and grit, appreciation and awareness. It is the opposite of the quick-fix hedonic happiness derived from external pleasures. Scientists at UCLA School of

"Pleasure is a subjective state. Happiness is a deeper and more rewarding condition. We act directly in order to achieve pleasure but we experience happiness as a by-product of living wisely."[8]

ANTHONY SELDON, CONTEMPORARY HISTORIAN AND POLITICAL AUTHOR

Medicine have found, by testing blood samples, that pleasurable hedonic happiness has fewer benefits than the more purposeful eudaemonic happiness (see Chapter One): those with a higher level of the latter had a greater immune response.[9]

Right: Savouring the good and coping with the bad requires balance. With balance comes acceptance, awareness and peace of mind.

"If you want to be happy, be."

NIKOLAI TOLSTOY, RUSSIAN WRITER

Opposite: True happiness is about sustaining a good quality of life that you are happy with, rather than fleeting feelings of pleasure, which quickly fade.

Pleasure is temporary

When it comes to that peaceful state of long-lasting happiness, many of us have been getting it wrong. We seek pleasure as a way to suspend and distract us from unhappy thoughts. Yet this merely replaces negative feelings with temporary happiness, which doesn't last. Fleeting feelings of pleasure do not equate with long-lasting happiness or a good quality of life.

Pleasure masks negative emotions, but also fades quickly, especially when it comes as a direct result of consumption. Yet we have long seen possessions and achievements as markers of happiness. But money matters less than we think. Yes, poverty can cause high levels of unhappiness, and for those without it having money can generate joy. However, according

to various *World Happiness Reports*, which measure the happiness of the richest and poorest countries, once we have sufficient money to get by, having more doesn't actually make us happier.

The problem is that, as humans, we are inherently dissatisfied with the status quo. We are driven to want more, buy more, achieve more. This leads to an "I'll be happy when..." mindset, and shifts our happiness to being dependent on the future and to external pleasurable stimuli. And yet the kind of hedonic happiness that comes from satisfying such desires has been proven not to last very long at all.

Studies have been conducted on lottery winners who were happier for a few months following their good fortune, yet soon returned to their habitual happiness set-point.

Adaptation and the hedonic treadmill

As we have seen pleasure, like pain, is temporary. Just as our lowest lows don't last, nor do our highest highs. We habituate to them, adjusting rapidly to both positive and negative events and returning to the same level of happiness that we enjoyed before we experienced the fleeting feeling of pleasure.

This ability to adapt rapidly to our circumstances is called "adaptation" and it keeps us on what psychologists call "the hedonic treadmill" – a perpetual loop of trading up and achieving or buying more and experiencing pleasure, which soon fades, causing us to desire more; and so on and on it goes, because we'll always "need another shot".[10]

According to the economic "law of diminishing marginal utility" devised by Prussian economist Hermann Heinrich Gossen in 1854, the more we have of something, the less happiness we gain from it. This, combined with our adaptation to material gains, explains why externalities – such as the next toy or achievement, or windfall or promotion – do not boost our happiness for long.

Adaptation impedes our quest for long-lasting happiness because no sooner have we experienced the joy of buying a new car or house, than we are back to our original set-point of happiness. Each new purchase gives us a shot of pleasure, but retail-related fulfilment soon wanes. And so we go on repeating this process over and over again, treadmill-style.

Focusing on the present moment

Evidently externalities do not make people lastingly happier. So thinking, "I'll be happy when…" is a fruitless exercise; it also explains why interventions such as gratitude and mindfulness (see the exercises on page 168) work well in enabling true happiness – that is, focusing on what we have *now* in the present moment, rather than what we hope to have in the future.

This doesn't mean that we should avoid setting goals altogether, for accomplishment is one of the pillars of wellbeing (see Chapter Four), as defined by positive psychologists, and is something that we'll explore further in Chapter Nine. Rather, if we balance our ambition to succeed in the future with our appreciation for what we already have, we are better able to maintain a stronger sense of wellbeing.

Experiences can generate happiness

We should also consider what we spend our money on. According to psychology professors at Cornell University, happy memories that we gain from experiences – such as travelling – last much longer than the pleasure we gain from purchasing "stuff".

Above: "I'll be happy when..." keeps us on the "hedonic treadmill". Once we get what we want, our happiness returns to the level before purchase or achievement and we're left wanting more.

They discovered that people's satisfaction with the items they bought went down over time, whereas their satisfaction with experiences they had bought rose over time[11].

This is because experiences enable us to connect with others who were involved in them, or who have undergone something similar. Furthermore, experiences evoke memories. We are better able to internalize experiences than objects. So experiences become a part of us and create good memories that we are able to store and readily access, in order to generate happiness.

How to step off the hedonic treadmill

To break this cycle and step off the hedonic treadmill, we can:

- **Buy experiences rather than things:** Ideally look for those experiences that involve others and are a long-way off, so that you can enjoy the anticipation of the event, savour the experience itself as it happens, then reminisce on your memory of the event as time passes – a wonderful way to amplify and enhance the pleasure of a single purchase.

- **Focus on being mindful of the present:** Be grateful for what is present right now, rather than for what you wish to be present in the future.

- **Buy products to celebrate happy milestones:** This maximizes their impact and ties the item to a memory of an event that matters to you, rather than purchasing something for pleasure's sake.

- **Seek out free fun with friends:** Read books in libraries, swim in lakes, go for a bike ride, camp on beaches.

- **See happiness as a journey:** View it as a by-product of the process, rather than as a destination or goal in itself.

The hedonic treadmill gives us another valid reason why happiness should be seen as a journey rather than a destination. Otherwise, once you've arrived at this destination called "happiness", what is next? Conspicuous consumption (our desire to keep up with the Joneses, and our human-centric trait of comparing what we have with others) is partially responsible for preventing us from stepping off the treadmill and for fuelling our desire for more. But this conspicuous consumption is futile.

As the financial author Dave Ramsey says, "We are spending money we don't have to buy stuff we don't need to impress people we don't like." As such, we ought to disconnect wealth and the accumulation of money from happiness, for happiness lies not in such accumulation. And this realization is a treasure in itself.

Opposite: Valuing the process rather than the product, the journey rather than the destination, gives us the chance to step off the hedonic treadmill and enjoy now.

GLOBAL GLEE

"Contentment is the only real wealth."
ALFRED NOBEL, SWEDISH CHEMIST AND INDUSTRIALIST

The world of wellbeing

The quest for happiness is an international one. Indeed, our mutual hope for a happy life extends to every corner of the globe. From East to West, the hallmarks of happiness remain remarkably similar. One of its key contributors involves other people: the support and generosity that we get from, and give to them and how much we trust in them.

In an effort to record happiness and "put people's wellbeing at the centre of Governments' efforts",[1] the annual *World Happiness Report* measures global glee based on six key factors:

1. Having someone to count on, in times of trouble

2. Healthy life expectancy

3. Income / GDP per capita

4. Freedom from corruption (trust)

5. Freedom to make decisions (equality)

6. Generosity (kindness).

Notably, three of these six factors – kindness, trust and having someone to count on – focus on supportive relationships, which have long been defined by positive psychologists as being a critical pillar of wellbeing (see Chapter Four). This social factor – a sense of belonging, community and togetherness – is seen as a leading contributor to happiness. Perhaps this is why, when we explore traditions from around the world, "connection" is the most prominent component of contentment, from one corner of the globe to another.

From the concept of Danish *hygge* and Swedish *lagom*, to Japanese *ikigai* and African *ubuntu*, "connection" is the common denominator. That said, connection with other people isn't the only type of connection that is encompassed by these traditions. Global happiness habits involve connection with:

• Our community (each other)

• Our natural environment (our planet)

• Our present moment (right now)

• Our true purpose (which brings meaning to our lives).

To join the dots of happiness across the world, connection unites them all.

Opposite: The pursuit of happiness is a global goal. Connection with others, our planet, the present and our true purpose are key components of happiness worldwide.

Ubuntu

This African concept focuses on community, kindness and an ethic of reciprocity. Roughly translated, *ubuntu* means "humanity toward others", and the idea that a universal bond of sharing and goodness connects us all. This guiding principle of pure "oneness" is about all of us being "in it together" – and the understanding that we can impact on others' lives, and the wider world, through our own actions, and by putting "we" before "me".

For example, African villagers practising *ubuntu* may have minimal furniture in their own homes, but will share their belongings with relatives and neighbours. For them, helping and being with other people are a priority. Togetherness and sharing are prioritized, whether that is sharing conversation and a cup of tea on the walk home from work or sharing food, possessions and comfort. This all stems from that guiding ethos of interconnectedness.

Perhaps the best example of *ubuntu* comes from the actions and attitude of Nelson Mandela, who had such "depth of empathy" that he invited his jailers to his presidential inauguration as honoured guests. Mandela both embodied and personified *ubuntu*. As President Barack Obama said at Mandela's memorial: "*Ubuntu* captures Mandela's greatest gift: his recognition that we are all bound together in ways that are invisible to the eye; that there is a oneness to humanity; that we achieve ourselves by sharing ourselves with others, and caring for those around us."[2]

Ho'oponopono

Translated from Hawaiian, *ho'oponopono* means "to make right". It is about forgiveness and connection with those who may have caused you grievance. Not only is this tradition about finding peace with others, but it's also about finding peace within ourselves, by disconnecting from unhelpful thoughts and reconnecting with more helpful ones.

Ho'oponopono originated as a principle of Huna, which is the traditional healing shamanism of Hawaii. The spiritual practice of *Ho'oponopono* was once a carefully guarded secret, but became

Above: Togetherness and interconnectedness are at the heart of the African concept of *ubuntu*, which means "humanity toward others" and celebrates that we're in this together.

available to the masses via the Hawaiian national treasure and healer Morrnah Simeona and her students, who helped spread the practice across the world. It involves communicating with our inner selves to reset and open the mind, cleansing errors and providing freedom from the past. It is based on the notion that we can connect with a deep spiritual power within us, to resolve both conscious and unconscious emotional baggage.

Like *ubuntu*, there is an element of "oneness" in *Hoʻoponopono* and the belief that, in being kind toward or hurting others, we are being kind toward or hurting ourselves. As such, this tradition is about vibrating love and compassion rather than hate and vitriol.

Fundamentally, *Hoʻoponopono* is a healing practice about forgiveness, gratitude and compassion. By repeating the *Hoʻoponopono* mantra ("I'm sorry, forgive me, thank you, I love you") several times, we can request forgiveness, accept responsibility, feel gratitude and move forward with compassion for others and ourselves.

Ikigai

This is a Japanese tradition of finding a purpose in life, which has been attributed to the lengthy life expectancy of the Japanese. Many centuries old, *ikigai* means "a reason for being", and it is our connection to this sense of purpose that gives our lives meaning.

Purpose doesn't stop when the Japanese stop working. The Japanese opt to keep both mind and body active, even after retirement. So they strive to maintain a meaningful and active life even when their working life has come to an end. For example, they keep their minds active by focusing on tasks that use their wisdom, rather than on tasks that require physical activity. In doing so, they remain active and valued members of their community.

Lagom

The core principle of the Swedish tradition of *lagom* is balance. Translated, it means "not too little, not too much, just right". Given the temporary nature of material pleasures, it's a wise concept to follow, as it seeks out a happy medium between decadence and deficiency, leading toward a balanced life. The *lagom*esque Swedish concept of *fika* ("a break from doing") also enables Swedes to prioritize their work–life balance, including social gatherings over coffee and "me-time".

Lagom nods toward the environmental joys of looking after the planet that we

Below: Feeling like a part of a community and having a strong purpose are central to the Japanese tradition of *ikigai*, so friendships are nurtured and passions cultivated.

Above: Pausing to share a pastry and a cup of coffee with friends is part of a well-balanced life and central to the Swedish concept of *lagom*.

inhabit, too. Mindfully recycling, living within our means and taking care of the environment enable us to feel better connected to the world we live in.

This connection to our planet further motivates us to live a balanced life, where we limit our consumption to just the right amount. As well as eating a balanced diet, lagom advocates foraging and growing our own fruit and vegetables, reflecting the changing seasons in Swedish cooking.

Keyif

Keyif is the real Turkish delight. When translated, it means "pleasure", yet it is specifically about the pleasure of *presence*. Feeling calm, relaxed and connecting to the present moment lies at the core of *keyif*.

Keyif moments are those when we are fully engaged with our surroundings and feel peaceful and relaxed. Cherishing what we can feel, hear and see in the present moment connects us to the here and now, rather than focusing on regretted past actions or future concerns. As such, *keyif* bolsters our connection with what really matters – what is happening right *now* in this moment.

In this way, *keyif* could be considered the Turkish version of mindfulness – enjoying peaceful relaxation and living in the moment: noticing the colours of nature change, watching fishermen from your window as they bob along on the sea, listening to birds tweet while taking pleasure in the taste of tea as you sip it. However, it is more than that.

Turks will tell you that, as well as promoting relaxing moments by yourself, *keyif* combines the notion of togetherness that the happiness traditions of so many

Nordic know-how

Most notable, perhaps, is how deeply-rooted *hygge* is in Danish culture – one of the reasons why Denmark, the southernmost Nordic country, has consistently topped the charts as the world's happiest nation for the past few years, only trading places with Norway in 2017. Meanwhile, the UK was ranked at number 19 in 2017, with the USA only a few places above.

The average differences between the top countries are so close that small changes can reorder their rankings from year to year. However, exploring *why* Denmark and Norway are happy chart-toppers gives us vital clues in our own quest for happiness.

In Norway, citizens and the government alike respect leisure time and its impact on people's wellbeing. So much so that time off is prioritized. Five weeks' vacation (25 days paid leave) is a compulsory requirement of employment, and parental/ maternity leave amounts to one year, fully paid. Meanwhile, in Denmark, *hygge* is ingrained in everyday life. It's a routine part of being Danish and, as such, means that the Danes have long paid attention to their wellbeing.

However, there's more to happiness than simply *hygge* or *jordnær*.

other countries incorporate. For example, enjoying a relaxed, lingering lunchtime meal with good friends, which gently meanders into the evening; laughing together and paying attention to each other's needs. Bringing pleasure, contentment and joy into each moment is *keyif* – whether you're watching the sunset from a serene evening boat cruise, eating mezes and savouring each sip of *raki* with friends or relaxing on a bench, listening to street musicians, chatting to locals and watching the world go by. The essence of *keyif* is a pleasurable state of idle relaxation, so whatever the *keyif* experience involves, it should be enjoyed at a leisurely pace.

Jordnær

Norwegians have a strong connection to nature and to their heritage. *Jordnær* translates as "nearness to the Earth" and is all about accepting and embracing your past and your environment. This connection to where you came from is celebrated annually on Norwegian Constitution Day, *syttende mai* (17 May), a national public holiday that celebrates all things Norwegian.

This nearness to the earth is also about being outdoors and connecting with nature, which is deemed as a Norwegian entitlement and is part of a law known as *allemannsretten*, meaning "everyone's right" to roam free. It enables Norwegians to camp respectfully anywhere they like, as much of the land is not owned outright.

Notably the Danish word *hygge* derives from Norwegian. Given that Norway knocked Denmark off the top of the *World Happiness Report* charts in 2017, it's no surprise that there are some synergies between these Nordic neighbours.

Hygge

Although there is no direct translation of this word, *hygge* suggests a cosy and calm feeling of wellbeing. It can be applied to your home environment, via toasty pyjamas,

Below: Taking a break the *hygge* way is about cherishing cosy moments, whether curled up with a good book or enjoying hot chocolate in front of a toasty fire.

warm blankets and lit candles; or it can connect you to the food you eat on a blustery autumn day, such as hot soup and grilled cheese on toast, or hot chocolate and marshmallows. It also relates to a wider commitment to being mindful of your surroundings, relationships and experiences. Essentially, the core principle of *hygge* is one of connection to good company, good food and the heartening experience of each moment.

"*Hygge* is about giving your responsible, stressed-out achiever adult a break. Relax."[3]

MEIK WIKING, CEO OF THE HAPPINESS RESEARCH INSTITUTE, COPENHAGEN

Equality emphasizes our interconnection

Knowing that their fellow citizens wish them well, and enjoying the sense of trust that fosters, factors high in the Danes' and Norwegians' happiness level. Indeed, the *World Happiness Report* criteria of trust and equality explain why Scandinavian countries that prioritize welfare consistently top the happiness charts.

In exchange for their generous tax payments, Norwegians are afforded mutual generosity from their government, via free college education, free hospital treatment and a healthy pension, on top of the ample annual and parental leave they are able to enjoy. And three out of four Danes report that they trust each other, as well as trusting their government, which is generous with its welfare distribution.[4] Not only that, but the poorer people in society are happier in Denmark than they are in most countries, meaning that there is more equality between the haves and the have-nots.

Similarly, in Norway there is a great sense of income equality. In a 2016 Unicef report, which compared the gaps in income, education, health and life-satisfaction between children at the bottom of society and those in the middle, Denmark, Norway, Finland and Switzerland all came out on top, with the lowest overall childhood inequality. And Norway, Iceland and Finland, are three of the most gender-equal countries, based on a 2016 World Economic Forum study.

The impact of inequality

Evidently, it's not just equality between
rich and poor that contributes to levels of
countrywide contentment; the existence
of inequality between ethnicities, gender
and social class negatively impacts on
our happiness. This explains why many
wealthy countries rank so low in the
happiness charts.

Inequality can affect freedom to make
decisions, while freedom from corruption
bolsters trust. The fall of the USA in the
rankings is testament to this, as it has sunk
in the rankings due to increased corruption
and declining social support. Conversely,
we naturally feel more content if we feel
safe and protected, with trustworthy
leaders and little perceived corruption.
Moreover, if we live in a country where a
diverse range of residents feel relatively

Opposite: Equality fosters trust, which begets
happiness. Societies where citizens feel equal trust
each other more, and that's a happy place to live.

equal and free to make decisions, overall
wellbeing is high.

Perhaps just as relevant to why the
Danes and Norwegians lead the way in the
happiness ratings is the fact that extreme
*un*happiness is less stigmatized in these
countries. Consequently, mental illness is
better handled. Danes recognize mental
illness and find ways to remedy and prevent
it, rather than simply ignoring the problem.

Meanwhile, in Norway pressure on school-
aged children is reduced, as they don't
receive any grades throughout elementary
school. This freedom to thrive and follow
individual interests in Nordic countries could
be seen as a useful preventative measure
for childhood and teenage anxiety, given
that exam pressures and an environment
of constant testing in British schools, for
examplle has been cited as a key reason for a
recent rise in childhood and teenage anxiety,
in a report commissioned by the National
Union of Teachers.[6]

Wealth is not wellbeing

The word "wealth" may originate from the word "wellbeing", but, as we've explored (see page 42), wealth is not a contributor to happiness. And while Norway may be one of the only countries in the world without a national debt, its wealth contributes far less to its happiness ranking than its people's openness to helping others, their desire for everyone to do equally well and their core sense of belonging.

Below: Social connections and supportive relationships have been proven to be much greater contributors to our happiness than income or wealth.

Various surveys, from the *World Happiness Report* and the *European Social Survey to The Happy Danes* report show that, while household income does impact on our level of life-satisfaction, it is "not the most important factor".[7] Indeed, a Danica pensions survey (which almost 10,000 Danes have answered since 2007, for *The Happy Danes* report) revealed that social relationships may be more important to our happiness, once our basic needs have been met by the income we have earned. The happiness scores of those who were most satisfied with their relationships were four points higher than those who were least satisfied, whereas the difference in "happiness points" between those with the highest and lowest incomes was only 0.5.[8]

Evidently, the quality of our social relations impacts on our happiness far more than the quality of our bank balances. And the fact that some of the wealthiest countries rank so far down the happiness list (with no increase in happiness, despite a dramatic increase in national wealth) further demonstrates this lack of connection between wealth and wellbeing.

Gross National Happiness

Over the past four decades, this lack of connection between wealth and wellbeing has gradually been observed by people in power (or those striving to gain power). Gross National Product is therefore not the final arbiter in a country's happiness stakes.

As presidential candidate Bobby Kennedy declared in 1968, "Gross National Product does not allow for the health of our children, the quality of their education or the joy of their play. It does not include the beauty of our poetry or the strength of our marriages, the intelligence of our public debate or the integrity of our public officials, it measures everything, in short, except that which makes life worthwhile."[9]

The Bhutanese example

A few years later, in 1971, Bhutan took the decision to replace GNP with GNH (Gross National Happiness). Rather than the country striving for a nation of happy people, GNH is – according to Bhutan's Minister of Education, Thakur Singh Powdyel – "an aspiration; a set of guiding principles through which we are navigating our path toward a sustainable and equitable society".[10] Those guiding principles are now part of the country's Gross National Happiness index, based on equitable social development, cultural preservation, conservation of the environment and promotion of good governance.

Four decades on, life expectancy has doubled in Bhutan, with almost 100 per cent of its children now enrolled in

> "We believe you cannot have a prosperous nation in the long run that does not conserve its natural environment or take care of the wellbeing of its people."[11]
>
> THAKUR SINGH POWDYEL, BHUTAN'S MINISTER OF EDUCATION

primary school. Those schools are now "green" schools, with GNH principles fully integrated into the education system. All school materials are recycled, as part of a national waste management programme, and daily meditation sessions exist alongside environmental protection and agriculture lessons. Consequently teachers have reported positive changes to the children's emotional wellbeing. For the Bhutanese, as for the Norwegians, Finnish and Danes, education is about more than achieving good grades; it's about preparing pupils to be good people, too.

Meanwhile, environmental protection is a huge part of constitutional policy in Bhutan. Caring for our planet, and each other, lies at the forefront of the GNH index, in a land that bans all private vehicles from its roads on a monthly pedestrian day.

Spreading the message

It seems that Bhutan's efforts haven't gone unnoticed and that world leaders are gradually taking note. Prior to the UN's first conference on happiness and wellbeing in 2012, and publication of the first *World Happiness Report*, the UK's then Prime Minster, David Cameron, called for measurement of progress based not only on economic growth, but on personal growth: "not just by our standard of living but by the quality of life".[12]

Shortly afterwards, the happiness portal Action for Happiness was established by the academic and economic leaders Lord Richard Layard, Sir Anthony Seldon and former Downing Street strategy chief Geoff Mulgan, to "create a shift in priorities in our culture by helping people take practical action for a happier and more caring society".[13]

Above: Taking care of the natural environment is a priority in Bhutan, a country which measures its Gross National Happiness.

Fortunately, as stated in the opening paragraph of the 2017 *World Happiness Report*: "Increasingly, happiness is considered to be the proper measure of social progress and the goal of public policy."[14]

That this goal exists, and is being prioritized, is of vital importance. However, even more crucial is what leaders and citizens of countries across the world actually *do* about it. How can we take what we know about worldwide wellbeing and blend it with scientific evidence from the field of positive psychology, to enable people to flourish?

59

POSITIVE PSYCHOLOGY
The science of flourishing

"What you do today can improve all your tomorrows."

RALPH MARSTON, AMERICAN WRITER

What is "flourishing"?

Flourishing is the opposite of languishing. To flourish means to thrive, grow and brighten, whereas to languish means to wilt, wither and fade.

Happiness research tells us that languishing amid long-lasting negative emotions is not good for our immune, endocrine or cardiovascular health. This is why "fixing people" has long been a priority for psychologists. However, positive psychology strives to do more than just fix us. It strives to enable us, too.

The "wellness model"

Whereas traditional psychology focuses on the "disease model" of fixing what is *wrong* with us, to alleviate human languishing and move people "back to neutral", positive psychology focuses on the "wellness model" of building what is *right* with us, to enhance human flourishing and help get people "north of neutral".

In the mid-1990s the founders of positive psychology (Martin Seligman, Mihaly Csikszentmihalyi and Christopher Peterson), began to focus on this wellness model, researching the conditions for flourishing, and creating evidence-based interventions that could enable those conditions. One of those founders, Professor Martin Seligman, defines positive psychology as "The scientific study of optimal human functioning. It aims to discover and promote the factors that allow individuals and communities to thrive."[1]

Above: Professor Martin Seligman created wellbeing theory and co-founded the field of positive psychology to focus on what is right, rather than what is wrong.

Opposite: Positive psychology focuses on creating the nurturing conditions to enable us to flourish and thrive in our lives.

The pillars of wellbeing

Having researched the key ingredients that comprise human flourishing, Seligman and his team created an anagram to summarize the five elements of flourishing: PERMA.

Some time later, Positive Psychology Masters graduate Emiliya Zhivotovskaya, founder of The Flourishing Center in New York, added a sixth element. Having studied mind–body medicine and the connection between the way a healthy body contributes to a healthy mind, Emiliya suggested a sixth "pillar of wellbeing", vitality – because even if we can tick the other boxes, without enough sleep, exercise and nutrition, we may struggle to flourish. This additional pillar of wellbeing has been widely accepted by the positive-psychology community, thus creating the PERMA-V model, which includes the following measurable elements of wellbeing:

- **Positive emotion**

- **Engagement**

- **Relationships**

- **Meaning**

- **Accomplishment**

- **Vitality**

Each pillar of wellbeing impacts on the others and feeds the next, creating a cycle of flourishing. For example, the more engagement and meaning our life has, the more likely we are to accomplish our goals, which causes positive emotions, which makes us better equipped to build healthy relationships, engage in our work and take care of ourselves, which in turn boosts our positive emotions, and so on.

Based on the PERMA-V model, happiness involves being:

- **At peace with our past:** by looking back with gratitude and forgiveness.

- **Optimistic and hopeful about our future:** with intentional, achievable goals.

- **Happy with our present:** savouring the current moment, feeling engaged in what we are doing and experiencing a sense of meaning and purpose in our lives *right now*. It also encompasses enjoying mutually supportive relationships, feeling grateful for what we have, with a healthy mind and body that give us sufficient energy to optimize how we function, think and feel.

The PERMA-V model

According to leading positive psychologists and the science of flourishing, in order to flourish we must have the following "pillars of wellbeing" [2]

1. Positive emotion: Happiness, joy, curiosity, serenity, hope, gratitude, awe and love are examples of this.

2. Engagement: This means using our character strengths to achieve a sense of "flow" through which we can lose ourselves in an activity.

3. Relationships: Strong, supportive and rewarding social connections.

4. Meaning: A purposeful life, which is valued, worthwhile and has meaning.

5. Accomplishment: Working towards and achieving goals, and thus growing and developing.

6. Vitality: Paying attention to sleep, physical activity, alignment and digestion, in order to feel alert with our available energy and be fully functioning and psychologically well.

Above: Supportive relationships are a key pillar of wellbeing. The sense of belonging, encouragement and support we gain from other people matters.

Set-point theory – our happiness is under our own control

Set-point theory suggests that we adapt to negative and positive life events (which only affect our happiness levels by 10 per cent) so that, over time, we return to our prior happiness set-point – that is, our level of happiness before the positive or negative circumstance occurred. Another 50 per cent of our happiness is determined genetically.[3]

As reported in a 2005 paper called *Pursuing Happiness: The Architecture of Sustainable Change* by happiness researchers Sonja Lyubomirsky, Kenneth M. Sheldon and David Schkade, this theory is based on a variety of scientific evidence gleaned from research spanning three decades, including twin studies, long-term panel studies and a 1978 study on the effects of life circumstances on wellbeing.

Based on a total of 60 per cent of happiness being accounted for by circumstances and genetics that are beyond our control, Lyubomirsky et al. concluded that the remaining 40 per cent is up to us. The fact that we each have the capacity to control this much of our happiness is great news. But how can we attend to this important percentage? Well, this part is attributable to intentional activities – that is, what we think, do and feel – and through our own efforts we are able to significantly raise and sustain our happiness set-point over the long term, because these researchers have discovered that "activity-based wellbeing change"

lasts, whereas "circumstance-based happiness change" does not.

The DIY solution

This means that lasting change to achieve a more sustainable, higher happiness set-point can only come about through habitual change of our thoughts, actions and feelings. So it is only through altering our habits and taking small, positive actions that we can raise our happiness set-point.

Whether we are innately grumpy or cheerful, happiness is equally available to all of us. We just need to take a DIY approach in attending to our thoughts, actions and feelings. But how do we intentionally control what we think, do and feel, given that these areas have the power to significantly raise or lower our happiness set-point?

The answer comes from Positive Psychology Interventions (intentional actions), which positive psychologists who were studying the science of flourishing in 2004–9 discovered can significantly enhance wellbeing and decrease depressive symptoms.

Above: Taking a DIY approach to our happiness by practising positive interventions can significantly raise and sustain our happiness set-point.

Intentional interventions: how to flourish

Professor Martin Seligman says in his book, *Flourish*, "If you want to have roses, it is not nearly enough to clear and weed. You have to amend the soil with peat moss, plant a good rose, water it, and feed it nutrients. You have to supply the enabling conditions for flourishing."[4]

The pillars of wellbeing (see page 64) *are* those conditions for flourishing. They are the good roses, the water and sunshine. And Positive Psychology Interventions are what enable those conditions. They are the watering can, the prime positioning for good sunlight and the nutrients.

Scientists have discovered a number of intentional activities that are proven to raise our happiness set-point and increase our life-satisfaction. If we can make habitual those activities that feel most natural to us, this can provide a sustainable boost to our wellbeing. While there are more than 50 activities in total, some of them are more powerful than others.

Generally speaking, the first seven interventions listed below have been the most validated in boosting wellbeing. However, positive psychologists and researchers agree that there is no "one size fits all" model, and that some interventions will work better for some people than for others.

Positive Psychology Interventions

1. Express gratitude: Count the blessings of what you have, in a journal or through contemplation, and convey appreciation in person or in a letter to someone you have never properly thanked.

2. Cultivate optimism: Practise optimistic thinking by considering the bright side of each situation and writing about your best possible future in a journal.

3. Savour life: Pay close attention to the little moments in life and take delight in daily joys. Replay these mini-moments of awe by writing about them, drawing them, sharing them or reminiscing about them in other ways.

4. Nurture social relationships: Schedule and invest time in relationships, both new and old. Practise strategies such as active listening.

Above: Supplying enabling conditions to flourishing is like tending to a garden. We need the right nutrients, perspective and care in order to thrive.

"Participate in absorbing activities that enable you to lose track of time and that engage you."

Right: There is much we can do to raise our happiness levels. Physically moving and stretching our bodies is just one such intervention.

Positive Psychology Interventions

5. Practise random acts of kindness: Do good for other people. This can be planned and direct or spontaneous and anonymous, for friends or strangers, or a combination of both.

6. Play to your strengths: Finding your character strengths and using them improves wellbeing and performance. Indeed, playing to your strengths can also have the knock-on effect of positively impacting on other interventions, such as helping you to achieve your goals (10) and making you more engaged (8) and physically energized (7).

7. Practise meditation and physical activity: Take care of your body by getting enough sleep, eating well, exercising, meditating, smiling and laughing.

8. Increase flow and engagement:
Participate in absorbing activities that
enable you to lose track of time and that
engage you. They should be sufficiently
challenging, but not so difficult that you lose
enjoyment of the activity. This intervention
can also tie in with using your character
strengths (6) – that is, those authentic
strengths that energize you and lead to
peak performance.

**9. Avoid over-thinking and social
comparison:** Minimize how frequently
you dwell on your worries and compare
yourself to others, using strategies such
as distraction, minimal social-media usage
and reducing worry-time when you gain
evidence for and against your anxieties
and judgements.

Below: Noticing and savouring the present moment is an important intervention. Becoming absorbed and engaged in a task can boost wellbeing.

Positive Psychology Interventions

10. Set – and meet – goals: Choose a few meaningful goals to commit to, and then devote effort to pursuing and meeting them.

11. Learn to forgive: Set yourself free of resentment by writing a letter to someone who has hurt you in the past, forgiving them by letting go of any residual anger that you may feel.

12. Develop strategies for coping: Consider how you have got through hardships in the past and practise methods to deal with stress, anxiety and adversity.

13. Practise spirituality: Read books on the subject of spirituality or get involved in local spiritual practices.

We'll explore how to put many of these interventions into practice in second half of this book. First, it's important to figure out which of these activities suits you personally best.

Determining your best-fit activities

Although Positive Psychology Interventions are evidence-based, which means they have been researched and scientifically tested, some of them will be more applicable than others to different people, based on how natural, worthwhile and enjoyable each activity feels. As such, it's worth carrying out the following survey, which has been loosely based on Lyubomirsky's more detailed "Person-Activity Fit Diagnostic",[5] to discover which six interventions make the best fit for *you*.

On a scale of 1 to 7 (with 1 being "not at all", 4 being "somewhat" and 7 being "very much"), rate how likely you would be to keep doing each of the 13 interventions listed below (and described above), based on:

A) How natural the activity would feel to you
B) How much you would enjoy and be interested in doing the activity
C) How much you would value and identify with the activity.

Then add up your scores. The highest scores determine the best-fit activities for you to practise as often as you can.

By picking the six interventions that feel most natural, valuable and enjoyable to you, and spreading them out over time, you will find that taking action seems less daunting than trying to incorporate all of the interventions in your life. You will also be participating in activities that you feel most motivated to try, based on your own personal values, lifestyle and interests. As such, they

Above: Floating paper lanterns or "sky lanterns" are often released for fun, as an expression of spirituality or hope and gratitude.

will be easier to sustain and will have the greatest impact. Later, you might choose a different intervention that you would find less enjoyable and more challenging. However, wisdom suggests that trying the most natural interventions first will have the most positive effect over the long term.

What are your own best-fit activities?

Activity	A	B	C
Express gratitude			
Cultivate optimism			
Savour life			
Nurture social relationships			
Practise random acts of kindness			
Play to your strengths			
Practise meditation and physical activity			
Increase flow and engagement			
Avoid over-thinking and social comparison			
Set – and meet – goals			
Learn to forgive			
Develop strategies for coping			
Practise spirituality			

Get in the driving seat

In order to change, we simply need to begin. And in order to experience happiness, we simply need to take control. Positive Psychology Interventions put us in the driving seat, so that we can control the 40 per cent of happiness that is up to us (see page 66).

By taking tiny steps using these interventions, we can create an upward spiral to flourish rather than languish; to cope with the bad and to cherish the good. And it is important to note that duality. For positive psychology is not merely a "happy-ology"; rather, it includes the entire sum of human experience and gives us "permission to be human" by equipping us with the tools to cope with negative experiences, while also enhancing positive ones.

"To maximize happiness, choose intentional over circumstantial change."

RICHARD WISEMAN,
PSYCHOLOGY PROFESSOR

Using the positive psychology toolkit

Life is a roller-coaster ride of ups and downs, leaps forward and setbacks. It isn't simply good or bad, happy or sad, easy or tough. It is each and every one of these things in varying degrees, across the whole spectrum of human experience.

Essentially, positive psychology and the science of flourishing equip us with a toolkit that enables us to respond well; to pay attention to what is right, and to take action when something is wrong. And because of the nature of life, hurdles will spring up and barriers to wellbeing will arise. Positive psychology provides us with the means to leap over them.

Below: With Positive Psychology Interventions in our toolkit (see pages 68–73), we can steer ourselves on our happiness journey and head in the right direction.

THIEVES OF HAPPINESS AND BARRIERS TO WELLBEING

"Worry does not empty tomorrow of its sorrow. It empties today of its strength."

CORRIE TEN BOOM, WRITER, WAR HERO AND ACTIVIST

Fighting the thieves

Worry, comparison, judgement and pessimism are perpetual thieves of happiness. They reduce our sense of self-worth, increase our anxiety and detrimentally affect our wellbeing. Yet they are wired in to our brains and are thus part of the human condition. Fortunately, we can reduce their impact.

In this chapter we'll explore what these barriers to wellbeing are, and why they exist. Then, in the following chapter, we'll learn exactly how to overcome them, by mastering our minds, reframing our thinking and gaining perspective.

The power of thought

The thoughts that we have are powerful. They can affect our mood, our choices and the way we view the world, and can lead to anxiety and depression (or to happiness and contentment, depending on how we think).

Essentially, according to a model created by Positive Psychology expert Emiliya Zhivotovskaya (see Chapter Four) in 2012 – after a decade of work studying her own mind-chatter and that of her students and clients – we have four types of thought,[1] and all our thoughts can generally fit into one of these clusters:

- **Factual** – e.g. I'm hungry.

- **Fantasy** – e.g. I wonder what we should have for tea.

Flourishing fact

"Learned helplessness" is a sense of powerlessness that both people and animals may feel, regardless of whether or not they have control over an experience. Whilst researching depression in 1967, Professor Martin Seligman discovered this psychological condition, in which a perceived lack of control over a situation's outcome exists, even when there is the potential to control and escape from the situation.

- **Future** – e.g. What if I burn the food again?

- **Judgement** – e.g. I'm always burning food. I'm such a terrible cook. Probably best to get a takeaway.

Factual and fantasy thoughts don't have as much negative impact as future and judgement thoughts. Future "what next?" thoughts can lead to "crisis-mongering", catastrophic thinking and anxiety. Judgement "why?" thoughts can lead to "learned helplessness", pessimistic thinking and depression.

Thankfully, through compassion, reframing and perspective (see page 110)

Above: Our thoughts have the power to greatly affect our mood. Understanding that we have the capacity to control our thoughts is a key lesson in living well.

we can regulate our future thoughts and judgement thoughts in order to reduce their effect. But why do we have a tendency to focus on what might go wrong or what we do wrong, rather than on what might go right and what we do right?

Negativity bias

The answer lies in what neuroscientists call our inbuilt "negativity bias", which means that we focus on – and react more strongly to – negative comments, situations or events than we do to positive comments, situations or events.

Indeed scientific research carried out in the 1970s by Dr Gottman and Robert Levenson discovered that it takes at least five good acts or "positive interactions" to repair the damage of one critical or negative one. These two researchers discovered that happy and stable relationships have five positive interactions to every negative one, after studying footage of married couples

"[our brains are] good at learning from bad experiences, but bad at learning from good ones. Your brain is like Velcro for negative experiences but Teflon for positive ones."[2]

RICK HANSON,
AMERICAN NEUROSCIENTIST

Below: Our brains react more intensely to pain than to pleasure and are better at remembering and focusing on the negative rather than the positive experiences.

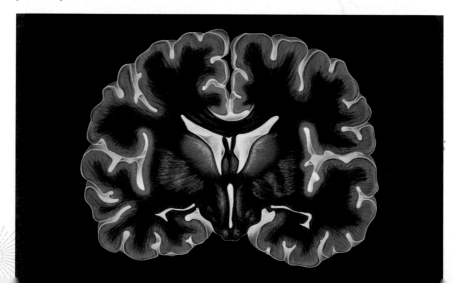

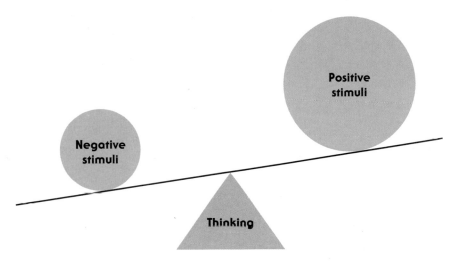

whom they had given 15 minutes in which to solve conflict. After following this up nine years later, they found that the balance between positive and negative interactions, particularly during conflict, made the difference between whether or not couples would stay together, having correctly predicted the couple's fate.

The right ratio for flourishing

In order to flourish, relationships ideally need between three and five positive experiences to one negative one. "Negative contaminates positive more than positive purifies negative," says Rick Hanson. "For example, a misdeed will harm a hero's

Above: Our inbuilt negativity bias means we respond more strongly to negative stimuli than to positive stimuli. To counter the balance we need to increase our positivity.

reputation more than a good deed will improve a villain's."[3]

To return to the analogy of our mind as a garden, and the need to nourish it with the right conditions in order for roses to grow (see Chapter Four), our brain is more "fertile" for negative thoughts, just as weeds are more likely to grow in a garden than flowers, because the ground is more fertile for weeds. Our brain "responds more intensely to unpleasant things than to equally intense pleasant ones."[4]

Danger detectives

It all comes back to human history. If our ancestors ignored dangers, then death was the likely result. Consequently, over the course of many millennia, we have evolved to look out for those dangers, remember them, react strongly to them and become increasingly sensitive to them over time. Once bitten, twice shy.

As a survival mechanism, dangers and pain were prioritized in our memory over joy and pleasure. Our brains have therefore learned to react faster and more strongly to negative stimuli than to positive ones; to learn more quickly from pain than from pleasure. That is how our inbuilt negativity bias originated, yet it continues to function as a survival mechanism despite our need for it having diminished in modern times, given that sabre-toothed tigers and other life-threatening dangers no longer lurk round every corner.

The "fight-or-flight" response

Humans remain on full alert to potential dangers, losses and injustices. When we are in "fight-or-flight" mode, adrenalin is pumped into the bloodstream, causing our hearts to beat faster and our breathing to quicken. Extra oxygen is sent to the brain, increasing our alertness as our senses sharpen. All senses, that is, except our common sense, which disengages, because all this happens before the visual centre of our brain has a chance to fully process what is happening, and our rational mind is

rendered relatively useless. In that moment, short-term survival is all that matters.

Whenever a potentially troublesome experience arises, our brain homes in on it and downplays everything else. This negative tunnel vision explains why we tend to focus on the single piece of criticism that we receive, even amid praise: the one negative comment among a plethora of positive ones. And because our brains have evolved to react more intensely to negative stimuli, those reactions last longer and end up in our implicit memory systems, ready to be called up again and again.

Ignoring the positive

Conversely, positive emotions don't make it to those all-important memory stores, simply because our brains have not been trained to react to them or remember them as vividly. So good news and opportunities get overlooked. We brush aside compliments and fail to notice or appreciate the positive, or at least not for long enough for it to be converted into a proper neural structure.

In order to reshape our brain chemistry and circuitry, and train it to react more

strongly to positive stimuli and to notice (and remember) positive comments and experiences more readily, we need to consciously and proactively focus our mind on them – and deliberately take them in (we'll explore this more fully in Chapter Eight).

Above: When danger lurked everywhere it was better to run away from something that wasn't there than ignore or "fight" something scary that was! Today our brains remain on high alert.

Worry

Worry can be defined as a chain of negative thoughts about what might happen next. Once the chain has begun, it can be difficult to stop it, especially when we fail to find a solution (as is often the case, given the hindering effect that worry has on our brains).

Stone Age tribal survival

We now know that during the Stone Age (which lasted for several million years, ending before 2000 BCE), when humans hid from sabre-toothed tigers and frequently used the fight-or-flight response, worry was useful. It served as a protection tool. With danger lurking around every corner, a brain that was able to quickly trigger an appropriate response to that danger (that is, run or fight) was of great life-saving importance. So was the need to imagine worst-case scenarios, in order to prepare for them. However, the evolution of this tendency means that we are now left with a constant fear of "what ifs?" – that is, what if this or that happens?

It is clearly far better to mistakenly perceive a threat when none exists, and endure the consequence of some needless anxiety, than mistakenly miss a threat when one does exist and endure the consequence of death. This is why our evolutionary biology has led us to do the former, over and over again, so that we never miss a potentially fatal threat. The result is a brain that overlooks opportunities and positive experiences, in favour of threats and negative experiences.

It's all about survival and prevention. And back when threats were prevalent, this made sense.

Busting the "worry is useful" myth

However, worry no longer benefits us as it once did. In the thousands of years that have passed since predators lurked, we've busted the worry myth. According to this myth, worry prepares us for danger and prevents us from harm, helping us to solve problems and perform well. But we now know that the converse is true, as the process of worry impedes – rather than assists – our thinking power.

The truth is that worrying induces a state of anxiety, which lowers our cognitive performance and makes us more likely to make emotional rather than rational decisions.

When our brain engages in a "fight-or-flight" response, our almond-shaped amygdala (the emotional limbic system of our brain, located deep within the temporal lobes) acts like a security guard, preventing logical thoughts from entering our pre-frontal cortex (the logical, decision-making zone). In this way, worrying fires up the emotional, irrational part of our brain,

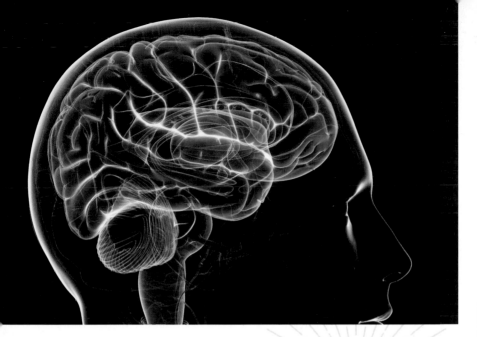

Above: Our amygdala is the emotional and irrational part of our brain. When on high alert it prevents reason and logic from passing through to our thinking brain.

which prevents important logic and reason from reaching the rational part. Evidently, worry is an unhelpful hangover of the "fight-or-flight" response.

The only caveat is if we are worrying about something short-lived and life-threatening, such as fast-moving traffic, which prevents us from stepping out into a busy road. We should care about real and imminent danger. Otherwise worry is not useful; quite the contrary. What's more, as well as preventing us from thinking straight, worry can prevent us from enjoying life.

"Worry doesn't stop the bad stuff from happening, it just stops you from enjoying the good."

LINUS VAN PELT IN *PEANUTS*

Flourishing fact
Studies show that worrying impedes our cognitive ability and makes us less able to find solutions for the problems we're worrying about.[5]

The snowball effect

Despite the irrationality of most of our worries, our brains and bodies perceive them to be real. There are two reasons for this:

1. The brain doesn't recognize the difference between observations and thoughts – that is, between what it sees and what it thinks about.[6]

2. The way we worry persuades our brain that the worry is real. Gradual layering of one thought after another (snowball thinking) helps the degree of worry to grow stronger, as each worrying thought builds upon the next, until we reach the worst-case scenario. This gradual process makes far more sense to our brain than going directly from one minor concern (e.g. "What if I fail this test?") to a catastrophic thought ("What if I end up with no qualifications in a dead-end job?").

Given that worries (and especially dwelling on them) hinder rather than help us, so implementing ways to improve our emotional regulation, control impulses and stop the snowball in its tracks are important steps in our happiness journey.

Right: Once we start to worry, our thoughts tend to snowball out of control, until we lose perspective and end up catastrophizing.

Social acceptance and comparison

Just as we are wired to worry, so we are also wired to care about what people think of us. Back when safety was uncommon and food was scarce, being part of a tribe was critical to survival. We needed to fit in, rather than stand out. As such, social acceptance was vital. Being disliked meant dismissal from the tribe and a high likelihood of death.

Below: In the past, belonging and social acceptance were vital to survival. So conformity was favoured over standing out, for fear of social disapproval.

We have therefore evolved with a fear of social disapproval and an obsession with what others think of us – which is, psychologists argue, as irrational and unproductive as our worries.

When being tribal was vital to survival, conformity was the priority. Nowadays, diversity is celebrated, possibilities and opportunities abound, and yet we're still ruled by an outdated fixation on external opinion and an innate requirement for social acceptance. We just want people to like us. But why?

"Us" and "them"

For our ancestors, rejection and criticism could result in dismissal from the tribe and potentially fatal consequences. Today the

Above: We've evolved, but our inbuilt need for social acceptance has merely been amplified by social media and our need for social validation via the "like" button.

stakes may be far lower, yet it still pains us to receive either, especially when we've based our identity on the validation of others.

And yet using other people's opinion of us as a compass for living our lives is not conducive to a happy life. Our true selves get lost when we constantly prioritize what "they" *might* think, ahead of who we actually are. I say "might" because it is often unlikely that the proverbial "they" even care. You see, "they" are too busy worrying about what we (*their* "they") might think of them!

Choosing to listen to external input rather than ourselves is draining. Not only because

it moves us away from our own internal values and insight, but also because we drown out the voice that tells us that we are enough, and we have enough. Instead, in seeking external validation, we constantly compare ourselves (and what we have) to others and what "they" have. The result is dissatisfaction over appreciation.

Indeed, as Theodore Roosevelt said, "comparison is the thief of joy". Upward comparison can lead to a sense of inferiority, whilst downward comparison can lead to guilt. Whichever way you look at it, the evolutionary tendency of comparing ourselves to others can leave us feeling depleted because we rarely measure up, as we never know the full story of other people's lives.

ANTs

Talking of stories, the degree to which we tell ourselves "we are not enough" is also determined by our beliefs – the mind-chatter that goes on within our own internal radio station. This mental chatter is determined by our ANTs (Automatic Negative Thoughts) and by own "explanatory style".

ANTs are "thinking traps".[7] They are the thoughts that automatically attribute blame, jump to conclusions and generalize. If left unchecked, they can create a situation where we automatically allow the cause of something to be permanent and global. These thinking traps narrow our perception, creating inaccurate assumptions and judgements.

ANTs include automatically:

- **Jumping to conclusions:** by believing in a certain meaning of a situation, without having any evidence to support your belief.

- **Mind-reading what someone else might think:** concerning something that you've said or done. This includes over-generalizing by making a decision on the basis of one situation or experience.

- **Having tunnel vision:** where you can't see the wood for the trees, and you focus on a minor negative detail of a situation and screen out the rest of the evidence.

- **Personalizing:** by blaming yourself, and your own actions or characteristics, for a problematic situation.

- **Externalizing:** by blaming other people, and their actions or characteristics, for a problematic situation.

- **Magnifying or minimizing:** where you magnify the negative aspects of a situation or minimize the positive aspects.

Can you recognize which of these "thinking traps" you tend to fall into the most?

Left and right: We all talk to ourselves to varying degrees. The committee in our head makes assumptions and judgements, often inaccurate ones.

> "Automatic Negative Thoughts are part of the destructive mind-chatter which informs us that we're not good enough."

Destructive mind-chatter

We all have ANTs to varying degrees. These Automatic Negative Thoughts are part of the destructive mind-chatter which informs us that we're not good / clever / slender enough; that we're a terrible mother / son / person, based on a single mistake; that "they must think we're stupid" or that we "should have", "would have", "could have" done something differently. We process this mind-chatter without pausing to reflect, consider more positive evidence to the contrary or honour ourselves with some self-compassion.

For example, if you automatically think you're never going to be promoted, because a promotion passed you by this time, then the ANTs might be: "I always miss out"

Left: Only when we become thought detectives and look for evidence to support or contest our assumptions, can we replace our destructive thought patterns with more constructive ones.

or "I'm not good enough". The danger is that this might lead you to conclude there is no point in trying, so you reduce your effort and create a self-fulfilling prophecy, by failing to get promoted due to your lessened effort, giving further weight to the inaccurate ANTs. Or perhaps you jump to a conclusion about what someone else must be thinking about something you've said or done, without having any evidence to support that assumption. Given that we can't read other people's minds, this is an unhelpful thing to do.

Simply being aware of these thinking traps can help to prevent us falling into them. And if we can catch them, name them and ask questions about them, then we can shift and reframe them – we'll explore exactly how to do so in the next chapter. Meanwhile, these ANTs can shape another key attribution of the way we think: our "explanatory style".

Explanatory style

Our "explanatory style" is the way we habitually explain why something (good or bad) has happened. So optimism is less about positive thinking and visualization, and more about how we view the causes of situations we find ourselves in. Optimistic and pessimistic thinkers will generally explain the cause of an event differently, based on the "three Ps" – personalization, permanence and pervasiveness.[8]

• **Personalization** is about whether we see setbacks and failures or successes and achievements as being down to us (internal) or not (external).

• **Permanence** is about whether we see setbacks and failures or successes and achievements as always happening to us and long-lasting, or not always happening to us and temporary.

• **Pervasiveness** is about whether we see setbacks and failures or successes and achievements as likely to affect everything we do or only specific things, isolated to a certain circumstance.

Let's say that both an optimistic and pessimistic person are struggling at work. The optimist might say, "The boss is in a bad mood today, but it won't last" or "I'm tired at the moment, but if I go to bed earlier, I'll be more productive." The pessimist facing the same situation might say, "I'm an idiot – the boss is always telling me off" or "I'm useless; no wonder nobody ever appreciates me."

Or say an optimist and a pessimist both try out for the football team. Neither gets selected. The optimist would probably say, "I didn't pass the ball very well this time. I'd better practise more. I'll try harder. Maybe next time?" The pessimist might say, "I'm terrible at passing. I'm never going to be any good at football. There's no point in trying. I give up."

The same event occurred to both people, but the resulting action was different. One person, based on what they believe caused the event, is going to give it another shot and put in more effort, while the other is going to give up and stop practising altogether.

How "explanatory style" works

Let's take an example of explanatory style:

Pessimistic thinkers tend to see failure or adversity as being due to their own fault (*internal – me*), long-lasting (*permanent – always*) and all-encompassing (*global – everything*).

Optimistic thinkers tend to see failure or adversity as being due to other factors that are involved (*external – not me*), unlikely to last a long time (*temporary – not always*) and specifically isolated to a particular circumstance (*local – not everything*).

The "three Ps" can conversely be applied to the pessimistic and optimistic explanations for achieving success:

Pessimists will tend to see success as a coincidence or fluke and not attributable to them (*external – not me*), unlikely to last (*temporary – not always*) and specific (*local – not everything*).

Optimists will see success as being due to their own efforts (*internal – me*), sustainable (*permanent – always*) and all-encompassing, in that it may positively impact upon other areas of their lives (*global – everything*).

"It's important to pay attention to the stories we tell ourselves, because they can positively or adversely affect our life decisions."

The domino effect

In this way our thoughts affect our beliefs, which affect our actions. This is why it's important to pay attention to the stories we tell ourselves (our "explanatory style"), because they can positively or adversely affect our life decisions, which can impact on our happiness and our success in life.

Negative judgements can create doubts and insecurities, which are highly disabling. They can prevent us from trying new, potentially enjoyable experiences or from bouncing back from adversity. Meanwhile, judging ourselves to be "not good enough" keeps us in a perpetual cycle of deficiency and dissatisfaction.

Above: Looking on the bright side of life depends on our explanatory style; on what we perceive causes our successes and setbacks.

Countering the barriers to wellbeing

Now that social media has catapulted comparison into a whole new level of joy-theft, and statistics reveal that we're more anxious than ever before, action is certainly needed to counter the thieves of happiness.

Thankfully, no matter which explanatory style we have, it has been learned and is not a trait, meaning that we can shift our explanatory style to become more habitually optimistic and, most importantly, more accurate and flexible. Accurate and flexible thinking represent the goal here.

Pessimistic thinking often is not based on fact, so it paints an inaccurate and inflexible picture of causes, which limits our perspective. Judging ourselves based on inaccurate information, and worrying about future events that are unlikely to happen,

is futile. Therefore if we can become more self-aware and notice our habitual thinking style, we can take steps to avoid getting stuck in that style. And there's a lot more we can do to counter our negativity bias and prevent the happiness-thieves that used to serve us by stealing our joy.

To reduce worry, comparison, judgement and pessimism, we humans have the capacity to master our minds, accept our emotions and then tweak our thinking. So let's explore how to go about it…

Below: Looking on the bright side of life depends on our explanatory style; on what we perceive causes our successes and setbacks.

MIND-MASTERY
Breaking down the barriers to wellbeing

"It is not what happens to you, but
how you react to it that matters."

EPICTETUS, GREEK STOIC PHILOSOPHER

Taking control

Self-judgement, worry and a pessimistic "explanatory style" (see Chapter Five) are all counter-productive. Fortunately – unlike life's circumstances – they are all within our control. We can literally master our minds and rewire our brains, to navigate the negative, strengthen the positive and cope better with life. Yay!

As the Buddha once said to a student: "In life, we cannot always control the first arrow. However, the second arrow is our reaction to the first. The second arrow is optional." This chapter is about that second arrow: how we respond not only to the circumstances beyond our control, but also to the aforementioned thieves of happiness (see Chapter Five).

Let's break these points down. First: how can we improve our response to that initial arrow – to the circumstances we cannot change and have no control over?

Below: We can choose our response; whether or not to fire the "second arrow", our reaction to life circumstances, symbolized by the first arrow.

Responding to what lies beyond our control

The best way to respond to circumstances that lie beyond our control is, as the Serenity Prayer below suggests, to cultivate acceptance:

THE SERENITY PRAYER

"God, grant me the serenity
to accept the things I cannot change,
Courage to change the things I can,
And wisdom to know the difference."

REINHOLD NIEBUHR,
AMERICAN THEOLOGIAN

Practising acceptance

Express your feelings by saying out loud how you feel. Psychologists say that accepting and expressing negative emotions in this way can help lessen their weight and impact. By feeling the emotions that come up, sitting with them and accepting them, we are able to experience what is, rather than being consumed by *what should be*. This clears the path for us to move forward.

Once we've accepted what we cannot change and have leaned into the negative emotions that have been stirred up, we can shift our focus toward finding the good within those circumstances.

Right: Acceptance, both in terms of accepting all the emotions we feel and accepting what we cannot change, is an important response as it helps us move forward.

Improving the responses we can control

But how do we tackle the automated negative responses and beliefs that fill our brains? That hard-wired negativity bias (see Chapter Two)? The tendency toward pessimism? Those judgemental thoughts that beat us up and get us down? How do we regulate what we are hard-wired to automate?

As we have seen, our tendency to "fight or flight" is inbuilt, automatic and immediate – rapidly triggered whenever we sense a problem. Meanwhile, we also have our ANTs (Automatic Negative Thoughts, see Chapter Five) and our deeply ingrained beliefs to deal with. If only we could hit the pause button *before* those automatic responses are triggered.

We can find that space, but it takes some effort. Meditation and mindfulness can both help. Yet there is more that we can do. Thankfully, although our beliefs – that is, the stories we tell ourselves – are automatic, they are not set in stone, no matter how deeply ingrained they are.

Our minds are malleable, so they can be moulded. The neuroplasticity of our brain (its ability to reorganize its nerve connections) means that new neural, or nerve, pathways can be carved out by reframing our thinking. This means that we can, with some practice and effort:

• **Override** the hard-wiring of our brain.

• **Tame and tweak** our judgements, our assumptions and other ANTs.

• **Put into perspective** our fears and worries.

We just need to practise.

This work of countering our negativity bias is essential to our happiness, because that negativity is a bias. This means it will always seek out ways to increase the negative and decrease the positive. We naturally over-learn from negative experiences and under-learn from positive ones – that's human nature. It was helpful during harsher times, but is debilitating today.

Opposite: We are automatically wired to "fight-or-flight" during threatening moments. But, like a radio-controlled aeroplane, we can assume control and learn to respond well.

"Between stimulus and response
there is a space.
In that space is our power
to choose our response.
In our response lies our
growth and our freedom."[1]

VIKTOR FRANKL, HOLOCAUST SURVIVOR
AND AUTHOR

Tackling our thoughts and responses

Thanks to scientific research, we now know that we can counter our automatic negativity bias using the following three mind-mastery techniques:

1. Taking in the good regularly and savouring it.

2. Practising giving ourselves the critical calm space that Viktor Frankl speaks of, through meditation and mindfulness.

3. Using reframing and other strategies to switch on our rational thinking, override our judgements (and other ANTs) and provide perspective.

We shall explore the first of these strategies in detail in Chapter Eight, and the second strategy in Chapter Thirteen. But for now let's explore the third mind-mastery technique mentioned above: how to tackle our thoughts and control our automatic negative tendencies, in order to train our emotional regulation and boost our wellbeing. To do this, we need to understand how our minds work.

Opposite: By savouring the good, giving ourselves space and reframing negative thinking, we can master our minds to feel happier.

How do thoughts and beliefs work?

- A thought consists of neurons – or nerve cells – firing.

- Thoughts become beliefs, which consequently become stories.

- Beliefs are simply thoughts that we've repeated often.

Each time we repeat a thought, the complex junctions between our nerve cells, known as synapses, transmit signals to other cells, strengthening the neural connections and carving out new linked neural pathways – a bit like when flowing water carves out a new river channel. So frequent thoughts become beliefs, which then become mental schemas – that is, the

stories we tell ourselves. Neuroplasticity
(the way our brain takes shape, based on
the repeated mental activity that it rests
upon) means that we can create new
beliefs by repeating thoughts more often.

We can either repeat inaccurate negative
thoughts or more accurate positive thoughts.
Either way, as the neuroscientists say,
"Neurons that fire together wire together",

creating new neural pathways and rewired
beliefs. So the more we think certain
thoughts and fire certain neurons, the more
hard-wired those neurons become. We can
take advantage of this neuroplasticity and
harness our ability to create new, more
accurate beliefs, which better serve us and
our wellbeing.

Thought-shifting is important work

We rarely question or dispute our mind-chatter. Instead, we accept our thoughts as truths. Yet, as we've learned (see page 99), pessimistic and judgemental thoughts and worries are rarely based on fact and are frequently inaccurate. Despite this, we often base our behaviour on them.

Yet our thoughts affect our feelings, which in turn affect our actions. As such, it can be life-changing to shift long-held beliefs. But how do we access those beliefs and carve out more accurate and useful ones? The answer is that by accessing our "mind-chatter" – the thoughts and concerns that created those beliefs in the first place – we can work on replacing old thoughts with new ones.

However, it isn't as simple as simply trying to push negative thoughts away. Worries and other negative thoughts are like an inflated beach ball. Ignoring them

completely is like trying to push the ball down below the surface of the water. They will simply resurface later on, perhaps while you're taking a shower or putting your child to bed. The only way to get rid of the proverbial beach ball is to pop it. And the only way to do that is to work on changing your thoughts, using the cognitive tools we're about to explore.

Above: Ignoring or pushing negative emotions down is like pushing a beach ball down under water. It'll soon resurface unless we pop it by reframing.

Choosing to replace thoughts that don't serve us

We can't just tell ourselves not to think a thought. It simply doesn't work. Let's try it out. Ready? *Don't think about a pink elephant.*

Did you manage it? I know that you thought about a pink elephant, because our attention bias naturally causes us to see whatever we are thinking about, even if we tell ourselves not to about it. This means that the only way for us to handle ANTs is *not* to avoid thinking about them (you can't *not* think about something, as the pink elephant exercise above demonstrates), but rather to *replace* them.

But how do we know which ANTs we need to replace?

• **Thoughts based on fact**, which we know to be certain and which help us feel how we want to feel and achieve our goals, **are useful**.

• **Thoughts based on false beliefs and judgements**, or irrational fears, which make us feel how we *don't* want to feel and prone to inaction, **are harmful**.

• **Thoughts that serve us** (by encouraging us to try harder and take action), and thoughts that are life-enhancing and help us show up in the world in the way we want to, **are useful**.

• **Thoughts that don't serve us** (by discouraging us and causing stress without action), and thoughts that are life-diminishing and prevent us from showing up in the world in the way we want to, **are harmful**.

Dwelling on things and ruminating are only helpful if they lead to positive action, which is rarely the case. So the best way forward is to replace the thoughts that don't serve you.

Overriding judgemental beliefs

This process of reframing helps you to examine the validity of your negative thoughts, gain a more realistic and flexible perspective on them and then quieten them.

1. Acknowledge your thoughts before taming them. Let your negative thoughts in. Tell yourself, "I'm obsessing about my assessment" or "I feel angry about this". Expressing your emotions – whether it's by speaking them out loud or using a strategy such as expressive writing in a journal – is healthy. Once you've accepted a negative thought, you can question it. In this way you can first own your thoughts, before moving on to challenging them.

2. Dispute your harmful thinking and take your thoughts to court. By identifying your beliefs and considering evidence both for and against them, you can adjust your thinking to create more accurate statements, which will serve you better. Judgemental beliefs tend to start with "I'm such a…", "He/she thinks I'm …", "I always…" or "I never…"

Let's say your belief is "I never get anything right". Dispute that belief by considering occasions when you did get things right. Look for evidence both *for* your belief and *against* your belief. If you have a shred of evidence against it, you have proven its inaccuracy and the need for a reframe. For example:

- **Inaccurate belief:** "I can never get anything right!"

- **Evidence for:** "I've made a lot of mistakes recently, and I didn't do this task right."

- **Evidence against:** "I'm required to do a lot of tasks, most of which I get right. I just didn't do well on this particular task, because I rushed it and lost focus."

- **Reframed accurate belief:** "I get most tasks right when I concentrate, and some wrong when I don't. I'll give myself more time to avoid this happening again."

Above: The way we frame our thinking can help us gain perspective and clarity, see the world through a more helpful lens and respond better to setbacks.

When we slow down, question our thoughts and consider the evidence – anything that our automatic thinking may have missed, plus other circumstances that may have contributed to the situation – the answers enable us to be more even-handed and balanced.

3. Check in with your intuition to assess whether that reframed thought feels right. If it's not too far-fetched (as "I'm right all the time" might be), then you'll be able to move on and feel better. This final evaluation of whether a new thought feels instinctively right is important, otherwise you'd create equally unrealistic positive thoughts, rather than more accurate ones.

The founder of The Flourishing Center in New York, Emiliya Zhivotovskaya (see Chapter Four) suggests reframing judgemental "why" thoughts as they come up (in real time) with specific sentence structures, such as "That's not true because…" or "Another way of seeing it is…" When we practise reframing, we give ourselves the space we need to access the rational part of our brain.

4. Give yourself permission to be human, rather than trying to be superhuman.

Human beings make mistakes. It's how we learn, achieve and grow. Remind yourself of that fact, and show compassion toward yourself when things don't go to plan. Learn from your mistakes and proactively consider what you'd do differently next time. In this way you can see mistakes as learning tools to be grateful for, rather than as disasters to be critical of.

5. Focus on what you *did* do, rather than judging yourself on what you *didn't*.

Far better to celebrate the fact that you went for a walk than judge yourself for not going for a run. Far better to send a friend a brief one-minute video message than beat yourself up for not having time for a proper phone chat. Far better to celebrate the one thing you managed to do from your "to-do" list than give yourself a hard time for not doing more.

Opposite: Trying to be superhuman without making any mistakes makes life harder than it need be. Granting ourselves permission to be human is important to our happiness.

How to reduce worries and get perspective

Worries are thoughts about something that has yet to happen, so you can't seek out evidence for or against them. However, there are many cognitive tools that you can use to catch this happiness thief, avoid catastrophic thinking and downward spirals, and boost your problem-solving capabilities.

1. Gain perspective. Consider whatever you're worrying about, and run through the worst-case, best-case and most likely scenarios. For example, perhaps you've missed a mortgage payment and worry about what might happen.

- **Imagine the worst-case scenario** – e.g. house repossession and homelessness. Identify the percentage likelihood of that happening. Probably one per cent likely, given that you'd need to miss lots of payments in a row and take no action, for that worst case to actually happen.

- **Consider the best-case scenario** – e.g. you get a sudden windfall and can pay immediately. Equally unlikely, odds-wise; perhaps one per cent?

- **Consider the most likely scenario** – e.g. you'll figure out a way through this and continue living where you currently do. About 99 per cent likely, given that you're already thinking about the possibilities. Use reframing sentence structures such as "The most likely outcome is..." and "I can..."

- **Create an action plan based on the most likely scenario.** In order to figure out a way through this, you'd need to talk to those involved. By having a conversation with your bank, it would most likely understand your situation and help you find a way to pay the arrears over time, without missing future payments.

Gaining perspective on the most likely eventuality often reveals that the issue isn't as bad as you think, and gives you a solid plan of action to help you find a way through. By taking you from the most negative to the most absurdly positive solution, you can see how unrealistic your worst-case scenario thoughts actually are. By considering the most likely scenario, somewhere in the middle of the two extremes, you get to see the most realistic (and less worrisome) possibility.

Furthermore it can be fun coming up with ridiculously best-case scenarios, and

Opposite: We can worry about all kinds of "what ifs" – our financial security and keeping the roof over our heads being common concerns.

this, in itself, can pull you out of a downward spiral into an upward one. That simple switch broadens your cognitive power to enable problem-solving, while furnishing your mind with more realistic thoughts about what will probably happen.

By using this cognitive tool you can make your worries serve you, by alerting you to a problem and helping you to solve it.

2. Calm down. Remember, when you are anxious or stressed, you can't access the logical part of your brain, because the amygdala security guard won't let rational thoughts through to the pre-frontal cortex. The only way to gain access and rationalize is literally to calm down first. So breathe; take three deep breaths, then try counting backward from 100 in sevens. Controlled breathing helps to lower our stress response, so that we can calm anxious thoughts. If you're still not calm, tap into

Above: Tuning in to our senses by focusing on what we can hear, see and smell can help us to become calmer and more mindful about our surroundings.

your senses rather than your thoughts, by focusing on what you can hear, see and smell. When we calm ourselves, we can focus and regain control of our minds.

3. Boost your confidence in your own coping skills. Remind yourself about what you've been through (and survived) before. Unless you've sailed through life thus far, you'll have been through some tricky stuff. You handled that, so you'll handle whatever it is that you are worrying about now. The fact is that even if a worst-case scenario *does* happen, you'll still have something to be grateful for (people who love you, future possibilities, a second chance).

If we worry about our fears, which then become debilitating beliefs ("I'm not good

"A happy life consists not in the
absence, but in the mastery
of hardships."[2]

HELEN KELLER,
AMERICAN ACTIVIST AND AUTHOR

at making new friends"), this affects our
behaviour (for instance, we keep quiet
when we meet new people). This, in turn,
affects the result and becomes a self-
fulfilling prophecy (so we don't make new
friends), thus throwing another log onto
the fire of our fear and furnishing our belief
by proving us right. Inaction enables fear,
while taking action – "feeling the fear and
doing it anyway" – disables it. This adds a
log to the "I can handle it" fire, and to the
bank of times when you coped well.

4. Designate worry-time. Sometimes
you'll be able to dispute and reframe your
mind-chatter in the heat of the moment,
as soon as the thought pops into your head
(this is known as "real-time resilience").
At other times you won't be able to. In such

instances, it's advisable to designate
worry-time: set aside a quarter or half an
hour to consider your worries. If a thought
pops up, you can tell yourself, "Thanks for
bringing this up, but let's think about this
later during worry-time" and get back to
what you are doing. In this way you can
create a container for your thoughts, and
allow the beach ball to resurface at a time
that suits you best.

**5. See the value in adversity, to lessen the
fear of bad things happening.** We worry
about bad things happening, and yet both
adversity and challenges can be useful.
When life gets tough, we learn. Anger can
be a catalyst for change, while insecurity
can be a catalyst for growth, and grief can
be a catalyst for gratitude.

The hardships that we go through often
teach us, always shape us and frequently
improve us. And we certainly learn more
from the hardships we experience than
from moments of life's rosiness.

MIND-MASTERY

Bear in mind that:

- **Knowing that bad things can be useful** may diffuse our fear.

- **Knowing that our worst decisions and poorest responses offer gifts** of experience and useful knowledge can dissipate our worries.

- **Knowing that we often make progress as a result of our challenges**, rather than despite them, can make us more likely to ride with them and to let them shape us.

This knowledge can move us from a place of fear to one of acceptance. Think about a hardship you've been through – something really tough. Now think about what that has taught you. How has enduring that hardship and emerging the other side shaped you? Consider how it might have improved you, as it probably has.

The realization that, even when worst-case scenarios do happen, we cope, learn and appreciate more reduces the weight of worries and makes them less scary, because we can handle it. And so we do.

"Ironically, had it not been for every disappointment, setback and detour in the road of your life, you wouldn't have come so far. Nice strategy."[3]

MIKE DOOLEY,
AUTHOR AND ENTREPRENEUR

Below: Challenges are useful as they equate to progress and we grow stronger because of them, rather than despite them.

Mastering your mind

Mind-mastery requires that we notice the types of thoughts we are having, then practise gentle questioning and reframing. Over time, as we continue to replace inaccurate harmful thoughts and beliefs with realistic statements, we reduce the power of negative emotions and expand that of positive ones.

This equips us to become more resilient in the face of adversity, so that we bounce back better when circumstances outside our control do occur. By mastering our minds, we assume control of that which we can control, so that we respond better to that which we can't.

Tuning into your mental chatter

Over the next few days, tune into your mental chatter. Do you habitually have more "what next?" (future) thoughts or more "why?" (judgement) thoughts? We are generally more prone to one or the other. Knowing which types of thought are more frequent helps when it comes to reframing.

Now the energy that you employed to judge harshly and worry unnecessarily can be used to live, connect and flourish. There are, of course, other ways in which this psychological hardiness can be further bolstered. One is by building a supportive and encouraging community of strong relationships around you. So, read on...

Right: By tuning in to our internal radio stations we can uncover which types of thoughts are most frequent, so we may gently question and reframe them accordingly.

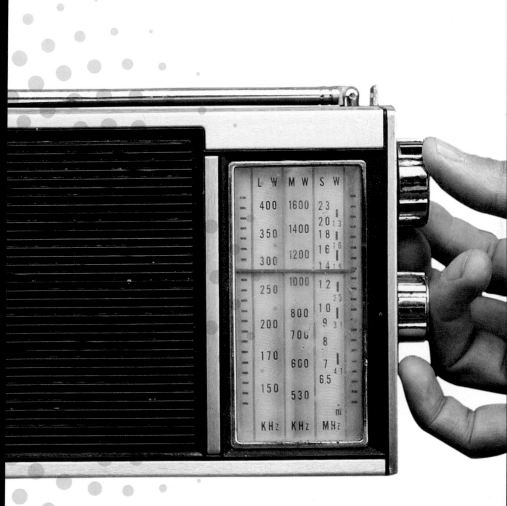

OTHER PEOPLE MATTER
Connection, community and communication

"Of all the things that wisdom
provides to help one live one's
entire life in happiness, the
greatest by far is friendship."

EPICURUS, ANCIENT GREEK PHILOSOPHER

Positive relationships

All of us need supportive relationships, and we are at our happiest when we feel connected with others. This is true even of introverts, who may tire of continued periods of social interaction and may cherish the solace of solitude. Indeed, the comfort we find – both in solitude and in social bonding – is very different from the pain that loneliness brings. Solitude is a choice. Loneliness is not.

Yes, good company is good for us. Strong, supportive relationships are an essential source of our happiness and mitigate stress, as both the ancient philosophers and modern scientists agree.

The need for love

Back in the 1940s, Abraham Maslow's "hierarchy of needs" revealed that once our basic safety and physiological needs have been met, the next most important requirements are love and belonging. Having someone (or something) who is

Flourishing fact
According to a study by the *Journal of Socio-Economics*, strengthening our social relationships would make us happier than an extra £85,000 ($120,000) per year![1]

Right: Abraham Maslow's "hierarchy of needs".

Self-actualization	Morality, creativity, spontaneity, problem-solving, lack of prejudice, acceptance of facts
Esteem	Self-esteem, confidence, achievement, respect of others, respect by others
Love/Belonging	Friendship, family, sexual intimacy
Safety	Security of body, of employment, of resources, of morality, of the family, of health, of property
Physiological	Breathing, food, water, sex, sleep, homeostasis, excretion

always pleased to see you, and whom you're always pleased to see, is a vital contributor to happiness, as is having people to rely upon for emotional support. This explains why, if you have at least one close long-term friendship, plus a relationship network of five or more key "confidant(e)s", you are – according to studies by Professor John Cacioppo of the University of Chicago, who's been studying the causes and effects of loneliness for 21 years[2]– more likely to describe yourself as "very happy".

As Dr Chris Peterson, a founding father of positive psychology, said: "For

Above: Other people matter to our happiness. Their support helps reduce our stress, bolster our sense of belonging and provide us with comfort and connection.

happiness, remember… *other people matter*."[3] A 75-year-long Harvard study of 724 adult men concurs with this, having proved that "good relationships keep us happier and healthier".[4] Specifically, brains stay healthier, nervous systems relax and emotional pain is reduced when we have someone we can rely on in our lives.

But why is that so?

Why do other people matter?

The answer comes partially from the impact that connecting with others has on our physiology. Of the four hormones that relate to happiness, two of these feel-good chemicals (oxytocin and dopamine) are directly connected to relationships.

Oxytocin

The neurotransmitter and hormone known as oxytocin is produced when we interact with others. As it flows, it incites social bonding behaviours, such as trust and eye contact. Hugging also optimizes our oxytocin levels. Oxytocin serves to calm us down, lift us up and open us to connection. It makes us more willing to be friendly, which in turn boosts oxytocin production in the person we're being friendly towards, triggering mutual connection and care.

While the amygdala part of our brain is responsible for our "fight-or-flight" response (see Chapter Five), oxytocin is part of our "calm and connect" response. When oxytocin is produced it moderates the reactivity of the amygdala, enabling us to think more clearly and become open to opportunities to connect.

Dopamine

Meanwhile dopamine is our inbuilt reward activator, which controls our brain's pleasure and reward centre by sending messages between the brain and the nerve cells. When we receive a reward, dopamine is released. Dopamine levels increase, and

"Micro-moments of positivity resonance build bonds, weave the social fabric that creates our community, promote health and can create micro-utopias in our day-to-day lives."[5]

BARBARA FREDRICKSON,
PSYCHOLOGIST AND RESEARCHER

stress chemicals decrease, when we have a massage or stroke our pets. And the knock-on effect of the dopamine boost that is induced by touch is improved sleep, energy levels and happiness.

Positivity resonance

Neurotransmitting brain chemicals aside, there's another reason why connection is so important to our happiness. Leading positivity researcher Barbara Fredrickson has discovered something called "positivity resonance", which reveals how and why connections with other people matter so much to our level of wellbeing.

When we engage in conversation and experience a "real-time sensory connection"

$$C_{43}H_{66}N_{12}O_{12}S_2$$

with someone (via eye contact, hearing their voice or feeling their touch), and we then share a positive emotion with each other, that positive emotion is, says Fredrickson, "unfurling across two brains and bodies at the same time".[6] This explains why connection via text or email doesn't lead to such positive resonance, because the connection has to be face-to-face or, at the very least, auditory via the telephone. It has to be sensory and in real time.

During these micro-moments of synchronized positive connection, a shared chain reaction occurs. "There is one state and one emotion," says Fredrickson. "A miniature version of a mind meld."[7] In this way, sharing a positive story and listening

to it becomes a single, shared process performed by two brains. The same parts of our brains are activated in parallel with each other. This is known as "brain-coupling" and causes us to literally be on the same wavelength at that moment of connection.

While mirror-neurons enable empathy (for instance, wincing when we see someone hurt themselves), brain-coupling opens us up to the other person, heightening our inclination to care about them. This positivity resonance is amplified back and forth between us, which increases how

OTHER PEOPLE MATTER

> "The more open we are to caring about and supporting each other, the more enduring and intimate our bonds."

willing we are to care about the other person's wellbeing. Deep connection that fosters caring: isn't that beautiful?

And the more open we are to caring about and supporting each other, the more enduring and intimate our bonds, and the happier we become. Evidently connection with other people is more beneficial than we think.

What connection offers us

Strong social bonds essentially provide us with what we need to feel good:

- **A sense of belonging and identity**

- **A sense of trust** and a comforting level of support, from having a network to confide in.

- **An opportunity to be altruistic**
  Feeling that we belong, and are able to both get and give support, enables us not just to survive, but to thrive.

Right: Feeling like we are a part of something gives our lives meaning, a sense of belonging and a reassuring feeling of trust and identity.

Belonging and identity

Our need to belong runs deep; it's instinctual and habitual. As intrinsically tribal beings, belonging forms a vital part of our existence. Inclusion has always been a key reason for our survival and a major source of happiness and security, while exclusion is an equally potent cause of unhappiness and insecurity.

This tribal instinct means that we tend to be drawn to those who are like us, and with whom we have something in common. Such people affirm who we are and strengthen our sense of identity.

Our family group is the first "tribe" to take care of us and provide us with protection. We then develop our own external families through our friendships. Then we grow our own families by welcoming new people into our family unit, joining theirs and having our own children. Within these units of family, and extended family, we feel safe.

Trust

According to *World Happiness Reports*, societies and organizations where a high level of trust exists are the happiest. The converse is also true. "The break-up of the family, fractured communities and a loss of trust"[8] are, according to the economist and happiness author Richard Layard,

responsible for the sluggish levels of happiness in the Western world.

Trust also plays a vital part in the quality of our close relationships. And it is the quality, rather than the quantity, of our friendships that matters. Supportive relationships are one of the "pillars of wellbeing" (see Chapter Four) and require a sufficient amount of honesty, encouragement and enjoyment. The quality of our connections also depends on how much we are able to be ourselves – how much we are able to be seen and valued for who we truly are; and how much we feel trusted and can rely on each other, with a healthy balance of give and take. For when it comes to other people, giving (and forgiving) is even more important than receiving.

Opposite: Human beings are driven by an inbuilt tribal instinct. This evolutionary need to belong is how we survive and thrive.

Altruism: good deeds beget good feelings

Supportive relationships are about give and take. However, being supportive is even better for our happiness than being *supported*. Service serves us more than those we serve.

From retirement studies of New Zealanders on the impact of volunteering,[9] to studies reported in the *Journal of Positive Psychology* and the *Journal of Happiness Studies* about the impact that kindness has on both givers and receivers[10] – and the positive feedback loop between pro-social spending and happiness[11] – scientific research repeatedly reveals that kindness results in more energy and laughter, and less anger and stress.

So whatever we spend on being kind – be it time, money, energy or effort – we also receive back, via boosted positive

> "The best way to cheer yourself up is to try to cheer somebody else up."
>
> MARK TWAIN, AMERICAN WRITER

emotions, a greater sense of meaning and improved social connection. This is what the Buddhist monk Matthieu Ricard calls "psychological economics". In terms of wellbeing, both giver and recipient win.

So if we want to be happy, we should look beyond our own personal wellbeing to that of others. For not only does making others happy make us happy; but altruism can help us live longer, too. According to Howard S Friedman's *Longevity Project*, a study that began in 1921 to explore who lives the longest and why, the clearest benefit from social relationships came from helping others, with those who supported and cared for other people living to a ripe old age.[13]

Flourishing fact

According to various scientists, such as Martin Seligman and E Diener in their 2002 *Psychological Science* study on very happy people, performing acts of kindness boosts our wellbeing more than any other exercise tested.[12]

Opposite: Performing acts of kindness has been proven to boost wellbeing more than any other positive intervention. Service serves us well.

The hidden benefits of giving

Why is helping other people so helpful to our own wellbeing? There are a number of reasons why it's beneficial to be good to others; from the release of feel-good chemicals and endorphins that occur when we are kind, to the sense of meaning and purpose altruism can generate. As we'll explore below – giving is as good for our own happiness as it is for the recipients of our kindness.

- **Helper's high.** Kindness acts activate the reward centre in our brain (our "nucleus accumbens", as it's known). In a study by University of Oregon researchers, the pleasure/reward centres in people's brains lit up and released endorphins (hormones that reduce pain, relax us or make us feel happy) during voluntary charitable giving, providing evidence of the "warm glow" that we feel.[14] This explains why performing, or even thinking about performing, acts of kindness produces a tangible high. Furthermore, kindness fosters togetherness and cooperation. So we are literally wired to feel good about doing something that aids the survival of the human race.

- **Virtuous circle.** The happier we are, the more likely we are to give, which makes us happier in turn, and so more likely to give more, and so on.

- **Sense of belonging.** Through generosity without expectation, altruism can help us root ourselves in our community. We are more likely to become a valued member of our community when we are kind to those within it.

- **That good feeling lasts beyond the good deed itself.** Dopamine levels (see page 126) increase not only when we give, but before and after our acts of kindness, too: during the planning stage and the "afterglow". According to the National Academy of Sciences, brain scans have revealed that planning a donation activates the mesolimbic pathway, which is associated with feelings of happiness and increased levels of dopamine.[15] Studies have also revealed that long after volunteering, many people feel an improved sense of self-worth and a lasting period of increased wellbeing, which reduces their stress levels. The benefits of kindness continue long after the act of kindness itself.

- **Kindness is meaningful.** Serving others gives our lives meaning (another of the "pillars of wellbeing", see Chapter Four). So kindness can impact on the way we evaluate our lives and our position within the wider world. Studies have revealed that people who volunteer have higher levels of happiness, less depression and anxiety and a greater sense of purpose.

Above: Giving is a meaningful action. It rewards not only the recipient of kindness, but the giver, and releases happiness-inducing endorphins.

Being kind incorporates two of the pillars of wellbeing: social relationships and meaning. No wonder kindness is an oxytocin-raiser and dopamine-inducer. So how can we be kinder? And what should we give?

How to give

As the great English politician Winston Churchill said, "We make a living by what we get. We make a life by what we give." And there are a number of practical ways in which you can give most effectively and beneficially.

- **Perform multiple kind acts in one day.** Studies have shown that "chunking" kindness (that is, carrying out five acts of kindness on one specific day per week, for a period of ten weeks) has a greater impact on our happiness than sprinkling kindness (that is, performing one act of kindness each day for 10 weeks).[16]

- **Mix it up.** Choosing a variety of kind acts over time is also recommended, rather than repeating the same ones. Acts of kindness that enable you to connect with recipients directly, or to see the impact of your giving, tend to have the greatest effect on the giver's wellbeing.

- **Pay it forward.** If you want to create a ripple of kindness, you might consider suggesting that your recipients "pay it forward". Just as 12-year-old Trevor did, in Catherine Ryan Hyde's novel *Pay It Forward*, you do a good deed for three people and ask each of them to forward it to three more people. Sometimes, because kindness can be contagious, your recipient may be kinder to others than they might have been, had you not performed the kind act. Either way, the ripple of kindness from one person to another can have an incredibly far-reaching positive impact.

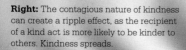

Right: The contagious nature of kindness can create a ripple effect, as the recipient of a kind act is more likely to be kinder to others. Kindness spreads.

"Sometimes, because kindness can be contagious, your recipient may be kinder to others than they might have been, had you not performed the kind act."

What to give

As well as gifts, flowers and charitable donations of money, clothing and food, you could donate your time, your presence and your expertise by helping a neighbour out, or through volunteering. Voluntary work offers a real sense of purpose and meaning. One of the reasons why the Danes are thought to be one of the happiest nations is that almost half of them volunteer, with 70 per cent being active in the last five years.[17]

Giving an experience is also proven to benefit the giver as much as the receiver. This kind of pro-social spending, where you buy concert tickets or pay for meals or spa days, has the added bonus of connection with those who join you in the experience.

And random acts of kindness, such as Sticking coins to parking meters or vending machines, baking cakes for neighbours and giving your support in other ways – by smiling, hugging and donating – can give you and your recipient a boost of happiness.

Below: From handing out flowers, home-made cakes and other gifts to volunteering time, there are many ways to spread kindness.

43 acts of kindness

I undertook a kindness marathon and performed 43 acts of kindness on my 43rd birthday. I wanted to do something to honour my kind-hearted mother, who passed away when she was 43 and I was 17 – something to counter the melancholy feelings that being the same age as my mother induced; something that would give me a boost; something that I hoped she'd be proud of.

My kindness marathon had a huge effect on me, and turned a day that was tough into a day that was tender; and a feeling of connection replaced the feeling of solitude that being a mum without a mum can create, no matter how surrounded by love you are. Both the planning and the "afterglow" boosted my wellbeing and

I couldn't stop smiling. It left me feeling replenished and more connected to humanity than I've ever felt.

During my own kindness marathon I gave home-baked biscuits, flowers and coffees to strangers and neighbours, and delivered baked goods and letters to friends. Such altruism works, no matter *who* you're kind to. But when it comes to building a network of supportive relationships, who you connect with and how you connect are of the utmost importance.

Above: For my kindness marathon, I dished out bunches of flowers to people at bus stops, chocolates to pensioners and biscuits to nurses.

Who to connect with

Other people have the power to make us incredibly happy or incredibly unhappy. As a prime source of both positive and negative emotions, the company that we choose to keep is critical to our wellbeing.

> "Living a quiet life among like-minded friends will more likely lead to the happy life."

EPICURUS,
ANCIENT GREEK PHILOSOPHER

Like-minded people who lift us up, inspire and encourage us are the best people to have on our "support team". Conversely, those who bring us down, demoralize and discourage us are not. As such, it is worth having a friend-audit once in a while to consider who – after having spent time with them – leaves you with such a warm feeling that you are glad and grateful to have them in your life. Cherish those people and their friendships.

As one of the founders of Positive Psychology, Dr Chris Peterson, said: "Bad friends aren't friends at all." So reduce the time you spend with people who drain your energy, and instead invest time in those who boost it.

Left: Gathering with positive, encouraging and supportive friends who make us feel good is an important source of happiness.

Flourishing fact

According to James H Fowler and Nicholas A Christakis, authors of *Connected*, each happy friend increases your probability of being happy yourself by 9 per cent.[18] That's due to what scientists call "emotional contagion", and partially explains why the people we spend time with can dictate our own mood.

Community counts

Today, with social media becoming all-consuming, we are more connected than we have ever been, in a virtual sense; but in reality, studies have revealed that many people still feel alone. All the more reason to make an effort to increase real-world connections. As well as forging strong bonds with those we are especially fond of, it's important to build "bridging connections" to unite different groups within a community.

> "Improving connections with people in our local community demonstrates a commitment to the notion that we're all in this together."

Consider ways in which you might bring people from different backgrounds together through a shared interest, to build what Harvard professor Robert Putnam calls the "social capital" of a community, to facilitate trust and impact positively on the wellbeing of the whole community. For example, you could:

- **Eat together round a campfire, BBQ or candlelit table.** Fire and food create that *hygge* feeling (see Chapter Three) of cosy warmth and togetherness.

- **Plant a community vegetable garden.**

- **Create a directory for your street,** listing names, occupations and resources that can be borrowed.

- **Make a "street library" cupboard** or fill an old phone booth with books, so that residents can donate and borrow books. Just make sure it's waterproof!

Improving connections with people in our local community demonstrates a commitment to the notion that we're all in this together, and that the common good is important for a good life. But what can we do to improve and *deepen* our connections with people, especially close friends and loved ones?

Left: Seeking ways to build connections within a community can have a significant impact on the wellbeing of everyone involved, especially if gathering to improve your shared environment.

How to connect better

As well as considering how the company that you keep makes you feel, consider how you make other people feel, and try some of the suggestions given below.

- **Notice the good in others.** Focus on what's right with people, rather than what's wrong. The "Losada ratio", named after Chilean psychologist Marcel Losada, states that in order to flourish you need to give/receive five positive statements for every critical statement. With that in mind, practise focusing on what your partner/family members/friends have done right, rather than on what they've done wrong. Praise and encourage rather than criticize.

- **Ask other people what's good.** What are they excited about? What's going well in their lives? Encourage them to talk about experiences that will lift them up.

- **Forgive others.** When we forgive people, we regain control over a situation that happened in the past. That time has gone. Forgiveness empowers us to move on with our lives and rebuild relationships with those we are forgiving, if that serves us. After forgiving, look for the good and practise empathy.

> "Other people matter. But few of them are mind readers. Let them know that they matter. They might benefit. And you certainly will."
>
> DR CHRIS PETERSON, A FOUNDING FATHER OF POSITIVE PSYCHOLOGY

- **Practise acceptance over annoyance.** Look for the good – even in traits that annoy you. For example, if your partner often grumpily shares their woes and you find that draining, then consider this: isn't it better that they feel comfortable enough to honestly share with you what's troubling them, rather than being dishonest or bottling up their emotions? See the value in that, and use it as a chance to practise empathy and help them find solutions.

Opposite: How we make people feel matters as much as how other people make us feel. Good connections are crucial to living a good and happy life.

> "Remind yourself that we're all just muddling through, and we all make mistakes."

- **Jot down positive traits that you value in each other.** And while you're at it, list traits that you value in yourself. In order to flourish, we need to love ourselves and our partners, just as we/they are, and accept our differences. The most effective teams have different traits that complement each other's: one person's strengths fill the gaps in another's weaknesses, and vice versa. So while you may have a good deal in common, try to celebrate and appreciate your differences, too.

- **Thank people more frequently.** And explain how whatever you're thanking them for has benefited you. For example, "Thank you for cooking today. It was really thoughtful of you, as it meant that I could finish the email I needed to send, which is a big weight off my mind. I appreciate your making time to help."

- **Practise a loving-kindness meditation regularly.** Loving-kindness is the desire for people, including yourself, to be happy – an opening of the heart. This has been proven to boost positivity resonance (see page 327), along with cognitive, social and psychological resources. We shall explore meditation in more detail in Chapter Thirteen.

- **Show empathy.** Consider other people's point of view before you respond. Or try viewing everyone as a vulnerable child, to minimize blame. Remind yourself that we're all just muddling through, and we all make mistakes. It's easier to judge and criticize than it is to praise and empathize. Yet the latter is far more rewarding and has a wide-ranging social impact. For example, teaching empathy in schools reduces bullying.[19]

- **Be present.** Give people your full attention, rather than just glancing up occasionally, with your attention darting between what you are doing and what they are saying. What message do you think that sends to them? How does it feel when someone does it to you? Stop multitasking and start listening.

Opposite: Meditation is not just about self-care, it can also be about building empathy and connection with humankind via a loving-kindness meditation, where you wish for other people's happiness.

Considerate communication

What we say, and how we say it, can directly affect the wellbeing of other people, but it can also impact on our own wellbeing. Similarly, how we respond to what other people say can have a powerful effect on how we make them feel. Practising empathy, active listening and constructive responding bolsters connection, which in turn positively influences our own happiness.

According to research, what distinguishes good and poor relationships is not how people respond to each other's disappointments, but how they respond to good news![20] There are four types of response:

- **Active constructive:** This involves enthusiastic support, using eye contact, smiles and nodding: you help the other person draw out, savour and optimize their good news with the questions you ask in response to it. For example, "That's brilliant! So how did you feel when…?"; "What happened next? What did he say then? And what about it are you most looking forward to?"

- **Active destructive:** This involves belittling the news by removing the joy from it. For example, "But you'll be really tired if you have to work longer hours in this new job. And what about childcare? Won't that cause you more of a problem than you have now?"

- **Passive constructive:** This is very common and involves minimal support that lacks enthusiasm, such as "Oh, how lovely…"

- **Passive destructive:** This is the worst kind of response, as it ignores the good news completely and shifts the focus onto the listener rather than the speaker.

Active listening and constructive responding are some of the most effective communication skills we can master to strengthen our relationships. By listening intently, you show respect and demonstrate that you are genuinely interested in what others are saying to you. Then, by asking them to relive the experience, tell you more about what happened and flesh out the details, you help them draw out the positive elements and capitalize on the good event.

Opposite: How we listen and respond to what other people say is crucial to our connections with others. Practising empathy and responding constructively creates a solid foundation.

The art of NVC

Another communication skill to improve connections is called "non-violent communication", or NVC. This is a process of clearly expressing how you feel, what you need and what would enrich your experience, without demanding, blaming or criticizing.[21] It works both ways, by empathically receiving what others are feeling, needing and requesting, too.

NVC was developed in the 1960s by Marshall Rosenberg, through his work as a civil-rights activist and mediator. It is based on the notion that we all share universal and non-conflicting needs and all have the capacity for compassion. It suggests that we only resort to culturally learned socially, psychologically and physically violent forms of communication (thinking and speaking) when we don't have alternative strategies to hand or when those strategies clash.

NVC is based on our natural state of compassion and empathy, where no violence is present. It assumes that physical and verbal violence are learned behaviours, and that we each share the same human needs and behave in certain ways in order to meet them. We often automatically get defensive or judgemental during communication, but NVC is about being able to express ourselves in a non-confrontational and non-defensive manner. For instance, "When I notice you tutting, I feel lousy. Would you be willing to bear that in mind?". How we communicate with other people matters, as does the amount of effort we put into our relationships with them.

Invest time and effort in your support team

One of the "Top Five Regrets of the Dying", from palliative-care nurse Bronnie Ware's book of the same name, is not having stayed in touch with friends. So it's worth putting effort into ensuring that golden friendships do not slip by.

Try devoting more time to positive relationships with your family and friends. Relationships will only last if you consistently put in the effort to maintain them. And while good friends understand that busy lives sometimes get in the way of getting together, it's important to stay in touch, so try the following:

- **Meet up with old friends:** Do this once or twice each year at the very least. Message them and get something in the diary for term breaks/holidays.

- **Send a letter to old friends:** Try to do this at Christmas or New Year, and again on their birthday (to go with their card).

- **Deepen existing friendships:** Take some one-to-one time with your favourite individuals from your group of friends: book an annual holiday or spa break that you can go on together.

Below: Committing to regularly getting together with old friends and current friends is a huge happiness provider.

- **Schedule social contact into your routine:** Make time for your relationships, both daily and weekly. Literally schedule in time for phone calls, video calls and texting, as well as meeting up – put it all in the diary. And when you don't have time, send a video message.

- **Do more together as a family:** Whether it's playing tennis, going for regular walks, popping to the park, finger-painting, kite-flying or playing Scrabble, create a routine that means you do at least one of those things together every week. It is all too easy to sit and watch TV together. But interaction generates laughter and positivity resonance, which strengthens bonds. Teamwork and team-play, especially of the family kind, boost positive emotions and enhance relationships.

Above: Investing time in family activities where we participate together gives us the opportunity to connect, be present and strengthen bonds.

- **Make one night per week "analogue night":** Deposit all your devices in a basket and enjoy a "no-phone zone" for at least a few hours. The kids can play outdoors or find something to do that doesn't involve a screen, and you can have extended talks round the dinner table or in the sitting room, read a book together or make something.

We are all leading increasingly busy lives, and although we shouldn't become overdependent on others or allow them to dictate our mood, we should invest sufficient time to build quality relationships with those in our support network. Because positive connection is key to our happiness.

HAPPY THINKING
Finding the good and navigating the negative

"Do not spoil what you have by desiring what you have not; but remember that what you now have was once among the things you only hoped for."

EPICURUS, ANCIENT GREEK PHILOSOPHER

Positivity matters

As we've discovered, given that our negativity bias leads us to respond more fervently to negative stimuli than to positive ones, it's in our best interests to pile on the positive so that we can counter this and give our wellbeing a chance.

This is not to say that we should suppress negativity, for doing so doesn't work. As we've already learned, it will simply resurface later. Rather, we should learn how to accept and deal with negative emotions, while simultaneously bolstering positive ones.

Mind-broadening

For the past two decades Barbara Fredrickson has been studying how positive emotions change the way our cells form and function, to keep us healthy and happy. Via MRI brain scans, scientific evidence has revealed that these positive emotions *broaden and build*, whilst negative emotions narrow and limit.[1]

The "broaden" part of Fredrickson's "broaden and build theory" has found that positive emotions enable us to think with greater clarity and accuracy, as we are more open to solutions when we're happy than when we're angry or anxious. Conversely, negative emotions shut down our logical neocortex (the part of the brain responsible for logical thinking, spatial reasoning and sensory perception), which restricts our thinking power and traps us in negative spirals of inaccurate perceptions and misinterpretation.

So it's in our best biological interests to find ways to boost our positive emotions so that we can think more clearly and become open to wider possibilities. In doing so, we can solve the problems and issues that we are worrying or angry about.

Mind-building

The "build" part of the "broaden and build theory" demonstrates that, over time, the more positive emotions we have, the more we can build up a well of positivity, which can be dipped into during times of adversity. The more we fill our positivity reserves, the more resilient we become. Our bank of positivity literally enables us to "survive well" as well as thrive well. As Barbara Fredrickson says, "Pleasant experiences, which can be so subtle and fleeting, can add up over time to change who we become."[2]

Ultimately, positivity improves our ability to deal with adversity, by putting us in a stronger position to cope and bounce back. So instead of glossing over negative thoughts or experiences or ignoring threats, topping up our reserve banks with positive emotions helps us to see them, process them and figure out ways to move past them rather than dwell on them.

Below: The more positive emotions we "bank" over time, the more resilient and able to overcome tough challenges we become. This is explained by the broaden and build theory of positivity.

Positivity

- **Boosts our problem-solving and cognitive capability** (enabling us to think with greater clarity and accuracy).

- **Improves our resilience** by bolstering our bounce-backability.

- **Limits our capacity for negative thinking,** due to there being less room for the brain to process negative thoughts if it is already focused on positive ones.

A toolkit for taking the good with the bad

In order to achieve optimum wellbeing and flourish, the best strategy is to equip ourselves with the right tools and inner strengths, so that we can both deal with inevitable hardships, anxiety and negativity and facilitate more joy, serenity and positivity.

Having Positive Psychology Interventions (see Chapter Four) at our fingertips is akin to having the right tools in our toolbox to enable us to navigate the downs and facilitate the ups. Through these tools or interventions – such as gratitude, mindfulness, kindness, acceptance and compassion, (which build not only our sustainable wellbeing levels, but also our inner strength and emotional regulation) – we are able to take the good with the bad. And that, according to scientific research, is what the happiest people do.

Contrary to popular belief, positive people don't wear rose-coloured glasses that filter out the negative. Rather, they have learned to hone in on and savour the good, whilst noticing and accepting the bad, without glossing over it. They take "an integrative view",[3] integrating a range of emotional processes to generate a unified response.

Below: The happiest people don't look through rose-tinted glasses or gloss over the negative, they focus on the good, get curious about the bad then respond in a measured way.

Flourishing fact

In studies published in the *Journal of Cognitive Neuroscience*, researchers reported that amygdala activation among happier participants was higher in response to positive images, compared with less-happy people. Yet the activity in that brain region was not lower in response to negative photographs, as the "rose-coloured glasses" perception might suggest. In fact, "amygdala activation among happier participants was equally high for positive and negative stimuli".[4]

This demonstrates that, as opposed to being "naïve or blind to negativity", happier people tend to be far more likely to "respond adaptively to the world, recognizing both good and bad things in life".

They notice and feel the negative, but are able to respond in a more measured way, due to their ability to savour the positive. As the report concludes: "Happy people are joyful, yet balanced."[5]

So, "while people do automatically attend to negative stimuli, given the proper ability and motivation, they can show the same sensitivity to positive stimuli".[6] This, and the fact that our brains are able to be reshaped, due to their neuroplasticity (see page 107), proves that it is possible to learn how to better navigate storms of negativity toward calmer seas.

Left: The neuroplasticity of our brains means we can train ourselves to respond adaptively to stormy waters and navigate our way to calmer seas.

How to navigate the negative

Heading in the right direction through life – onward and upward, rather than backward and downward – depends on knowing how and when to replace inaccurate and harmful negative beliefs (via reframing); and how to lean into negative emotions (via acceptance and labelling). In short, it means knowing how and when to let negative emotions go or let them flow.

Letting them go is about adjusting your sails so that you can better navigate stormy seas as negative beliefs arise (reframing). *Letting them flow* is about riding the waves, before coming out the other side, stronger yet weathered (accepting and labelling). The former offers clarity over irrationality; perspective over inaccuracy. The latter offers the gift of experience and greater self-awareness.

For the former, see page 110 to remind yourself of when and how to replace and reframe negative beliefs that are clouding your judgement, limiting your cognitive capabilities and hindering rather than helping you.

Below: Navigating onward and upward, rather than backward and downward is about knowing when to let emotions go or let them flow.

Riding the waves

When it comes to the latter solution – riding those waves – there are two approaches:

1. The first is to *label negative emotions* (see below) to take the sting out of them.

2. The second is to *find the good in the bad*, by recognizing that setbacks can strengthen and the hardships can help. For instance, adversity often acts as a catalyst for creativity, enabling us to make beautifully resonant art and meaningful music. We've already explored why

Above: When faced with challenges we have a choice: to either accept or ignore how they make us feel; to ride the wave or let it pull us under.

unhappiness matters (see Chapter Two), and how it is our response to negative experiences that matters most. We can either do something about the experience or, if it's outside our control, accept it.

However, before we seek out the silver lining or accept the feelings and let them flow, there's something else we can do, when we're feeling angry or sad, envious or guilty.

Letting negative feelings go

Studies have revealed that simply labelling an emotion in a couple of words reduces the feelings associated with it. This descriptive tool is used in mindfulness, and is also employed by FBI hostage-negotiators to calm situations down.

According to an fMRI (Functional Magnetic Resonance Imaging) study called "Putting Feelings into Words",[7] which assessed amygdala activation by detecting changes associated with blood flow, the emotional reaction of participants who had been shown images of emotional expressions reduced when they were invited to name the emotion they saw. Deliberately identifying and describing the emotions activated the pre-frontal cortex and reduced the arousal of the amygdala, decreasing the emotional impact.

Above: Releasing negative emotions once we've addressed and accepted them can be incredibly freeing.

"We all make mistakes, so just as forgiveness of others helps us to move on, so does forgiveness of ourselves."

Using forgiveness

Another way to deal with negative emotions is through forgiveness, for it addresses how we feel about others and ourselves, and enables us to accept these feelings and move forward. Just as reframing is one way to "let it go", by replacing negative thoughts with more accurate ones, so forgiveness is all about letting experiences go, removing blame and, most importantly, putting yourself back in control of a situation, as master of it, rather than victim. Forgiveness feels good. We all make mistakes, so just as forgiveness of others helps us to move on, so does forgiveness of ourselves. This helps us to move past guilt.

How to forgive

Judgements about ourselves or others stem from a feeling that all is not as it should be. In order to move from judgement to forgiveness, we can take the following steps:

1. Acknowledge that whatever you need to forgive happened in the past, so you cannot change it now. You can only learn from it.

2. Identify the issue that you are about to forgive by spelling out what happened.

3. Label your emotions about it. To heal, you must first feel, so define how the actions make you feel. If you need to release the feeling, do whatever is necessary, whether that is screaming, yelling, crying or even hitting a pillow to get the emotion up and out.

4. Devote some time to empathizing with the person (or yourself) by considering why they may have acted in a certain way. Perhaps a bully was bullied themselves? Perhaps someone lashing out has struggled to control their temper since they needed to defend themselves as a child? This isn't about finding excuses, but about considering, human-to-human, why someone has made a mistake or an error of judgement, just as we ourselves sometimes do. Asking why enables us to cultivate compassion and reduce blame.

5. Write a letter to the person you wish to forgive (even if that person is yourself). It's not necessary to send the letter, but writing your feelings down helps to release and purge them, and to get them out. You might choose to read the letter to the person in a calm state; or to send the letter; or you might simply prefer to read the letter out loud and imagine them saying sorry.

6. Forgive them (or yourself), then move on. Say, "I forgive you" and experience the freedom that doing so generates. This may take time, but going through this process will help to release the blame or judgement and enable you to get on with life.

As we'll explore in the final chapter of this book, self-compassion is just as important as compassion for others. We need to show ourselves, in addition to the wider world, loving-kindness. We are the sum total of all the experiences that we enjoy and endure throughout our lives: the ups and the downs, the accomplishments and the mistakes. If we removed any of those successes or failures from our journey, we wouldn't be us. This realization can be powerful in warranting forgiveness.

Opposite: The cultivation of compassion and the reduction of blame are useful when we want to foster empathy, forgive and move on.

How to facilitate the positive

According to neuroscientist Rick Hanson in *Hardwiring Happiness*, and various studies on brain activity and morphology carried out by the University of California and the University of Miami, when people intentionally practise gratitude, the flow of favourable neurochemicals in the brain multiplies and the neural structure of the brain is literally resculpted.

Whether we focus on regret and resentment or on gratitude and appreciation, new neural substrates build up, new blood flows and new synapses grow.[8] By giving good stuff more of our attention, we can – little by little, synapse by synapse – develop happier brains.

Gratitude

If kindness ranks as the most effective intervention for boosting wellbeing, then gratitude – actively seeking out stuff to appreciate, then feeling grateful for it – ranks alongside altruism as a top-notch feel-good strategy.

Often happiness is right here, under our noses, if only we noticed. Sometimes we are so caught up in striving for what we want to have in the future that we forget to appreciate what we already have right now; we miss the *presents* in our present. At other times our negativity bias means that, regardless of how wonderful things might be, we tend to focus on one negative thing – that critical remark, that typo, that difficult relationship; that is, what's wrong rather than what's right. It's the way we're wired.

Right: Giving thanks is a gift to ourselves and the recipient. Gratitude makes us feel happy for what we have right now – the presents in our present.

"What a wonderful life I've had,
if only I'd realized it sooner."

COLETTE, FRENCH NOVELIST

Flourishing facts

Studies by the HeartMath Institute
and the University of California reveal
that changes to the brain instigated
by gratitude practices create an
optimal state, whereby our systems
function more efficiently with
"increased mental clarity and brain
function". Those who habitually feel
and articulate gratitude perform
better, sleep better and see health
and relationship improvements.[9]

Health-wise, heart-health professor
Paul Mills from the University of
California surveyed 186 people with
heart conditions and discovered
that the more grateful participants
were also the happiest and healthiest
ones. On following up two months
later, blood tests revealed lower
inflammation and improved heart
health for those who had undertaken
a "gratitude journal" practice.[10]

Yet rather than seeking out things to *fix*, gratitude is the process of seeking out things to *appreciate*. And it works! Practising gratitude has been shown to be the most effective way to reprogram our negatively biased wiring. Gratitude biologically affects the brain and has been called "nature's antidepressant", given the way it boosts dopamine and oxytocin even more successfully than antidepressant drugs. Yes, gratitude is a simple, natural, yet tremendously effective way to lift your spirits and cultivate happiness.

Gratitude has the power to literally pull us from our downward spiral into an upward one; to take us from our future yearnings to our current blessings. But how can we flex our muscles of appreciation more readily?

Joy detectives

We've been wired to look out for, remember and react strongly to dangers in order to survive. So it makes sense that we should also train our brains to look out for, remember and react strongly to that which brings us joy, too. And while feeling grateful and expressing gratitude is important, the simple act of seeking and noticing the good is also effective.

But to really change our brains for the better, it's not enough to have – and enjoy – positive experiences; we need to sustain those positive experiences and grateful feelings and do what neuroscientist Rick Hanson calls "taking in the good".[11] The key lies not just in seeking and finding the good, but in sustained attention to what is good. As such, to have the greatest impact, gratitude is a four-step process:

1. Seek out the good. Look for it – notice it. Searching for the good has been proven to be as effective as finding and appreciating it.

2. Express gratitude. Be, and feel, grateful for the good that you've seen and found.

3. Savour feelings of appreciation. Stay with that appreciative feeling for longer than you ordinarily would. A good five or ten seconds longer of taking in the good will maximize its positive impact. Soak up the feelings that you experience in your body and mind, then turn up their volume, so that you feel and picture the gratitude sinking into and flowing through you.

4. Reminisce about those good moments and memories. Look back on them, share and reflect.

Above: An Indian girl at the festival of Holi which celebrates gratitude and thanksgiving for a good harvest, the joys of Spring and the triumph of love and goodness.

"Gratitude is a simple, natural yet tremendouly effective way to lift your spirit"

Appreciation interventions: practical actions to become more positive

Now let's explore in much greater detail how we can take each of those four gratitude steps and integrate them into our lives.

1. Seek out the good

Remembering to look for stuff to be thankful for is an important type of emotional intelligence, which numerous studies by university researchers into grey matter, synapses and brain activity have shown to bolster neuron density, making the nerve cells more proficient. This means that the more we look out for stuff to be grateful for and build our emotional intelligence, the more we flex our gratitude muscles and find that it takes less effort to be grateful.

- **Be curious.** This helps to stimulate brain cells, spark fresh ideas and develop neural pathways. So be open to learning, and ask questions such as "What if I…?" and "Why not?" to prompt your inquisitiveness. Curiosity has been shown to improve memory; and learning fuels self-esteem and inner growth. And try taking part in a curiosity-prompt photo challenge, such as #MyCuriousEyes, via https://www.curiosityinc.com. Participating helps train your eyes to pay more attention to your environment, before taking quick photos to share. Paying more attention is an important skill to hone, especially nowadays, when our attention is pulled in so many directions and is subsequently diluted.

- **Search for the good,** even when you feel there's nothing to be thankful for. The searching counts, too. Before you know it, you'll be more alert to the beauty in autumn colours, a child's giggle, the closeness you feel to someone, or the clean water and other good stuff that you might ordinarily have taken for granted.

- **Practise mindfulness.** Doing so enables us to slip from automatic gear into manual, so that we can really see and experience each moment with bright intensity, delight and wonder. (There is more on mindfulness in Chapter Thirteen.)

Opposite: Being a gratitude detective by noticing what there is to be grateful for and seeking out the good in every situation is an effective way to boost your wellbeing.

2. Express gratitude

- **Keep a gratitude journal.** Jot down three good things that went well today. Next, consider why those things happened. This will help you to focus on the actual sources of goodness, and on how each good thing made you feel. Some experts suggest gratitude-journalling daily. Others, such as researcher and author Sonya Lyubomirsky,[12] suggest playing around with the practice to see what works best for you, and to avoid it becoming repetitive and subsequently losing its power. If daily journalling becomes less effective, try doing it on a weekly or fortnightly basis instead. More than 500 participants of Martin Seligman's online "Authentic Happiness" website study (2005) who regularly recorded three good things reported that their moods improved, and they felt happier and less depressed, for up to six months after they began the intervention.[13]

- **Organize a gratitude visit.** According to Professor Martin Seligman, this is one of the most effective happiness-boosting exercises anyone can do.[14] Consider who has made a genuine difference to your life in some way – someone you've never properly thanked. If they live or work close enough for you to visit them, write a letter thanking them in detail for the specific positive impact they have had on your life. Arrange to visit them, without revealing your intention, and when you visit, read out your letter to them. As soon as you can, record how this experience made you feel.

Gratitude, recognition, acknowledgement and praise are a powerful combination.

- **Keep a gratitude jar.** Jot down experiences that you're grateful for in a single sentence on Post-it notes or scraps of paper. Do this either as they happen or at the end of each day, then pop them into a jar. This allows you to capture fleeting moments that will soon pass and could disappear from your memory.

- **Create a gratitude photo album** and/or a gratitude board to display on your wall.

Gather together photographs, pictures and words that provide a snapshot of moments, things, people and experiences you are grateful for, to serve as a powerful reminder of what you already have to appreciate.

- **Thank others well.** Whether you thank people in person or via email or text, in order to optimize your gratitude, tell the recipient specifically what you are thankful for, and describe how what they have done was beneficial to you. Acknowledge the consideration and effort they put in.

Above: Displaying images of people and places, moments and memories that you are grateful for serves as a reminder of what is good in life.

- **Be genuine.** Focus on what you are truly grateful for in this moment, rather than listing everything you think you ought to be grateful for, or that you feel guilty about taking for granted. For it is the genuine feeling of appreciation created by gratitude interventions that has the most impact. So look up and around you, and consider what makes you feel truly alive and thankful. Ponder on those genuine gratitude-inducers.

3. Savour feelings of appreciation

Savouring is a vital part of gratitude, as it helps us carve out positive memories that stay with us. "The problem with positive thinking is that it sometimes just stays up 'in the head' and fails to drip down to become a fully embodied experience,"[15] says Barbara Fredrickson. This is why neuroscientists suggest that we go deeper and savour our feelings of gratitude, to take our appreciation from our minds to our bodies and back to our minds again – thereby optimizing the experience. They have discovered that the longer we spend savouring good experiences and positive feelings, the more our neurons fire and wire together, to reshape our brains for the better.

To fully relish your reality, experts suggest that you focus your attention on your feelings of appreciation for as long as you can (at least ten seconds) and let those feelings sink deep into your body. Notice where in your body you feel that emotion. How does it feel? Savouring in this way installs the positive experience into your memory bank, whilst also giving your current wellbeing a healthy boost.

"Sometimes you will never know the true value of a moment until it becomes a memory."

ANONYMOUS

Right: Soaking up all that is good in our lives is a powerful contributor to happiness. We can savour the good by letting feelings of gratitude sink into our bodies.

- **Feel gratitude as well as writing it down.**
Focus on *feeling* gratitude rather than
just recording it. Take your gratitude
journal, letter, jar or display and read out
what you are grateful for. Then turn up
the volume on your emotion. Close your
eyes and *feel* that gratitude seeping
through you; *feel* your heart beating with
appreciation for what you have.

- **Go on a gratitude walk and recognize
sources of joy.** Pay attention to what you
can see, hear, smell and touch as you walk
– from the magnificence of the sky to the
smell of pine trees and a heartfelt smile.
Feel gratitude for everything you notice
on your walk, and take time to absorb why
you are grateful for it. How does it make
you feel? Why is it so beautiful? What is it
about that sky, that smell of pine trees or
that smile that delights you so? Studies
report that people who took savouring
gratitude walks each day for one week
significantly boosted their happiness levels
compared to those who walked as normal.

4. Reminisce about good moments and memories

The amount of attention we pay to our
happiest moments determines whether
that happy moment is amplified and
optimized, or fleeting and soon forgotten.
By first anticipating a happy event, then
savouring and enjoying it as it happens,
and finally recalling that happy memory
by reminiscing, we can amplify a solitary
magical moment and get the most from

the experiences we are grateful for. The
recollection of happy moments focuses our
attention on them and therefore enhances
them, giving them the chance to last longer
– milking them for every last drop of joy
available. Looking back at photographs that
captured happy times, sharing them with

others and reminiscing on happy memories boosts positive emotion.

Another way to use recollection to ramp up our level of gratitude is to use a method that psychologists call the "mental subtraction of positive events".[16]

Above: Taking a daily "gratitude walk", by considering all you are grateful for as you walk, has been proven to significantly boost happiness levels.

Be thankful that it happened

We take so much for granted as we get used to our current existence. Hence the phrase "You don't know what you've got till it's gone". As soon as something or someone is no longer there, we realize the strength of our appreciation for it or them. Rather than waiting until it's too late, try the exercise below, which uses the imagination to give you that realization while you still have the target of your gratitude:

1. Look back at happy memories, such as a job promotion or work achievement, the birth of a child or an exciting adventure, and consider the circumstances that helped make it happen.

2. Ponder how things might have turned out differently and imagine what your life might be like, had those positive events not happened.

3. Feel the overwhelming sense of gratitude that they did indeed happen.

Reminiscing about a positive event, with the added insight of imagining the absence of it, can really heighten how thankful we feel that it happened. It helps us to feel grateful for key parts of our life that we may otherwise start to take for granted and adapt to. Participants of this "mental-subtraction intervention" reportedly felt more gratitude than people who have reminisced on past happy events without picturing an absence.

To further amplify your feelings of gratitude through reminiscing:

• **Keep memories alive and provide opportunities to relive them.** Create photo-books, family adventure scrapbooks and memory boards; establish new family traditions of looking through them together at regular intervals.

• **Schedule monthly gratitude mornings.** Invest time in reflecting on all that you have. Read your gratitude journal and sift through the notes in your gratitude jar, so that you can revel in a feeling of luck, rather than of lack.

• **List your achievements as far back as you can.** A medal for netball when you were ten? 400-metre cup winner? Sponsored swim? Being made a sixer at Brownies, or a prefect at school? Getting *that* job? Having the guts to leave that job when you started your own business? Having the guts to leave that man when he treated you badly? Getting an award for something? Helping to nurture your child so that they won an award for something? Get it all down on paper and cherish all that you have achieved on your journey so far.

Above: As well as savouring what we have to appreciate while we still have it, imagining its absence can amplify our gratitude and stop us from taking it for granted.

You should be so lucky

Gratitude has many benefits, including the fact that being grateful makes us luckier. By raising our awareness about all that we have to be grateful for, we begin to see ourselves as blessed and lucky.

According to research by Richard Wiseman, Professor of the Public Understanding of Psychology at the University of Hertfordshire, this becomes a self-fulfilling prophecy, as we literally open our brains up to possibility. Following a 2003 study of 400 people,[17] Wiseman concluded that people's thoughts about how lucky they considered themselves to be, and their subsequent behaviour, determined much of their fortune. People who counted their blessings and considered themselves lucky had positive expectations. They created their own luck as they noticed more opportunities for good fortune, and were able to transform bad luck and rejection into good fortune and learning opportunities by adopting a resilient attitude (a direct result of their positive expectations).

So considering yourself lucky becomes a self-fulfilling prophecy. That's plenty to smile about.

Right: Feeling blessed can become a self-fulfilling prophecy. The more we count our blessings, the more we notice blessings to count and create our own luck.

Just smile

Talking of smiling, curving our mouths upward is another way to instantly boost positive emotion. Being smiled at also has a tremendous affect. According to Ron Gutman in his 2011 "TED Talk", "Smiling stimulates our brain reward mechanism in a way that even chocolate, a well regarded pleasure-inducer, cannot match."[18] And research by Hewlett Packard and Dr David Lewis reveals that "just one smile can generate the same level of brain stimulation as 2,000 bars of chocolate or receiving £16,000 in cash!"[19]

We smile in the womb. And a smile is a uniform expression across all humanity – the same in any language. And yet as we leave childhood, we smile less. While one third of us smile more than 20 times a day and laugh around 17 times, children smile as many as 400 times a day – the same number of times that they laugh.[20]

As we grow older, life may become more serious, but we can still strive to increase the amount we smile, even when we don't feel like smiling. For even fake smiling has the capacity to boost our happiness.

Smile for your health

The act of smiling makes us feel better, whether or not we experience the emotion behind the smile. Furthermore it's not only good for our wellbeing, but it's great for our health, too. Smiling can help reduce our stress-enhancing hormones like cortisol and adrenalin, and increase the level of mood-enhancing endorphins, while also reducing blood pressure.

> "Even the simulation of an emotion tends to arouse it in our minds."
>
> CHARLES DARWIN,
> ENGLISH NATURALIST

It's contagious, too, and according to a Swedish study, it's very difficult to frown when you're looking at a smiling face.[21] As well as having the power to brighten other people's days, smiling also enhances how positively others see you. And as smiles grow into laughter, it becomes even more beneficial, boosting immunity, lowering blood pressure and reducing anxiety.

Furthermore, when laughter takes place within a group of people, the number of endorphins released is enough to significantly increase people's pain threshold.

Opposite: Children smile more than adults but, as adults, we should endeavour to smile more. Smiling releases feel-good chemicals and reduces stress-inducing ones. And it's contagious too!

Give yourself a reason to smile

Sometimes we may struggle to notice how lucky we are, or even to find anything good. Despite that, we can choose to smile and to keep looking; we can also be more proactive by scheduling enjoyment into our lives.

If you've been struggling to find the good, create some: source your own satisfaction. Rather than catching up with paperwork or chores on a day off, your time could be better spent doing three enjoyable activities:

- **Do something on your own that you enjoy,** where you are likely to lose track of time – be it dancing to music, meditating or reading a book.

- **Do something meaningful,** such as volunteering your time, donating to a charity shop, helping a neighbour or friend with something they're struggling with.

- **Do something with people you enjoy spending time with.** You could meet up for lunch, go out for a bike ride or visit an art gallery together.

Psychiatric patients with suicidal thoughts who took part in this exercise reported, in a 2014 study, that they felt less hopelessness and more optimism as a direct result.[22]

Sometimes we really do need to create our own sunshine and, by doing three smile-inducing activities that are linked to the core "pillars of wellbeing", we can give ourselves plenty to be grateful for.

Left: What we choose to do with our time impacts our happiness. Dancing and listening to music is a great smile-inducing activity.

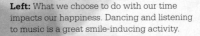

GOALS AND GROWTH

"The grand essentials to happiness in this life are something to do, something to love, and something to hope for."

JOSEPH ADDISON, ENGLISH ESSAYIST AND POLITICIAN

Why accomplishment matters

Goals, like purpose, give us focus: targets at which to aim, enabling us to direct our energies toward a specific achievement via inspired action. This is the definition of accomplishment, which is, according to positive psychologists, one of the six "pillars of wellbeing" (see Chapter Four), leading to a flourishing life.

Rather than aimlessly ambling through our lives, goals give us the chance to become the archer with targets in sight; the author of our own story, with a storyboard mapped out. And while we may sometimes miss the targets or find that life delivers its own unexpected plot twists, if we approach our goals as steps in the right direction and use failures as learning opportunities, our goals will feed our growth.

Indeed, given how little control we have over our lives during childhood, autonomy in adulthood is pleasing. By considering what matters to us, then accordingly setting and working toward goals, we can approach our lives with a satisfying sense of control.

"If you want to live a happy life, tie it to a goal, not to people or things."

ALBERT EINSTEIN, GERMAN-BORN THEORETICAL PHYSICIST

Right: Achievement is a core pillar of wellbeing because aiming for targets gives life a sense of purpose and direction and helps us to grow.

Decisions and direction

As a result of deciding precisely where to devote our energy, rather than drifting astray, we gain clarity over uncertainty and our lives can become more meaningful. This purposeful approach to living induces positive emotion because we've made a decision and we're in the driving seat of our lives.

Our neural circuitry likes both decision-making and destination-setting:

- **Making decisions and setting intentions** have been shown to positively engage the pre-frontal cortex, calm the limbic system and overcome activity of the striatum, which influences movement and balance. The combination of these factors pulls us away from negative impulses and reduces our anxiety.

- **Being in the driving seat** means knowing where we are heading, so that we are better able to enjoy the journey, rather than aimlessly driving in all directions, not knowing which is the right path or where we might end up.

  Feeling in control, rather than in chaos, reduces stress and increases pleasure simultaneously. This is because deciding to take action toward achieving a goal releases dopamine (see Chapter Seven). So we feel better when our decisions lead to good stuff happening rather than when this happens simply by chance or obligation.

The benefits of voluntary action

This explains why it can be tough to motivate ourselves to visit the gym or make decisions that we feel we *ought* to be making, but aren't making voluntarily. When we voluntarily decide to do something that results in a positive effect, our brains get a boost of pleasure. Conversely, when we do something because we feel obliged to do it or are forced to do it, we may feel stress. And when a positive effect occurs by chance, with no direct link to an action we have chosen to take, we feel nothing.

This also explains why accomplishment is a "pillar of wellbeing". Choosing to set goals and take action to achieve them is a pleasurable experience. The converse is also true, because having no aims in life – or not bothering to try and achieve them – can leave us feeling bereft and disappointed.

Opposite: Choosing a desired destination gives us control over moving forward in the right direction, whatever obstacles may get in our way.

Dreams unfulfilled

Time flies. And so, without any goals (or without trying to achieve anything), we can feel as if life is passing us by. Indeed, unfulfilled dreams can be a cause for regret when we reach the end of our lives, as recorded by Australian palliative-care nurse Bronnie Ware in her book, *Top Five Regrets of the Dying*.

"When people realize that their life is almost over and look back clearly on it, it is easy to see how many dreams have gone unfulfilled," says Ware. "Most people had not honoured even a half of their dreams and had to die knowing that it was due to choices they had made, or not made. Health brings a freedom very few realize, until they no longer have it."[1]

On the contrary, we end up thriving when we are striving toward something. But what about "the hedonic treadmill" (see Chapter Two) and adaptation? Doesn't it suggest that we ought to focus more on what we already have, rather than constantly strive for more? The truth is that in order to optimize our happiness, gratitude and growth go hand-in-hand.

Right: Life can pass us by without a dream to pursue. It's important to pause sufficiently to appreciate now, whilst also having something to strive towards.

Balancing gratitude and growth

Working toward goals brings meaning to our lives, while reaching them brings accomplishment. Yet in order to flourish, both gratitude for what we already have and growth toward that which we hope to achieve are of equal importance. Balancing both allows us to enjoy the journey.

When our intentions and hopes come from a place of contentment, they have far more power than when they come from a place of lack. Thriving with intention always trumps striving in desperation. Hence the importance of cultivating gratitude in our lives as a foundation from which to dream.

On the one hand, it's important to have a clear vision of what we'd like to accomplish during our lifetime, as this spurs us on and gives our lives purpose and meaning. Meanwhile, intentional action toward such a vision becomes a yardstick for measuring our growth. Hence "meaning" and "accomplishment" are two of the six "pillars of wellbeing" (see Chapter Four).

The joy of the journey

Striving to achieve things only becomes problematic if we stop enjoying the journey toward it. It's time to redress the balance, if our fixation on future gratification reduces our pleasure within the present – if we find

"Striving to achieve things only become problematic if we stop enjoying the journey toward it."

ourselves focusing so intently on the end result that we forget to cherish our current contentment. The "I'll be happy when..." fallacy simply postpones happiness, in lieu of achievement; especially given how quickly the novelty wears off, once we've grown accustomed to what we've achieved.

Opposite: Balance is one of the most important contributors to happiness. Balance between appreciating what we have and growing towards what we hope to achieve is key.

Our flourishing garden

Thankfully, we can offset adaptation by creating an environment of growth; by tending to our dreams, just as we might water our plants – enjoying them not only once they blossom, but also while they (and we) grow.

"Happiness is neither virtue nor pleasure nor this thing nor that, but simply growth. We are happy when we are growing."

WILLIAM BUTLER YEATS, IRISH POET

Gardeners don't wait until every flower is in full bloom to enjoy their gardens. They delight in each new bud and cherish the time they spend tending to each blossom, step-by-step. Similarly, we shouldn't wait until we've achieved our goals to enjoy our lives. Instead, let's delight in each small step we take toward bringing our goals to fruition, for each little action has meaning and significance and is worth celebrating immediately.

The planting cycle

Let us stop and smell the roses, then keep watering them; marvel at their growth, then enjoy the floral tapestry in full bloom before the petals begin to wither. Then, with each new season, plant fresh seeds and tend them, too. This is the process to enable flourishing.

In this way, our life is a flourishing garden and our goals are like flowers or vegetables planted within it. With our intentions we plant seeds and, with each action, we water those seeds so that they may grow and blossom. As the flowers bloom and we harvest the vegetables, we feel a wonderful sense of accomplishment. Presently the petals fall off the flowers and the garden looks bare, so we plant new seeds and tend them, so that our garden (and our lives) may continue to flourish.

Opposite: Stopping to smell the roses along our entire flourishing journey is crucial: from idea to accomplishment, from seeds of intention to blossoming dreams in full bloom.

How to relish the path to achieving your goals

Reaching our destination by achieving our goals offers a great sense of achievement, which boosts our wellbeing for a while, until it fades. As such, the vital part of striving to achieve is the actual process of working toward it. It's the steps taken, the small actions carried out and seeing the value in them that counts. It is the journey that nourishes our wellbeing, so try the following suggestions:

- **Reward yourself** along the way for mini-milestones.

- **Celebrate the meaning** and sense of direction that having goals gives you.

- **Revel in the anticipation** of achievement.

- **Remain grateful.** Cherish your current reality and stop to smell those roses.

Of course before you can enjoy the journey, you need to know where you are heading and map out how to get there.

Defining the destination: where do you want to go and why?

Our goals are anchored in hope, in what we desire and wish to achieve in our lives. So how do we tap into those hopes, in order to travel in a direction that aligns with them?

1. Figure out which parts of your life require some growth. You can use a "wheel of life" approach to establish which life areas need the most attention, giving a mark out of ten for work, finances, personal environment, personal growth, health, love, family and friends, fun and recreation. Then consider what a "10/10" might look like for each, and what you might be able to do to increase your rating of those life areas.

Alternatively, you could figure out which "good life buckets" to fill. For example, as Jonathan Fields says in his book *How To Live a Good Life*, vitality, connection and contribution are the three areas that constitute a good life.[2] Each can be considered to be a bucket, which needs to be constantly topped up. If the level in one of these buckets goes down, this affects your ability to live a good life. You need all three buckets to really thrive:

- **Vitality** includes meditation, activity, food and sleep.

"Considering what effect the goal will have on your life, and why it's important, makes you more committed to it"

- **Connection** includes self-awareness, family and friends, community and nature.

- **Contribution** includes your "actionable values" and how you might bring them to life in the service of others.

Once you know which of your buckets needs attention, you can set your goals accordingly in order to fill them. (We'll be exploring all three in the following chapters.)

Opposite: Knowing where we hope to head in life and what happiness looks like for us can help us figure out which areas of life might need a little attention.

2. Assess what matters most to you.

Consider the following:

- What would you wish for, if money/time/experience were no object and successful achievement of your goal was guaranteed?

- What would you wish for if you knew you might – and probably would – fail? Would you still go ahead and try anyway, because trying and failing would be better than never trying?

Your answers to these questions will reveal what you most hope to achieve in life and what you can't *not* do.

3. Consider what makes you feel envious or inspired.

Often envy occurs when we see someone with something we want to have. It's a completely natural negative emotion, but it can serve a purpose in alerting us to areas in our life that we'd like to change or improve, and to what we might wish to achieve. Sometimes, rather than feeling envious, we feel inspired, by a lifestyle, a job role, a relationship, an individual's character traits or style. Both envious and inspired feelings give us clues as to what we hope for, and are worth noting.

Opposite: Considering what we might do if success were guaranteed (or if failure were likely, but we'd still be keen to do it) can help uncover what matters most to us.

4. Work out your motivation and the emotional trigger behind your aims.

The value of your goals is an important factor affecting goal commitment.[3] Considering what effect the goal will have on your life, and why it's important, makes you more committed to it. For example, Nick Grantham, Performance Enhancement Specialist and former coach of Great Britain's basketball team, says of their reason for competing, "It's never just to win, it's to fulfil a dream, like making their family proud or overcoming adversity."[4]

Consider why you hope to achieve your goal. What would attaining it give you? A sense of warmth and belonging? A feeling of security? The ability to impress family and friends? Pride and confidence in yourself and your abilities? Peace of mind? Your motivation shapes why this goal is so important to you, but also gives you a plan B. If you are unable to achieve your goal within the timescale you planned for, there may be other ways to create the same feelings.

For instance, if your goal is to save for a deposit on your dream home and your "why" is to give you those feelings of warmth, security, pride, peace of mind and belonging, by listing other ways you can feel those feelings right now (such as joining a community group, moving your furniture around to feel more homely, stocking up on candles and cushions to create a more *hygge* home) you can enjoy the journey and experience similar feelings that attainment of your goal would provide.

Goal-setting 101

Goals tend to be about increasing, decreasing or improving something by carrying out certain actions. Specificity is the key. So having assessed what matters most to you, having considered the areas of your life that you wish to improve and having focused on what is motivating you to make these changes, it's important to set goals in the right way to give yourself the best chance of success.

When we achieve our goals, especially challenging ones, our belief in our abilities and our performance improves. So it's in our best interests to give ourselves the greatest chance of achieving them. Here's how:

1. Set SMART – Specific, Measurable, Attainable, Realistic and Timely – goals.
To have the best chance of achieving our goals, research reveals that they should be specific and challenging, rather than vague and subjective. For example, "Do ten press-ups a day and increase by three press-ups per week" is better than "Lose weight". Similarly, "Organize a fortnightly get-together with my favourite people" is better than "Improve relationships".

• **Specific goals** are clearly defined and vague goals that lack specificity, such as "doing my best", "increasing income" or "losing weight", are harder to achieve and more likely to cause procrastination. Participants in one German study, which involved 120 people solving brainstorming tasks under different group goal conditions, revealed that they were more likely to meet goals when those goals were specific rather than vague.[6]

• **Measurable goals** enable us to know precisely when we've achieved them, when we need to persevere further in order to attain them and how far away we are from completion.

• **Attainable goals** are reachable, taking the skills, resources and time required in which to achieve them.

• **Realistic goals** are sufficiently challenging to make them worthwhile but realistic enough to successfully achieve.

Right: Dreaming big and flying high gives us something significant to aim for. This gives us a sense of direction, while accomplishment bolsters our self-belief and confidence.

- **Timely goals** should have time-specific target deadlines and be measurable, to enable focus. In this way, it is clear how you will achieve your goal through the actions you take, and it is easy to know when you have achieved that goal or how far you have to go until you do so.

2. Frame goals using positive terminology.
This makes them "approach goals" rather than "avoidance goals". For example, turn "Stop eating junk food" into "Eat healthy food, including five portions of fruit or vegetables each day". Goals should be framed in the positive because, according to author and coach Caroline Adams Miller who has studied eating disorders for decades, approaching a goal in this way uses less mental energy than avoiding it.

3. Set goals that balance attainability and ability.
Goals can cause anxiety if they are beyond your ability, and boredom if they are below it. So goals should balance your skills and should be realistic.

Mapping out how to reach your desired destination

Once you know your intended destination, you need to plot a map of your goals and the steps you need to take in order to reach them.

"A journey of a thousand miles begins with a single step."

LAO TZU, ANCIENT CHINESE PHILOSOPHER

- **Set the goal: write your intentions down.** Get your goals down on paper, to clarify your destination. If we keep our intentions inside us, they can't grow. Only when we plant them, like seeds, and tend to them, like seedlings, can we expect them to flourish.

- **Break the goal into small stepping stones.** Develop an action plan, listing the step-by-step sequence toward your goal, with clear deadlines. Define what you will do and when, to get you from where you are now to where you wish to be. This process simplifies your goal and makes it more likely to be achieved. Breaking up goals in this way motivates the unconscious mind to accomplish them, as the emotional part of the brain prefers small, easy actions that provide immediate feedback. And if you create mini-celebrations as you take each step successfully, you'll enjoy the journey even more.

Opposite: Figuring out the steps to take on our journey toward our goals gives us a clear plan of action to work from.

How to achieve your goals

Dreams remain in your head, or on the page, until you take action. Those seeds need watering. So once you know where you're heading and have created a route map to get you there, it's time to move. Taking active steps toward your destination – even one small step – means that you are heading in the right direction rather than standing still.

You are much more likely to achieve the goals you set yourself if you:

- **Write a self-contract to seal your commitment to the goal.** According to a behaviour modification study in *Creating Your Best Life: The Ultimate Life List Guide* by Caroline Adams Miller and Michael B Frisch, participants who wrote a contract were more 86 per cent more likely to meet their goal, and students who contracted to complete all assignments did more work than students who didn't.[6] (For a template of a goal self-contract, see page 211.)

- **Set primers to support your goal.** "Primers" are cues or reminders that are paired with your goal, to create a change in behaviour and keep the goal fresh in your mind. They act as stimuli to impact upon your behaviour. For example, a charm bracelet or well-worded password; a Post-it note on the fridge; a book beside the bed; workout gear on a bedside chair; meditation bells next to the coffee; vision boards or screensavers. Researchers have

found that our unconscious reaction to external cues directs the majority of our activity,[7] so words, scents and sights can have a significant impact upon how likely we are to take specific actions. An example of this is provided by Adams Miller and Frisch in *Creating Your Best Life*,[8] when students seated next to a scent of lemon cleaner were more likely to clean up the crumbs of the intentionally crumbly biscuit they had been given than were those students without any scent nearby. In another study, performance was enhanced after seeing an image of a runner crossing a finishing line and winning a race.

- **Create implementation intentions to help prevent pitfalls.** "Implementation intentions" are statements outlining what you will do, should a pitfall arise. To use them, you simply consider what pitfalls might arise during your journey toward your goal and set out the response, ahead of the situation arising. This method of reframing negative possibilities into positive ones can triple the likelihood of challenging

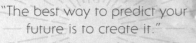

"The best way to predict your future is to create it."

ABRAHAM LINCOLN, AMERICAN STATESMAN AND LAWYER

goals being achieved, and uses far less energy (and willpower).[9] For instance, "If I feel hungry after 9pm, I will have a herbal tea." Or "If I ignore my alarm clock for meditation practice, I will sit up in bed and list all the benefits of meditation, as written on a notepad on my bedside table."

- **Share goals and report progress.** Accountability reduces our excuses and reminds us that other people care. Consequently, having someone to hold us accountable can make us 243 per cent more likely to achieve our goals.[10] If nobody knows that we are *not* taking the steps we're meant to be taking, it's easier not to bother. Being answerable to someone else is a motivating factor.

Right: Setting goals is important, but it is the process of working towards them and then achieving them, which has the most impact on our wellbeing.

Self-fulfilling prophecy

This method of affirmation has repeatedly worked for me. In 2003 I affirmed my goals of having a bestselling book and of meeting Dame Anita Roddick. My *Small Business Start-Up Workbook* was published two years later, with a foreword written by Roddick after I not only met her, but ended up working for her, too. In 2013, within the pages of my *Flourish Handbook*, I affirmed that I would buy my dream home by the end of 2014. We moved in at the end of November that year.

- **Affirm goals in the present tense.** This may seem "woo-woo", but stating goals as if they've already been achieved is a way to use the neuroplasticity of the brain (see Chapter Six) to our advantage. Every time we repeat our affirmed goals, the neural pathways around that thought strengthen into a belief. For example, I might affirm: "My book is a global bestseller and has sold hundreds of thousands of copies by the end of 2020."

- **Reward yourself.** Whenever we achieve a target, a pat on the back is important. But so too is planning for a future reward. Just as planning a holiday induces happiness almost as much as going on one, due to the sense of anticipation it affords us with,[11] so planning the rewards you'll give yourself when you accomplish your goals can provide a significant spike in your happiness and motivation levels. You can even set primers (see above) to remind you about those rewards, and to help you enjoy – rather than endure – the journey toward achievement.

- **See failure as feedback and go again.** When you don't achieve what you set out to, you learn. That's useful because, in learning, we grow. This is why there's no such thing as failure, unless we fail to learn from our mistakes, which can always be rectified by trying again. Successful inventors are testament to this notion that their successes are attributed to as much as "99 per cent failure". From Eddison to Dyson, the ability to galvanize oneself and learn from those failures ultimately leads to success – which wouldn't have happened without the lessons learned from the mistakes made en route.

Right: Our brains are powerful tools. When we affirm, imagine and then picture ourselves achieving our goals, our brain perceives this as having happened.

- **Visualize achieving your goal.**
  Visualization takes place in the cerebral cortex – the same area where our thinking, language and problem-solving happens. For this reason, the brain can't tell the difference between what it thinks about and what it sees, so it reacts to *visualized* images as though they are real.

"The ability to galvanize oneself and learn from those failures ultimately leads to success"

The power of visualization

When we imagine something we fear, our heart rate quickens as if we were facing that fear for real; the same is true when we visualize something positive. So seeing our desired future in our mind's eye, as if it's already happening, is a powerful exercise – especially if we also focus on how we might feel once we've accomplished our goal.

When we vividly picture ourselves enjoying our achievements, we gain confidence, feel positive and show our brain that it's possible. To the brain, our achievement becomes real. So if your goal is to buy your dream home, create a mental picture-and-emotion combination: see yourself living there, enjoying coffee in the kitchen or watching your family play in the garden; and feel the emotion that accompanies the image. If your goal is to write a book, picture yourself walking into your local bookshop and seeing your book on the shelf; pick it up and feel the cover; experience the emotions you would feel, should that be true.

Visualization is a great motivator. It excites us about our goal and opens us up to opportunities around us that may help bring it to fruition. Scientifically, visualization works because it:

- **Activates the placebo effect,** because we become more confident in the possibility of our goal, which primes us for action.

- **Activates the attention bias,** by deepening awareness concerning whatever supports our belief about achieving the goal.

- **Induces positive emotions** more than verbally discussing the goal does.[12]

There are three ways to maximize the positive effects of visualization:

1. **Visualize the process of achievement as much as the outcome.** Scientific studies by Shelly Taylor from the University of California (1999) have revealed that we should use both outcome visualization (seeing the end result of our achievements) and process visualization (seeing ourselves

Above: Seeing yourself in your mind's eye moving in to your dream home can make it more likely to happen, as visualization is a great motivator and possibility generator.

working toward the goal) in order to maximize the benefits of visualization.[13] After all, we still need to put in the effort. So in addition to picturing yourself in your dream home, see yourself viewing the house and making an offer, shopping for furniture and carrying out the tasks that provided you with the deposit. And in addition to picturing yourself with your book published, see yourself signing the contract and submitting chapters to your publisher. Visualize the process just as much as the final outcome.

2. Create a vision board as a primer, to capture what your vision looks like. Get a load of magazines and cut out images that appeal to your vision. Gather photos or graphics of sunshine, beaches, or homewares that symbolize your dream home. Include images that capture your dreams, goals and purpose, and also things that make you smile. Pin it in a place where you will look at it frequently.

3. Visualize your best possible self, where everything is going as well as it possibly could and you have achieved all you set out to achieve. See yourself literally living the dream. Then *write* about it: when you wake up, what do you see? What do you do next? What's for breakfast? Then what? How do you spend your morning, lunchtime, afternoon and evening? Describe what you are doing, who you are with and how it makes you feel. Get specific. Write non-stop for a few minutes about what you see, feel,

hear and smell. *Picture* your future desk and examine your environment. What colours catch your eye? What sounds? Breathe in your surroundings. Now focus on what you're doing: Who is there with you? Why are you smiling? What are you enjoying? Imagine yourself telling someone else how proud you feel about achieving this goal. See your success. Feel it.

Goal self-contract

My specific goal is to: _____ by _____

Action steps include: _____

_____

_____

_____

_____

I will measure my progress and reward myself to celebrate my wins.

I will use the following primers: _____

_____

_____

_____

I will share my goals with: _____

_____

_____

_____

I want to achieve this goal because: _____

_____

_____

_____

This is my commitment contract to myself.

Signed _____

Dated _____

The benefits of accomplishment

Accomplishment isn't just about providing us with what we hoped for. As we know, the happy feelings arising from it don't last long. Accomplishment earns its place as a "pillar of wellbeing" due to the many other benefits it provides us with.

Accomplishment boosts our self-esteem and our self-efficacy, as goal-achievement gives us greater awareness of what our strengths are, which boosts our belief in our abilities. This, in turn, helps us to see tough tasks as challenges to be mastered rather than feared. Additionally, the process of celebrating and savouring our wins helps us to become our own cheerleaders – an important role for us to assume in life – to encourage ourselves to participate fully in every moment and to grow.

"You are never too old to set another goal or to dream a new dream."

C S LEWIS, BRITISH WRITER

Opposite: We can become our own cheerleaders by celebrating and savouring our accomplishments. Such achievements help us to boost our belief in ourselves and our capabilities.

NOURISHED BY NATURE

"Climb the mountains and get their good
tidings. Nature's peace will flow into you
as sunshine flows into trees. The winds
will blow their own freshness into you,
and the storms their energy."

JOHN MUIR, SCOTTISH-AMERICAN NATURALIST AND AUTHOR

Mother Nature nurtures

The wilderness does wonders for our wellbeing. The mind-clearing, life-affirming power of nature has long been explored, from Henry David Thoreau's 1854 book *Walden; or, Life in the Woods* to more recent scientific evidence. All of these clearly conclude that spending time outdoors in nature makes us happier and healthier.

There is a delicious duality in the restorative effect of nature, which both invigorates and relaxes us; stimulates and soothes us; and lifts us up and calms us down. Immersion in nature engages our senses, giving us an increased feeling of "aliveness" and a strong sense of wellness. It also induces feelings of awe.

Just as essential to our vitality as sleep or meditation, exposure to nature has the capacity to improve our creativity, our attention span and our energy levels. It can even enhance our ability to connect with others and our tendency toward kindness. The natural world also diminishes stress, reduces anxiety and improves our brains and bodies. If nature were a drug, it would be a wonder drug, such is its healing power.

Flourishing fact

Researchers in Finland discovered that just 20 minutes outside in natural environments, rather than urban ones,[1] has the power to lift mood, open the mind, improve memory and catalyse creativity. As we breathe in the fresh air and soak up the sights, sounds and smells of our natural environment, the positive impact that nature has on our brains and behaviour is profound.

Opposite: Being outdoors in nature has a profound impact on our wellbeing. Rivers, mountains, woodland and green space restores, heals and engages us. Nature makes us feel better.

Tree glee: the tonic of forests

The Japanese practice of *shinrin-yoku*, or "forest bathing", involves making a connection to nature by combining the presence of trees with mindful breathing and walking. The practice is so beneficial to health and wellbeing that this ancient tradition has been part of a national public-health programme in Japan since 1982; it is now a national pastime.

Scientific evidence from a study by the Centre for Environment, Health and Field Sciences in Japan's Chiba University has shown that forest bathing reduces blood pressure, heart rate and cortisol production, whilst boosting the immune system and levels of wellbeing.[2] As such, nature is not just incredibly good for our physical and mental health; it's also a veritable feast of wonderful goodness.

No wonder the Wildlife Trust in the UK is advocating a Nature and Wellbeing Act, to encourage investment in nature, "because wildlife and wild places need it, and because our health, wellbeing and prosperity depend upon it".[3]

But why exactly is nature so good for us, and how does immersing ourselves in it make us feel happier and healthier? As we shall explore below, nature has the power to:

- **Protect and boost our physical health**

- **Protect and boost our mental health**

- **Spark our creativity and boost our performance.**

So let's explore the nourishment of nature in more detail.

Opposite: Nature nourishes us. Specifically "forest bathing", mindful walking among trees, has been proven to have many health benefits.

Protecting and boosting our physical health

Natural outdoor settings impact on our wellness in all kinds of ways. First, trees and other plants give our immune system a boost.

Our immune system is our inbuilt defender, protecting our body from infection and illness by destroying any disease-causing bacteria, viruses and parasites – that is, cells it doesn't recognize. When we breathe in fresh forest air, we inhale essential oils called "phytoncides" that are emitted by trees, plants and some fruit and vegetables. Trees emit phytoncides to protect themselves from parasites, insects and germs and yet, in doing so, they also help to bolster our nervous system and improve our immune-system function.

So not only do trees provide us with the air we need to breathe, but according to a 2009 study by a Tokyo medical school,[4] they also boost our natural killer-cell activity for up to a month after we have visited woodlands. These cells are linked to cancer prevention and immune-system functionality. After a $4 million investigation by Japanese officials into these and other benefits of forest bathing, 48 *shinrin-yoku* trails were developed in Japan to maximize the healing power of our natural world.

Enhancing vitality

In addition to powering up our body's protection against illness and boosting our resistance to infection, being around natural elements has been shown to enhance our vitality, too – even after taking into consideration the vitality-inducing effects of physical activity and social interaction that can arise while out in nature.

For example, in a study carried out on undergraduates for the *Journal of Environmental Psychology*,[5] in which the participants were led at the same pace on a 15-minute walk, half on a tree-lined path along a river, and the other half on a 15-minute underground walk through tunnels, those walking in nature had significantly higher vitality-change scores. Their baseline state vitality scores were measured using a 7-item "Subjective Vitality Scale" where participants were asked how vital, energetic, energized and alert they felt. Similar results were achieved from a green-walk-in-nature vs shopping-centre-walk study, carried out in 2007 by the mental-health charity Mind UK. "The green walk left 53 per cent of people

surveyed feeling more vigorous whereas 45 per cent of respondents felt less vigorous after the shopping centre walk."[6]

So walking in nature works. It invigorates and energizes us more than walking anywhere else for the same length of time and at the same pace. This explains why regular outdoor breaks are important for both children and adults, and why outdoor learning has been proven to boost concentration. Some studies, such as those

Above: When walking through woodland, we breathe in the essential oils released by trees which boosts our immune and nervous system.

carried out by researchers at Uppsala University in Sweden, have shown that nature can significantly restore attention deficits that arise from overwork or over-concentration, and can enable people to think more clearly.[7] Outdoor learning has even been shown to help raise standardized test scores.[8]

The power of wow!

According to University of California, Berkeley research, another factor that impacts on our immune system is awe, which positively affects healthier, lower levels of core inflammatory proteins known as "cytokines".[9] These cue the immune system to work harder, and may explain the effects of forest walks on health, given that walking through woodland has the capacity to inspire awe.

Indeed, awe is a powerful and intense emotional response, which is defined in the dictionary as "rapt attention caused by the sight of something extraordinary".[10] The unexpected beauty of natural wonders represents one of the most prevalent promoters of awe – glorious sunsets, panoramic views, magnificent skies and magical forests all inspire feelings of awe within us. In doing so, recent research carried out by the University of California, reveals that awe inspired by nature not only helps to protect our physical health, but can also boost "cognition, interpersonal perception and social behaviour"[11]. And as if improving our physical health, mental health and cognitive ability wasn't enough, experiencing awe from natural environments may also help us to be more kind, trusting and generous.

Nature as a promoter of trust and generosity

The level of trust and generosity that participants displayed whilst playing two economics games has been measured in a series of experiments at the University of California, Berkeley. Those who were exposed to beautiful, awe-inspiring scenes of nature before playing the games experienced increased positive emotion and subsequently behaved in a more trusting and generous manner, compared to those who saw less beautiful scenes.[12]

In another study at the University, those who looked upward to stare at a row of tall trees for one minute "experienced measurable increases in awe, demonstrated more helpful behaviour and approached moral dilemmas more ethically", in comparison with those who stared up at

a tall building for the same duration of time.[13] Researchers have concluded that this greater tendency to helpfulness is due to the corresponding notion of being inspired by something bigger than ourselves. Such feelings can lead to an increase in "prosocial behaviours".[14]

Such is the power of nature to induce positive behaviour that it has resulted in

Above: Awe is a special positive emotion. Marvelling at extraordinary sights can positively impact our kindness, happiness and thoughtfulness.

a whole field of treatment for improving mental health and lifting people out of debilitating depression, as we shall explore below. This moves away from the "medical model" toward the "wellness model", is accessible to all and costs nothing.

Protecting and boosting mental health

The discovery that forests and open countryside, parks and allotments, gardens and beaches are therapeutic landscapes has led to the rise of eco-therapy – treatment programmes that aim to improve mental and physical wellbeing by connecting us with nature.

Such landscapes foster mental wellness and engage the parasympathetic nerve system ("rest-and-digest") rather than the sympathetic nerve system ("fight-or-flight", see Chapter Five)). Consequently, outdoor natural environments help to lower stress, diminish depression and alleviate anxiety – the three main issues that affect our mental health. As such, nature has been found to be a natural (and free) antidepressant.

In 2015, 61 million antidepressant prescriptions were written in England, at a cost of £285 million,[15] up from 27.7 million such prescriptions ten years beforehand.[16] But eco-therapy – a free and accessible treatment with no side-effects – offers a natural and cost-effective addition to existing treatments. Bearing in mind that (according to the World Health Organization) one in four people suffer from mental-health problems, this is a notable consideration.[17]

Below: Eco-therapy has been proven to improve both mental and physical wellbeing by tapping into the healing qualities of nature.

Meeting the PERMA-V model

Getting out into nature more often is so good for our mental wellbeing that certain types of eco-therapy tick every single box of the PERMA-V "six pillars of wellbeing" model (see Chapter Four)! We've already seen how "green exercise", by means of outdoor walks in nature, can bolster energy and impact upon our vitality, compared to indoor walks (see page 220). However, depending on what activities we undertake outdoors, the benefits can be even more substantial.

For example, carrying out conservation or voluntary work in a group setting, while

Above: Group gardening or conservation work ticks all six boxes of wellbeing, providing positive emotions and engagement, improving relationships and vitality and providing meaning and accomplishment.

working toward shared goals, facilitates social connections, provides a source of meaning and purpose, gives participants a sense of accomplishment and brings people together, thereby improving social bonding. As such, these outdoor activities tick the "Relationships", "Meaning" and "Accomplishment" boxes of the PERMA-V model. Furthermore, given that we are more likely to experience a sense of flow

and intense engagement of our senses while enjoying nature, the "Engagement" box can also be ticked, as is the "Vitality" box, given that moving in nature makes us feel more energized.

Perhaps the most profoundly impacted contributor to happiness, though, is the "Positive emotion" box, as being in nature activates many emotions (including awe, gratitude and joy). And this is the pillar of wellbeing that has the greatest impact on mental health. By providing a restorative environment in which people can recharge, green space improves psychological health and mental wellbeing, provides a buffer from depression and anxiety, and improves mood.

Proof positive

Recent studies, described below, prove once and for all that nature is a clinically

Above: Green exercise, from cycling to canal boating, has been proven to decrease negative emotions and boost self-esteem.

valid treatment for improving mental health. For example:

• A Japanese study by the Centre for Environment, Health and Field Sciences in Japan's Chiba University, which compared biometrics of participants who spent a day in the city and those who enjoyed a 30-minute visit to a forest, revealed those who enjoyed the forest-bathing activity measured "lower concentrations of cortisol, lower pulse rate, lower blood pressure, greater parasympathetic nerve activity, and lower sympathetic nerve activity".[18]

• Multiple studies comparing "green" nature walks in varied landscapes (such as woodlands, grasslands, lakes and urban parks) with tree-free urban street walks in city centres (by Swedish researcher Terry Hartig[19], or indoor walks in shopping centres (by MindUK),[20] arrived at the same conclusion: participants walking in nature showed significantly lower depression, perceived stress, blood pressure (72–94%) and rumination. These walks also positively impacted a number of mood factors[21] and cognitive measures, such as short-term memory and performance ability.

- Studies by the University of Essex, which measured the effects of various green exercise activities, from cycling and horse riding to canal boating and conservation,[22] found participants to be significantly less angry, depressed, confused and tense, with higher levels of self-esteem and positive emotion. In addition, as a result of the green exercise, 94 per cent of those surveyed by MindUK felt an improvement to their mental health.[23]

- Studies of 4,529 Dutch respondents to the second Dutch National Survey of General Practice revealed that green space can act "as a buffer between stressful life events and health",[24] having explored how people living with a large amount of green space within a 3-km (1¾-mile) radius were "less affected by experiencing a stressful life event, had less health complaints and better physical and mental health than respondents with a low amount of green space in this radius".[25]

Flourishing fact

We know the health benefits of nature because of the firm scientific evidence from a wide array of classic eco-therapy studies that have taken place over the past few decades. In the 1980s studies carried out by environmental psychologists revealed that post-operative hospital patients with views of trees recovered far quicker, with less medication, than those whose rooms overlooked a brick wall.[26] And studies in Michigan have shown how prisoners in cells overlooking trees and farmland had 24 per cent fewer sick visits than those in cells facing the prison yard.[27]

Inside / outside benefits

Evidently, we respond well to nature – whether we're immersed in it outside, walking through it briefly or even just surrounded by images of it. For instance, patients in a 2003 hospital study who were shown an image of a natural landscape, while listening to nature sounds of birdsong and a babbling brook, demonstrated 50 per cent higher pain control than other patients who hadn't been shown the nature images.[28] And in a laboratory experiment by Roger Ulrich, co-founding director of the Center for Health Systems and Design at Texas

AM University, participants who were shown film footage of nature, following a stress-inducing movie, recovered quicker than those who watched film footage of urban settings.[29]

Furthermore, according to research by University of Wales Trinity Saint David (UWTSD) academics, low-impact eco-therapy activities, such as indoor gardening, instilled feelings of positivity, hope and control in cancer patients who had cultivated and cared for their own indoor garden-bowl for a three-month period.[30]

In such instances we don't even need to get outside to benefit from nature. And when we do, it's not only lengthy, unplugged sessions away from technology that do us good. Even tiny doses of nature, from visits to tree-lined urban parks, can relieve stress. Indeed, whether it's immersive or brief, exposure to greenery has been shown, by researchers for the journal *Environment and Behavior*, to have a positive effect on city-based children with attention-deficit disorders.[31]

Let the children play (outside)

Being out in nature is good for us at any age, but during our development it is especially crucial. A 2010 study of British forest schools (which use a specialized learning approach within the context of outdoor and woodland education)[32] revealed how outdoor learning and play enable children to develop their resilience, confidence and physical skills; boost concentration levels, improve behaviour

Below: Outdoor play and learning via woodland adventures, climbing trees and pond-dipping have been proven to improve self-regulation, resilience, concentration and behaviour among children.

Vitamin N

Richard Louv, author of *Last Child in the Woods*, refers to nature as "Vitamin N" and urges paediatricians to prescribe it. Having noticed, from his research, a societal disconnect from the natural world, which he calls 'nature-deficit disorder', Richard Louv has launched an international movement, The Children and Nature Network. The network aims to reconnect children and their families to nature, which he sees as an antidote and elixir to this increasing deficiency in everyday connection to nature.[34]

Louv speaks of a "deficit" because of the rather alarming statistics about how, according to Unilever, prisoners spend more time outdoors than the average child.[35] This was based on a survey of 2,000 parents, which revealed that 74 per cent of the children of those surveyed spent less than an hour playing outside each day. Sixty minutes of open-air exercise is the minimum recommended amount for prisoners, based on UN guidelines.

Certainly, with screen time replacing "green time", today's children are often limited to playing and learning within the confines of four walls. This could be part of the reason why we're seeing a rise in mental-health issues in children across the world.

and foster environmental stewardship and an affinity with nature.

From a parental perspective, getting children outdoors more, and giving them more freedom to explore their natural environment, is of critical importance to their current and future health and happiness. Woodland adventures, enabling children to run through meadows, splash in muddy puddles and climb trees not only sparks their awe and delight in nature, but also, according to psychologists at Cambridge University, enables them to better self-regulate, which is "a better predictor for how well children do later in life than reading and writing".[33] In urban areas where big stretches of grass are less common, children can still sow seeds in egg boxes, go on treasure hunts and find trees to climb and puddles to splash in.

As we have seen, outdoor play is a huge factor in wellbeing, enabling children to figure out their strengths and be fully engaged in what they are doing. But it isn't only important for children — play and creativity are huge contributors to our wellbeing as adults, too, because nature is a wonderful catalyst for creativity.

Sparking our creativity and boosting performance

Bombarded by information as we are, in today's always-on society, it's no wonder that our attention suffers. Feeling overwhelmed and mental fatigue are the consequences, and creativity is the victim. Thankfully, nature has the power to relieve our attention fatigue, stimulate learning and creativity, restore our attention and improve our problem-solving skills.

Constantly using our phones to call, text, email, take photos and watch videos is distracting us from what is around us and is sapping our cognitive resources. Conversely, according to EEG (electroencephalogram) readings of the brain, in a University of Edinburgh study,[36] nature activates our brains in a way that puts us into a more "open, meditative mindset" and allows for what psychologists call "attention restoration". Putting our phones down and taking an outdoor break enables our pre-frontal cortex to reset and recover.

Given this immense and growing evidence for the positive effect that time spent in the natural world has on our health and happiness, it's a shame we are spending more time indoors and online than ever before. Doing so is incompatible with our pursuit of happiness and good health.

In good company

Not only does walking in nature improve our mood and energy levels, but it helps us to think with greater clarity and sparks creativity. Charles Dickens, Charles Darwin, Steve Jobs and Ludvig van Beethoven are all cases in point; each of them is reported to have walked for many miles each day. I, too, can testify to the mind-opening power of walking in nature. I've been taking daily "gratitude walks" for the past decade and have found that opportunities show themselves and ideas are formulated. With each step there is creative progress.

Above: Being out and about in nature stimulates our creativity and our cognitive abilities. We literally think better when we're out in nature.

We're doing the opposite of what is conducive to optimum wellbeing. Perhaps it's time to do something about this.

Flourishing fact

According to a Stanford University study, we are between 60 and 80 per cent more creative when we walk, compared to when we sit still.[37] And this effect can last long after we have returned to a sitting position, following a walk. Being active rather than static has a lot to do with this, but our surroundings matter, too.

How to be nourished by nature

Here's what we know for sure: the natural environment is refreshing and essential to our wellbeing. Not only does it give us the air we breathe and the water we drink, but nature also makes us feel better, think better, perform better and connect better.

If the restorative qualities that nature begets could be bottled, it would be flying off the shelves for significant amounts of money. Yet we frequently dismiss this free and accessible natural wonder.

We lead increasingly busy lives, with so much else demanding our attention that it's easy to see why we may take nature for granted, and why we forget to press pause, to look up and out, to soak up nature's nourishing wonder. Yet nature can help us better cope with our increasingly demanding and fatiguing lives, and we needn't spend long in it to benefit from its restorative powers.

Yes, unplugging and escaping into the wilderness for days on end may do us the world of good, but even five minutes here and there, getting outdoors and interacting with nature, is beneficial. Rather than sleepwalking through life, actual walking in the fresh air wakes us up to life's rich treasures.

Experiencing the healing tonic of nature

Here are a few ways we can all experience the healing tonic of Mother Nature, no matter how much time we spend being nurtured by it. Remember: even 20 minutes makes a huge difference.

"Walking is man's best medicine."

HIPPOCRATES, ANCIENT GREEK PHYSICIAN

• **Take a 20-minute "forest bath".** Slow down, inhale deeply and absorb the nourishing essence of nature surrounding you. Pay attention and just breathe. Look at the website of your national forestry/woodland association to discover local woods to explore.

• **Go on a "gratitude walk".** Walk away from worries and into fresh ideas, creative solutions and immense appreciation for what you have. As Friedrich Nietzsche said in his 1888 book *Twilight of the Idols*, "All truly great thoughts are conceived by walking." As you stroll among nature, say "thank you" (out loud, in your head or into a voice recorder or notepad). Say thank you for the natural world surrounding you and for all that it gives you, then list everything in your life that you feel grateful for – from good health for you and your family to your work/home/friendships. This is especially useful if you are too

Above: When we commit to getting curious about the natural world around us, we pay more attention to tiny treasures, which brings more joy to our days.

tired to record your gratitude in a journal before bed. It offers an alternative that combines the wonder of walking in nature with the wellbeing boost that gratitude provides.

- **Use each of your senses whenever you're out in nature.** Listen to the wind in the trees, the snapping of twigs and the different tones of birdsong. Feel the crunching of leaves underfoot, the roughness of the tree bark, the softness of green moss. Smell the scent of pine trees and the earthy aroma of the woodland

floor. Watch the sun's dappled light dance from branch to branch.

- **Choose a tree to focus on, and revisit it time and again.** You could even give it a name. I have a yew tree in my local woods that I'm especially fond of. Sit beneath its protective branches, examine its bark, feel its leaves and get to know your tree.

- **Notice tiny details.** Look out for bugs, tree bark, ladybirds, weeds emerging from the soil, drops of rain dripping from the leaves.

- **Pay attention to change.** Notice the changing seasons and the natural cycles of night and day, sunshine and rain.

Experience the uniqueness of each
season. Jot down your findings.

- **Decide to witness blazing sunsets and
  meteor showers.** Schedule this in your
  diary. Feast your eyes on awe-inspiring
  natural environments on a regular basis.
  Visit http://earthsky.org/astronomy-
  essentials/earthskys-meteor-shower-guide
  for a calendar of meteor showers, so that you
  can wrap up warm and lie down on blankets
  to watch the wonder of shooting stars.

- **Marvel at vastness.** Visit the ocean; or
  simply stop, look up at the sky, wherever
  you may be, and get marvelling.

- **Go to your favourite green space and
  watch the goings-on all around you.**
  Just sit and observe.

- **Notice how nature makes your body
  feel.** Pay attention as you watch, listen
  to and feel what is going on *outside*, and
  to what is going on *inside* your body –
  how the wind in the trees and the vast,
  tall trees make you feel *inside*. Where
  does your body experience that feeling?

- **Wrap up and go outside, whatever the
  weather.** As they say in Scandinavian
  countries (a sentiment observed by my
  daughter's forest-school teacher): "There

Right: Each day the sun rises and sets and it
is up to us whether we witness or miss this
marvellous sight.

> "If you think back to your childhood, it's likely that many of your memories originate from outdoor fun."

is no such thing as bad weather, only bad clothes." Rain and cold don't diminish the therapeutic effect of a woodland walk. Often they enhance it, for there is gratification in that discomfort. So venture outside on blustery, rainy days and feel the rain on your skin and the wind in your hair. You may come back windswept and soaked, but you'll feel more alive than ever.

- **Go on micro-adventures and create unique memories.** If you think back to your childhood, it's likely that many of your memories originate from outdoor fun. Go on treasure hunts. Track animals. Sleep under the stars. Skate at a skatepark. Build a woodland den. Plant flowers for bees and butterflies, and vegetables for your family to enjoy. Take picnics. Drink hot chocolate on countryside benches. Explore.

- **Learn about the flowers in your garden and the birds that visit.** Get books from the library, to look up species of birds and plants that surround you on a daily basis.

Rather than failing to notice the nature on your doorstep, this gives you the opportunity to get to know what's out there.

- **Consume less.** As we've discovered, nature has a much greater positive impact on our wellbeing than material wealth and possessions ever could and provides us with a high happiness ROI (Return on Investment). Yet, ironically, the more we consume, the more we put natural ecosystems at risk and the more the natural environment suffers.

Evidently, natural ecosystems have an important role to play in our happiness. If you take one message from this book, let it be the notion of consuming less and getting out into nature more; in doing so, we can protect and boost the very ecosystems that our long-term happiness and health depend on, just as they protect and boost us.

Opposite: Paying attention to the nature on our doorstep is the first step to appreciating the great outdoors.

FIND YOUR FORTE
AND GO WITH THE FLOW

"What did you do as a child
that made the hours pass like
minutes? Herein lies the key
to your earthly pursuits."

CARL JUNG, SWISS PSYCHIATRIST

What's right with you?

It's human nature to want to fix what's wrong with us and strive for betterment. Self-growth and personal development give our lives meaning – an integral ingredient in the recipe for living a good life. Yet if a good life is our goal, it's equally important to know, and build upon, what's right with us, too. Focusing on what's already working is just as crucial as improving what's not.

Fixing the sails of the boat

To journey through the choppy seas of life, we need a sturdy boat with a good sail. In his book *Practicing Positive Psychology Coaching*,[1] Robert Biswas-Diener describes our weaknesses as holes in the boat, and our strengths as the sail. We need to patch

holes and fix leaks to prevent the boat from sinking. However, fixing leaks alone won't move us forward. We need our sails in order to do that. Ultimately, even if we fix the leaks (our weaknesses), we can't go anywhere without the sails (our strengths). It is the sails that will take us wherever we hope to go.

Yet many of us sail through the ocean of life with our sails clipped – our capabilities untapped, our potential wasted. So says John W Gardner in his book *On Leadership*, where he suggests that many people with strengths in leadership never actually lead. But how do we figure out what our individual strengths are?

Founding fathers of the positive psychology movement, Christopher Peterson and Martin Seligman, defined 24 signature character strengths in their 2004 book *Character Strengths and Virtues: A Handbook and Classification*. Within its pages, these strengths provide an antidote to the mental-health profession's prior focus on what is *wrong* with us, and serve as a reminder about what is *right* with us. We'll explore what these 24 character strengths are, and how to discover yours, on page 246, for knowing and using them is incredibly beneficial.

Below: Just as a sailor cannot survive on the seas without a strong sail, we cannot flourish without harnessing our strengths.

Play to your strengths

Finding our forte and deploying our signature strengths (our top character strengths, which are most essential to who we are) has been proven to boost our wellbeing, mood and performance. Various studies reveal that knowing, naming and using our character strengths increases our life satisfaction.

Not only that, but playing to our strengths has the added bonus of buffering us against the negative effects of stress and enhancing some of the core "pillars of well-being" (see Chapter Four). For example, using our strengths can have the knock-on effects of giving us more vitality, improving our relationships, of us becoming more engaged and achieving our goals.

Flourishing facts

In 2015 the researchers and authors Scott Barry Kaufman and Spencer Greenberg collected data on 517 people and found that 23 of the 24 character strengths defined by positive psychologists were predictive of wellbeing.[2] (According to their research, humility was the only exception.) And a randomized controlled diary study of strengths and mood-repair on a relationship group revealed that using these character strengths impacted on positive mood the following day.[3]

Research has also proven the link between knowing and using our strengths and boosting our wellbeing. A 2016 Argentinian study of 687 adults found that character strengths were a crucial part of life-fulfilment.[4] Meanwhile, a study carried out in 2005 by Professor Seligman et al. revealed that deploying one's signature strengths in a novel way each day for a week increased happiness and decreased depression and stress for between three and six months.[5] These results were corroborated by later studies by researchers from the University of Manchester in 2011.[6] And a Human Resource Management study of 442 employees across 39 departments in eight organizations revealed that a strengths-based psychological climate was linked with improved work performance.[7] Evidently, strengths strengthen our happiness levels.

Signature strengths

Importantly, our character strengths are different from our skills, talent or spark; they are the collection of traits that form our individual nature; the hallmark of our character that guides our thoughts and actions. Aristotle believed that the more we act in accordance with our character, the better people we become.

Some observers report that we are in danger of losing our character strengths, as the social-media juggernaut and 24-hour newsreels have shifted our focus from character to image; from our worthy values to a projected personality. Meanwhile schools' emphasis on exam results is also reportedly shifting the focus away from character values and individual strengths, such as kindness, courage, hard work and loyalty, as Anthony Seldon notes in his book *Beyond Happiness*.

The good news is that we all possess every single one of the 24 character strengths to varying degrees, so we each have a unique character-strengths profile, which ranks our own signature strengths in order.

Right: Sharing edited filtered versions of ourselves and our lives via social media has led us to care more about how people perceive us than who we truly are.

VIA character strengths

Instead of finding flaws with yourself, find your forte.
Consider what is *right* with you, rather than what is *wrong*.
By using our top-ranked strengths regularly, and in new
ways, as often as we can, our wellbeing is boosted.

The scientifically validated "VIA (Values in Action) Inventory of Strengths" survey is a free online test featuring 120 questions and providing incredibly accurate results about what our own individual signature strengths are, ranked in order. Below is a list of all 24 signature character strengths.

Reprinted with kind permission from: www.viacharacter.org

Appreciation of beauty and excellence
You notice and enjoy beauty in many places (nature, art, music, etc.).
You notice, and enjoy watching, people who are talented or very skilled at what they do.

Bravery
You do not avoid challenges or difficult situations.
You speak up for what you think is right, even if others disagree with you.

Creativity
You think of new and original ways of doing things.

Curiosity
You are interested in many things.
You like to explore and discover new things.

Fairness
You give everyone a fair chance.
You treat others in a fair and just way.

Forgiveness/mercy
You forgive those who have done wrong.
You give people a second chance.
You do not seek revenge against those who have wronged you.

Gratitude
You notice and appreciate the good things that happen.
You take the time to express thanks to those who do nice things for you.

Hope
You expect good things to happen in the future.
You work to make good things happen.

Humour
You like to laugh and make jokes.
You like to bring a smile to people's faces.
You see humour in many situations.

Opposite: We each have unique character strengths; from bravery and curiosity to hope and creativity. When we do work which utilizes our strengths, we flourish.

Integrity

You speak the truth.
You allow others to see the "real you".
You are true to yourself.
You take responsibility for what you do
and say.

Kindness

You enjoy doing favours and helping others.
You enjoy taking care of other people.

Leadership

You like to work with others and help them
to get things done.
You like to organize group activities and
see that they happen.

Love

You like being close to other people.
You like to give love to others.
You like receiving love from others.

Love of learning

You enjoy learning new information.
You enjoy learning how to do things.

Modesty/humility

You do not like to draw attention to yourself.
You let your accomplishments speak for
themselves (rather than pointing them out).
You do not view yourself as better than others.

Open-mindedness

You like to think things through before
making a decision.
You look at all "sides" of a situation.
You are able to change your mind (if there

is a good reason to do so).
You listen to other people's ideas.

Persistence

You finish what you start.
You find ways to overcome obstacles.
You enjoy completing tasks.

Perspective

You are able to give other people good
advice.
You are able to see the "big picture".

Prudence

You are careful in making decisions.
You avoid taking unnecessary risks.
You avoid doing or saying things that you
later regret.

Self-control

You avoid "overdoing" things (losing your
temper, eating too much, etc.).
You are able to keep things balanced in
your life.

Social intelligence

You know what to do to get along with
different groups of people.
You know what makes other people "tick";
you know why they do what they do.
You are aware of other people's thoughts
and feelings.

Opposite: Kindness and love are just two of the
24 character strengths defined in the VIA character
strengths assessment tool.

Spirituality

You believe that you are part of a larger plan or purpose.

You believe that your life has meaning and/or purpose.

Your beliefs about life's meaning/purpose give you comfort and help to guide your actions.

Teamwork

You work well as a member of a group or team.

You always do your share of the work in a team or group.

You are loyal to the groups or teams to which you belong.

Zest

You do what you do with energy

Knowing what our character strengths are is an emboldening experience. For each time we use them, we strengthen our character, which in turn boosts our well-being and puts our stamp on the world. This allows us to live a virtuous life rather than a virtual one. And a virtuous life is, according to Aristotle, the ultimate route to happiness.

Right: Team players thrive when given the opportunity to work as part of a team, just as those whose top character strength is leadership flourish when enabled to lead.

Strength training

In order to flex your character-strength muscles, try some of the following suggestions and see which ones work best for you.

1. Notice when, where and how your top strengths are used, and write a paragraph about this. In a Chinese education study,[8] this exercise was found to boost life-satisfaction over the short and long term.

2. Consider how you might use your strengths to help you overcome a challenge that you are facing, or have faced in the past, and to help other people. List the ways and endeavour to do so on a regular basis.

3. Use your signature strengths in new ways more frequently, and integrate them into your daily routine if possible. Here are some ways to do so. If your top strength is:

- **Appreciation of beauty and excellence** – Notice and savour one or more examples of natural beauty every day for 30 days. Do this by drawing a picture, writing a poem or taking a photograph of it. From sun shining through trees to birdsong, beautiful flowers and sunsets against the clouds, consider how these instances of beauty make you feel. Consider ways you may attract more of these examples into your life, such as by putting up a bird feeder or travelling on a regular basis to a specific spot to watch the sun set or rise.

- **Bravery:** Write a plan of action about how you might influence change in some way, and read books to collect stories of bravery to inspire you.

- **Creativity:** Take a new creative class, such as painting, stained glass or photography, then use the skills you have learned to transform a room, a piece of furniture or a wall in your home and to make personalized birthday cards for your friends. Perhaps you could illustrate their character strengths on the card?

- **Curiosity:** Attend an event with a person from a different culture, and connect with people at that event from whom you can learn. Find out what books, magazines and other media they choose, and expand your knowledge of their culture through various mediums.

- **Fairness:** Consider ways that you might take action to counter human-rights injustices on a regular basis, such as writing letters to editors to speak up about specific issues, joining peaceful activism groups or volunteering to work for a human-rights organization using your skill set.

Above: Forgiveness and gratitude are powerful, especially when we express those to someone, as human connections are vital to our wellbeing.

- **Forgiveness/mercy:** List any grudges that you hold. Write a few sentences, as if writing a letter to the other person, explaining why you held that grudge, considering their reasons for doing whatever they did to offend you, and committing to forgiving them. Also list potential responses to future offensive remarks, and respond as planned whenever possible.

- **Gratitude:** Consider something you tend to take for granted. Perhaps being cared for or cooked for? Or the ability to walk or run? Spend the next week focusing your appreciation on those things. And devote one day per week or month to practising gratitude by "chunking" it, as in the kindness exercise (see page 254). Write down three good things that you are grateful for about the week or month; write a note to someone expressing your gratitude for helping you in some way;

write an email to the editor of a magazine thanking them for writing an article that has helped you; make a conscious effort to thank everyone you meet who gives you a reason to be thankful; look through photo albums and feel gratitude for the moments captured within the photographs

- **Hope:** Make a list of adversities that you've experienced in your lifetime and jot down anything positive that came from them, in terms of how they shaped you, strengthened you or showed you what you are capable of. What strengths or values did experiencing those adversities demonstrate? Create a list of books or films that demonstrate triumph over adversity. Spend time working on a vision board of your hopes for the future, by cutting out images and words from magazines that inspire you. Create some "hope" cards, depicting hope in words and images, and send them to charities.

- **Humour:** Set aside some time to learn ten new jokes, and time to watch your favourite comic characters. Consider what you find funny about them. Schedule time to visit a comedy club on a regular basis with your favourite people.

- **Integrity:** Check how much the next three decisions that you make match your values. Note down any discrepancies.

- **Kindness:** Schedule in a "kindness day" each week or month, when you "chunk"

lots of kind acts together. For example, send copies to friends of your favourite books wrapped in brown paper and tied with string, accompanied by handwritten notes; buy a magazine subscription for a friend; donate clothing to a charity shop or food to a food bank; volunteer at the charity shop; phone an elderly relative for a chat; or babysit for a friend who could do with a night out.

- **Leadership:** Organize an intergenerational family event and assign small roles to various members of the family, depending on their own strengths. Offer to mentor one of the family members who attends the event. Consider using your skills and leadership strength to coach individuals, or a team, on your topic of expertise; start up a communal garden and rally support from your local community.

- **Love:** Make gifts for friends and family members that demonstrate how much you know them and their individual strengths, and how much you love them. Write a poem or note to capture this.

- **Love of learning:** Commit to either attending an exhibition or visiting your local library once a month (perhaps alternate between the two) and learn something that you can share with your friends and family.

- **Modesty/humility:** Commit to keeping your accomplishments to yourself for an

entire month. If you wish to record them to enable you to look back on them, do so in a personal notebook or computer file, rather than sharing them on social media. Additionally, list mistakes you may have made in the past few weeks (ask close family/friends to help you with areas you might need to work on, if necessary). Learn from them, apologize for them and move on.

- **Open-mindedness:** Find a blog post written by a person with a view that contradicts your own. Consider how you might ordinarily respond, and then put yourself in the writer's shoes. Why might

Above: If one of our top strengths is persistence and another is teamwork, we might gain great joy from training with a group of friends to run a marathon

they feel that way? How do you think they've arrived at their conclusion?

- **Persistence:** Consider a goal that you've struggled with in the past, then write a contract to yourself that you will persist until you achieve it. Announce the goal to a supportive group of friends, then make it happen. Break the goal down into small, specific actions and tackle one or two of those each week. Monitor progress and keep at it.

255

- **Perspective:** Find inspirational quotes that might apply to some challenges that you and/or your friends face, and jot down action steps that you or they could take, based on that wisdom. Then seek out quotes that provide alternative perspectives, which may also help. Consider how, based on these various pieces of wisdom, you might counsel a friend facing such a challenge in the future.

- **Prudence:** Make a conscious effort to pause and take a deep breathe before responding. Practise. Record the effects of doing so at the end of each day. And try pondering on what the long-term effects might be of decisions you're considering. How might the decision impact on your life in two or five years' time?

- **Self-control:** Create a schedule of routines for exercise, work, domestic care, texting or writing to friends, preparing meals, and so on. Base this schedule on when you are most and least alert. For example, schedule exercise and work duties for when you are most alert, and domestic duties and texting friends for when you are flagging. Commit to sticking to these routines for 30 days and reward yourself for doing so. Note down any times that sticking to them was more difficult, and why. Use this information to improve your ability to stick to them in the next 30 days.

- **Social intelligence:** Seek the good in offensive remarks by trying to find a positive motive or reason for them. List positive attributes for everyone in your life, including anyone you may be experiencing difficulties with. Pay attention to those people who seem to demonstrate the most empathy. Consider what you could learn from them.

- **Spirituality:** Meditate on a daily basis, even if only for a few minutes. And devote time to getting a basic understanding of a few different religions. Consider the synergies and similarities between each of them. Create a reading list of spiritual books and schedule time to read them each week. Note down the key lessons that you learn from them.

- **Teamwork:** Volunteer for a community project that interests you – whether that's helping the local forestry commission, planting a community garden or picking up litter. Use this experience as the seed to start your own community project.

- **Zest:** Consider the activities you used to love doing when you were ten years old, and engage in them with the same sense of enthusiasm. This might be roller-skating, tree-climbing, bike-riding or skate-boarding.

4. List times when you have been useful to others. Perhaps a friend asked you for advice, listened, took it and benefited as a direct result? Perhaps a work colleague or boss asked you to carry out a certain task and was suitably impressed by your input?

In doing this exercise, you may uncover character strengths and abilities that you previously took for granted.

Above: Meditation is a useful activity for anyone, but it especially utilizes the strengths of those with top character strengths of spirituality, prudence and perspective.

5. Consider how it feels to have those strengths, and exercise them. Feel the positive effects and think about what it's like when you are using them, and when others see you using them. How does it feel?

6. Find literature and films to identify real-world examples where people use various character strengths. Consider what those strengths are, how they use them and how you might be able to do the same.

As well as boosting our wellbeing, deploying our character strengths helps us to better enjoy what we do. When we participate in activities that are attuned to our character and harness our capabilities, we feel more engaged and alive. So it makes sense to do more of what we're good at – to use our skills as well as our strengths. In so doing, we can raise the level of enjoyment to a whole new level.

Optimize enjoyment by increasing "flow" and engagement

A happy life is an enjoyable one. When we improve the quality of our individual experiences, we improve our enjoyment of life itself. We can optimize each experience by choosing activities that absorb and engage us. Duing so enables us to enter a state of sustained involvement known as "flow".

Flow, or "optimal experience" as it's otherwise known, is a heightened level of engagement; a deeply involved state where we are so absorbed in what we are doing, and enjoying the experience so much, that nothing else matters – for example, when musicians feel they "become one with the music", or when athletes lose all sense of the crowd being there. During experiences of flow we forget our everyday worries, feel no sense of self-consciousness and often lose track of time.

However, "flow" is not the norm. Entropy – randomness or lack of order – is. We tend to continually interrupt our activities and thoughts with questions and concerns: "Should I be doing this now? What about such-and-such? ... I wonder how so-and-so is? I must remember to put the rubbish/dog/recycling out", and so on. This "entropy" is our regular state of mind, where we automatically think about current problems, grudges or frustrations and give those thoughts precedence.

Right here, right now

Conversely, flow carries us forward through the engaging activity in a timeless bubble, where everyday concerns and thoughts momentarily leave us. Our focused absorption in the activity leaves no room for other stimuli. When we are in the zone, fully engrossed in the experience, our attention is consumed by it; we are engaged in nothing else other than being in the moment, engaging in the now. The past and future become momentarily irrelevant. *Right here, right now* is all that matters.

Flow enables order, to quieten the chaos of our everyday minds while optimizing our experiences. This is why "engagement" is one of the pillars of wellbeing (see Chapter Four). Engagement begets flow, which begets intense satisfaction.

Opposite: We lose track of time when we are in the "flow" zone, absorbed by activities that we have strong capabilities in, yet which sufficiently challenge and engage us.

Flourishing fact
According to research by Hungarian psychologist Mihaly Csikszentmihalyi, flow can bring deep joy and satisfaction, even over the smallest experiences. Numerous academic studies collected in his book *Optimal Experience: Psychological Studies of Flow in Consciousness* reveal that frequent flow correlates with improved creativity, self-regulation, achievement and, subsequently, better life-satisfaction and well-being. As such, what we choose to spend our time doing – and how we do it – matters.

The flow zone

To "get into the zone" and find flow, we can: *get engaged*, immersing ourselves in absorbing activities and engaging experiences; and *grow with the flow*, challenging and stretching ourselves sufficiently in order to improve and grow.

Both engagement and improvement are important criteria for flow, as they enrich our experience and actualize our potential. In doing so, the activity and experiences themselves are their own reward. Intrinsically rewarding experiences set us free to enjoy the gift in the present moment, rather than – as Csikszentmihalyi, the author of *Flow* says – "being held hostage to a hypothetical future gain".[9] But how do we know which activities to absorb ourselves in?

Get engaged

Cast your mind back over your life thus far and consider which have been the best moments: the most enjoyable experiences of your life. For example, I'd include giving birth to my daughter, abseiling for charity, receiving the first copy of my first book, interviewing some of my idols, downhill roller-skating with friends and blissfully floating in the clear Mediterranean Sea.

Each of these moments was active. They involved either accomplishing something that stretched me to use my strengths or an activity that caused me to lose track of time. Surprisingly, they do not include any passive moments of pleasure.

Indeed, the most memorable moments of our lives tend to be those that are active rather than passive – the result of activities that we completely immerse ourselves in. Passive moments may bring many positive emotions, such as joy, serenity and gratitude, yet we are unlikely to count them as the best experiences of our entire lives, with perhaps a few exceptions. Rather it is those activities that took courage or persistence – and when we deployed our strengths – that generate the gratification to be stored in our memories as the best times of our lives.

It is not only through immersing ourselves in sporting activities or

competitive games that we can find flow. Yes, tennis, dancing, football, climbing and chess are prime inducers of the flow state, as are artistic and creative endeavours that involve escaping from reality or making something. Yet mundane tasks too, such as queuing for a theatre show or mowing the lawn, can be transformed by implementing these flow criteria. For example, in focusing

Above: Active moments which took courage or persistence tend to be the most memorable. But there are many ways to get engaged in our everyday activities and find flow.

your attention on mowing the lawn, setting a time limit within which to mow a certain area and scoring points for accuracy, the act of lawn-mowing becomes engaging and thus more enjoyable.

261

> "Flow-inducing activities should be achievable, controllable and focused, with the potential to receive feedback during participation."

Grow with the flow

Stretching ourselves to rise to challenges boosts our confidence in our own capabilities. When we invest effort in goal-oriented activities and achieve our targets, we "grow with the flow" – we improve. En route we gain feedback to keep us on track. According to flow expert Mihaly Csikszentmihalyi, flow-inducing activities should be achievable, controllable and focused, with the potential to receive feedback during participation.

They should be sufficiently challenging to enable improvement and sustain interest, but not so challenging that enjoyment in the activity is lost. That is, there should be the right balance between challenge and ability: a little outside the comfort zone, to escape the tedium of repeating the activity at the same level over and over, but not so far outside the comfort zone that the activity becomes a chore. Too easy or too tough has a diluting effect on the flow feeling. We disengage.

For example, a dancer focused on moving seamlessly through moves in a new routine that taps into their dancing abilities will gain feedback from the instinctive feeling that tells him he got the move just right. He'll most likely find flow if the routine isn't too easy or too hard, so it pushes him just enough. The same might be said of a footballer during a match. She'll gain instant feedback with each kick of the ball, letting her know whether she is on target or not; and if she sets herself a personal challenge of 80 per cent accuracy, she'll probably get into the zone. Equally, a mother enjoying the experience of reading to her child will gain feedback from the warm smile, gentle squeeze of the hand and shared laughter between her and her child.

Opposite: When a dancer moves seamlessly into the "flow" zone they feel so engaged in dancing and so euphoric, they can lose track of time.

How to optimize experiences and engage in flow-full activities

When we are fully immersed in an activity and momentarily lose touch with the outside world, we are experiencing flow. And if we can create opportunities to become more deeply engaged in the activities that we choose to participate in, we can optimize our enjoyment of life and, therefore, our happiness.

1. Find your own personal flow. Which activities get you "in the zone" where your focus is fine-tuned and your engagement is intensified? As you go about your daily life over the coming week, pay attention to those activities that enable you to lose touch with the outside world, no matter how momentarily. Then plot to engage yourself in more of those activities.

2. Turn mundane activities into flow experiences; turn tasks into a game. All you need are clear rules, immediate feedback and time pressure. Ideally, as your ability grows, so should the level of challenge. For example, if you are packaging products, figure out ways you could get further, do more, improve your performance each time or perform the task within a certain timescale.

3. Create more; make more stuff. Trust in the moment and let the words, paint or glue flow. Finding flow during the creative process gets you more attuned to your inner monologue of feedback and what feels instinctively right. You don't need to be in a state of flow to create, but creativity may induce that feeling in you – and even more besides.

4. Play more; source more fun. Grab a pen and write three lists, then schedule in time to do more of the following:

- **Activities that you could happily talk about (and engage in) for hours.** For example, fishing, dancing or camping.

- **Activities that require skill and concentration,** and which you find gratifying, yet challenging. For instance, writing, drawing, sporting activities such as netball, football or ice-skating.

- **Activities you loved doing when you were ten or eleven years old.** Tap into the enthusiasm that you had when you

Above: Leaping from one optimal engaging experience to the next is only possible when we know which activities get us into the "flow" zone.

were a child. For example, rolling down grassy hills and jumping through sprinklers with friends, roller-skating, den-building, tree-climbing or doing dance routines.

Just as happiness is about enjoying the journey, so flow is about engaging in the process rather than the end result. By finding sources of engagement and leaning into them, we can flow from one optimal experience to the next, and make the most of the moments that make up our life.

Flourishing fact

A New Zealand diary study of 650 young adults[10], which measured the correlation between creativity and wellbeing, discovered that small acts of daily creativity boosted flourishing and a general sense of wellbeing the following day. Participants reported feeling happier and more energized, with a positive mood, during and after they had embarked on creative activities. Creativity on one day predicted increased wellbeing the next day.

MEANING & PURPOSE
What matters most and why?

"He who has a why to live for,
can bear with almost any how."
FRIEDRICH NIETZSCHE, GERMAN PHILOSOPHER

What matters most to you?

So far we've explored what matters most when it comes to maximizing happiness. We've discovered that positivity matters, other people matter and achievement matters – along with a good deal more. Now it's time to get a little more personal and focus on what matters most to *you*, and why.

The values you hold dear, the things you love to do and the contribution you hope to give to the world – these fundamental essences of who you are, and what you care about, spell out your "why" and give your life meaning, along with the experiences that life gives *you* and the way you respond to them.

Imagine for a moment your 90-year-old self reminiscing. What do you hope you'll be able to look back on with joy and say, "I'm glad I did that" – rather than "I wish I'd done that"? Whatever it is, that's the important stuff. Focusing on what is uniquely significant to *you* matters. Being a good parent/sibling/friend perhaps? Treating others as you wish to be treated? Taking care of people? Accumulating material items isn't so vital, when you view life in this way. Watching TV, getting the latest gizmo and making sure you know all the gossip becomes less meaningful. Sharing your life with someone – being loved, and loving back – following your most meaningful path in life and staying true to who you are: that's important. Trying not to lose sight of

"Doing more of what is important to us, and learning from our daily experiences, gives our lives meaning."

what is meaningful to us helps us not to "sweat the small stuff". When our daily lives are aligned with our values, our strengths and our interests, we are less likely to get caught up in the woes of the car failing its saftey inspection, burning the toast again or worrying about what people think of us. Because none of that really matters, does it?

Doing more of what is important to us, and learning from our daily experiences, gives our lives meaning; but "meaning" is more than that. Essentially, meaning is a sense of comprehension that our life has inherent value and significance, based on what we do, what we give, what we

MEANING AND PURPOSE

Above: What matters most to you? Taking part in challenges? Raising money for good causes? Spending quality time with quality people? Contributing to the wider world in some way?

experience and how we respond to life. "Meaning" is the M in the PERMA-V model of wellbeing (see Chapter Four). As such, it matters significantly. But why does a purposeful life with meaning make for a happier life?

Purpose makes us function better

Back in 1963 the Austrian psychologist and neurologist Viktor Frankl first suggested that people function best when they possess a central purpose to build their life's meaning around.

Having endured life as a Nazi concentration-camp prisoner, Frankl realized that fellow prisoners with a sense of purpose were more likely to survive. He noticed that those who lacked a sense of purpose gave up and died sooner than those who looked back on their lives with fond satisfaction, and those who looked forward to future accomplishments yet to come. Prisoners who were able to dream of something in the future, such as finishing a book or being reunited with family, did not give up. Hope gave them a directional sense of purpose, which gave their lives meaning.

For Frankl and his fellow prisoners, whose lives were made unbearable, having purpose – and thus meaning – made their lives sufficiently worthwhile not to give up. Frankl's own purpose was to help fellow prisoners find theirs, which gave meaning to his life during extreme suffering and demonstrated that our response to situations is often where the nucleus of meaning exists. He chose to respond to his experience by using it to serve others.

Ever since providing his own example, and creating a framework to help us cultivate meaningful lives, hundreds of research studies have been carried out that concur with Frankl's ideas, and which

cement the notion that the more focal our purpose is in influencing our actions, the more we benefit from having one.[1] But what exactly is purpose, and why is it so integral to our level of life satisfaction?

Above: When we spend our days doing what we love, abiding by our values and contributing in some way, we feel purposeful, which enables us to flourish.

Flourishing facts

A wellbeing and personal-growth study of 338 university students in 1996[2] revealed that optimism is easier to cultivate, and obstacles easier to rise above, when we are committed to a set of values, a cause, a purpose. Other studies have further demonstrated how purpose enhances wellbeing and decreases depression and anxiety, including the 2008 "Meaning in Life" Questionnaire, which enabled Michael Steger, Professor of Psychology at the University of Colorado, to assess meaning in life and its correlation with positive affect.[3]

Meanwhile, in a 2012 scientific study of 222 college students, which measured how purpose, mood and pleasure predicted life-satisfaction, researchers discovered that those with a strong sense of purpose had higher levels of self-esteem and felt more satisfied with their lives.[4]

The power of purpose

Having a purpose gives us a sense of direction. It strengthens our resolve to persist during tough times, because it's far easier to have the courage of our convictions if those convictions are woven into an overarching guiding intention.

Researchers P E McKnight and T B Kashdan define purpose as "a central, self-organizing life-aim",[5] while purpose-expert Carin Rockind defines purpose as "the driving force behind who you are and the active way you uniquely impact the world".[6] But whatever the definition, "purpose" is intrinsically motivated by what sparks our interest, engages our empathy and motivates us to act. And it is one of the prerequisites that give our life meaning.

Meaning and purpose feed on each other: investment in a purpose gives life meaning, and living a meaningful life offers a sense of purpose. However, there are, according to Viktor Frankl, two types of meaning:[7]

1. Ultimate meaning: purposeful direction that we are headed toward, defined by what matters most to us/our values, rather than by an achievable goal. For example: serving, inspiring or teaching others.

2. Meaning of the moment: the choices, responses and decisions that we make in each moment.

Flourishing fact

Research by Nansook Park, Myungsook Park, and Christopher Peterson[8] explains the distinct differences between the subjective "meaning" (which makes us feel that our lives are significant, important and worthwhile; that they fit into a larger context and therefore make sense) and "purpose" (a sense of direction and statement of intention, based on what matters most to us) and reveals how strongly correlated and important both are.

Opposite: Feeling like we have a sense of direction and know where we are headed can help us to enjoy the journey a whole lot more.

Giving, receiving and responding well

In a nutshell, we can gain meaning from what we give, what we receive and how we respond. In 1964 Frankl framed these three core values into a "meaning triangle", to illustrate how anyone can cultivate meaning in their lives.

- **The first value, "creativity",** is about what we love to do and how we contribute: that is, what we give the world via our self-expression – be it through our work, art, good deeds, inventions, writing, music, volunteering, charitable efforts, and so on. This affects the "ultimate" type of meaning.

Below: Holocaust survivor and psychotherapist, Victor Frankl devised a "meaning triangle" to help people to identify how to live meaningful and purposeful lives.

- **The second value, what we receive from the world via our experiences,** can also create "meaning of the moment", and includes our interactions, relationships, nature, culture, spirituality, and so on.

- **The third value, our attitude** – in terms of how we respond to situations, circumstances and other life-conditions via our own perspective and mindset – can also generate the second type of meaning.

Victor Frankl's Meaning Triangle

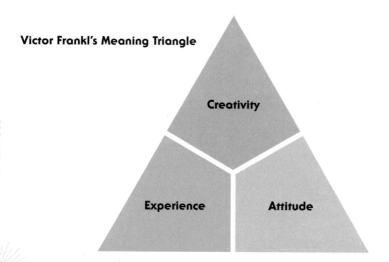

Creativity

Experience

Attitude

Above: Making something can help us to make something of our lives. We can create meaning through how we contribute creatively to the world.

Based on this and a wealth of additional research since the 1960s, there are three key prerequisites to living a meaningful life:

1. Our contribution: Contributing to something bigger than ourselves that positively impacts on the world, or giving creatively to the world through our self-expression, gives life meaning.

2. Our compass: Why we do those things (based on our curiosity, our spark and our values) tells us what matters most to us. This provides us with an inner compass that guides our direction – our purpose in life. It is this purpose that further gives our life meaning and a consequential sense of enthusiasm, satisfaction and fulfilment. For when our purpose is in congruence with our values and goals, we are happiest. Conversely, when it is not, we may experience discord.

3. Our response: How we respond to, and interpret, the events that life gives us – that is, the perspective and attitude that we choose to take, in reaction to our circumstances – can give our life meaning. For example, when we consider how we might view situations differently, what we can learn from the circumstances we are given and the challenges we face, and how we might use those experiences to benefit ourselves or others in the future, we can make each moment of our lives meaningful. Especially when we consider how we might serve others, as a result of the meaning we have gained from our own life experiences.

In this way, "meaning" is a two-way street. It is about both what we give and what we receive. It is the former, however, that can cause a great deal of head-scratching and soul-searching. After all, "What is your purpose in life?" is a big question, and such questions can leave us feeling small.

The pursuit of purpose

It's all too easy to beat ourselves up when we don't reach our goals or don't feel we have a purpose. Just as the pursuit of happiness can backfire when unrealistic expectations get us down, so the same can be said of the pursuit of purpose. The pressure to find our calling and pursue our true passion in life can lead to "purpose-anxiety" and can hamper our happiness.

- What if we have no idea what our purpose in life might be?

- What if we're not particularly passionate about any one thing?

- What if we don't feel called to anything specifically?

- What then?

- Who are we meant to be?

- What are we meant to do?

The answer, of course, is: We are meant to be ourselves and do what feels right for us. *Uncovering our purpose in life shouldn't be about who we one day hope to become, but about listening to who we are now and becoming more of that.* Yet the pressure to find our calling, and to contribute to the wider world, can be deafening. There are two ways to deal with this.

Opposite: Tuning in and listening to how we wish to live gives us a way to live a purposeful life with intention and without the pressure of pursuit.

1. Listen to life, and remember that a meaningful life isn't only about purpose. As Viktor Frankl's two types of meaning suggest, a meaningful life is also about how we create meaning from the choices we make and the responses we give to each and every moment – even the difficult experiences that we face. Paying attention to what we learn through our hardships, disappointments and failures gives our lives just as much meaning as what we learn from our successes. When we know that whatever is happening to us is worthwhile and useful – even when we are faced with adversity – this can provide us with inner strength and serenity, and can bolster our resolve to continue along the route we are on. That in itself is meaningful, especially if we can use what we learn in order to serve others.

2. Shift how you view purpose. Rather than seeing purpose as something you should seek and find, it is better to view it as a way to be and to live – that is, to be purposeful and live intentionally. You can do this by making "purpose" into a verb or adjective, rather than a noun.

"Challenges are what make life interesting; overcoming them is what makes life meaningful."

JOSHUA J MARINE

Viewing purpose as a verb

Shifting our perception of what purpose actually is releases the pressure of expectation around it. Rather than trying to find our purpose (and risk feeling disappointed or frustrated if we are unable to do so), we can shift our focus to being *purposeful* – to living with intention; seeing purpose and passion as something we *do* rather than something we *have*. Living life with a sense of purpose gives it meaning enough.

Purpose-expert Carin Rockind says that we often struggle with the expectation to find a purpose when we view the word as a noun, or a series of nouns,[9] such as "teacher", "mother", "writer" – as something we want to be, or have. Rather, we should see purpose as a verb – a "doing" word that explains our overarching mission and is prefixed with the word "to": for instance, to inspire, to teach, to build, to support, to heal, to create, to care for.

For example, rather than having the purpose of being a teacher, your purpose might be to teach with a sense of purpose – that is, to inspire people to keep fit and stay healthy, or to show introverts how to speak with confidence. There are many ways you can do this, rather than having the purpose of becoming a teacher.

Likewise, rather than having the purpose of being a mother, your purpose might be to care for children and equip them with the tools they need to cope and flourish. Rather than being a writer, your purpose might be to empower people with guidance to help them live more appreciatively, or to support vulnerable people by providing

information they can use to improve their lives. These reframings widen the net of what we might do, in line with an overarching aim, and make the possibility of following such a route more achievable.

Turning the future into now

Indeed, by framing our purpose as verbs, we can find opportunities to take those actions *right now*, rather than seeing purpose as something to strive for in the future. As such, instead of dreaming of becoming a teacher/writer/entertainer, we can seek out opportunities to teach, write and entertain others *right now*, by using the qualities and skills we already have. So we could teach work colleagues something that will help them; write down some advice and pass it on to those who might need it; or find ways to entertain a few people each day And in doing so, we can teach, write and entertain sooner rather than later.

In this way we can enjoy the journey, find more balance and stress out less about achieving some ultimate end goal. For when our sense of purpose is central to our daily

actions, we will find harmony between what we want to achieve and who we already are.

Life needn't live up to the lofty ideals and high, purposeful standards set by the game-changing Gandhis and Luther Kings of this world. Changing the world *was* their purpose, but it might not be yours. Rather than trying to imitate those who inspire us, we should "listen" to our own lives, to figure out what we wish to give, contribute and learn, whom we wish to represent and how we wish to behave and respond.

How to live purposefully

So how can we turn our purpose into a verb and live it each day? While many of us might have self-defining activities that end in "-er" (writer, painter, runner, blogger,

Above: We are better able to overcome hurdles of false expectations in life if we live our lives purposefully. Being purposeful guides our actions and gives us focus.

speaker, mother, and so on), we should explore how we already impact on the world and how we wish to do so in the future.

Our aim is to become *us*, more rather than to become something else. There is no point living a life that's been suggested for us, rather than living our own. Living a purposeful and meaningful life gives us the chance to become ourselves more fully. And that means tapping into the values and truths about what really matters and who we actually are, rather than the expectations and standards that we feel we ought to live up to.

Curiosity, creativity and contribution

Rather than viewing purpose as something external that must be found, it is better viewed as something internal that we can uncover – something that comes from within: from our individual values, our interests and our spark.

Purpose lies at the intersection of the following:

- **Your curiosity:** what you're interested in.

- **Your spark:** what you love doing.

- **Your skills/talent/wisdom:** what you do well.

- **Your strengths:** the essence of your character.

- **Your values:** what causes and qualities most matter to you.

- **Your contribution:** how you use the above to impact positively on the world around you.

Deploying your strengths, skills and spark in accordance with your values and interests, to contribute intentionally, is the epitome of living a purposeful life. And doing so need not be a lifelong quest, but rather a series of daily authentic, intrinsically joyful actions.

> "The important thing is not to stop questioning… Never lose a holy curiosity."
>
> ALBERT EINSTEIN, GERMAN-BORN THEORETICAL PHYSICIST

Your curiosity

Simply cultivating your curiosity, and cherishing the process of uncovering more about a certain topic, is a meaningful pursuit. Living purposefully is partly about fanning the flames of what fascinates you – whatever ignites your interest. "What are you curious about/interested in/fascinated by?" is a far lighter question than "What is your purpose in life?"

Adding a sprinkle of curiosity to our lives is an achievable aim, yet the benefits can be profound. Curiosity inspires gratitude. It gives us permission to notice and savour more. It opens up opportunities to explore and learn and thereby fosters growth. As a

result, curiosity leads to greater meaning and life-satisfaction. And pondering what we'd like to know more about is the first step in sparking our curiosity.

Above: Getting curious about our interests and learning how to improve what we love and do well is helpful in cultivating a purposeful life.

- **What questions do you yearn to have answers to?** What are you curious about? Are there any problems you are keen to solve? Your quest to find the answers to

these questions, and the solutions to those problems, could become the way you earn your living, or it could simply be something you do to add a splash of meaning to your life. Either works.

- **What fascinates you so much that you are keen to learn more about it?** If you didn't need to earn money, what topics would you pay someone to teach you more about?

- **What inspires or amuses you?** What do you get excited by? What are you in awe of? What do you take pride in? When are you happiest? When do you feel most hopeful? Keep questioning, to dive deeper into what you are most curious about. Your answers to these questions will demonstrate what topics and quests you might wish to investigate further.

- **What lights you up?** Which engaging activities do you love to immerse yourself in so that you lose track of time? When are you in your element and most at ease with what you're doing? What do you love doing so much that you don't even mind failing at it? Consider those activities for which simply participating in the experience provides its own intrinsic reward. Write them down and commit to doing more of them.

- **Why do you love participating in these activities so much?** What is it about them that you enjoy? Your answer can provide a major clue to what living purposefully might look like. For example, you might

Right: Certain activities fire a spark in us and light us up. Those activities enable us to feel so at ease that our experience is optimized.

enjoy teaching because you love watching people glow with pride when they master something you've encouraged them to learn. You might enjoy writing because you love the process of choosing the right words to communicate something that is important to you, and love the feeling of accomplishment when you read the finished version. You need not become a teacher or writer professionally to experience these feelings – you can teach or write anyway and find other ways to cultivate those same feelings of pride, joy and accomplishment.

- **What do you want to master?** What do you love to do so much that you want to become better at it?

- **What did you love doing as a child, and what did you want to be when you were older?** Consider ways in which you might revisit those activities. It's never too late.

Your skills

- **What are your core capabilities? What are you already good at?** We are all good at something. It may not always seem obvious, but it's there. What do people get from us, or admire in us? It might be a calming effect, or a sense of positivity that we inspire people with; or it might be a skill or a talent, such as drawing, writing or sewing. Write down

the competencies you'd list in your work CV. Then list the competencies you'd include in a life CV (if there were such a thing). Perhaps you're good at asking for help? Remaining calm in a crisis? Speaking up in defence of others? Encouraging, cheerleading or empathizing with people? Ask other people what they'd come to you for, thank you for or know you best for. Their answers might surprise you.

Above: By devoting time to activities we loved to do as children and to whatever we're keen to improve, we can do more of what we love and thrive.

Your strengths

- **What are your top character strengths?**
  Read the novel ways in which to use your strengths (see page 252) and brainstorm other means of putting them to use in a meaningful way.

  Sussing out our own strengths helps us to get on with the business of living purposefully, with immediate effect. We don't need to make grand gestures, such as leaving our jobs to build a business of our own, or leaving our suburban home to travel the world. We can start *today*. We can honour our purpose by finding possibilities in our existing lives for us to use our skills and enjoy whatever it is that lights us up.

  For example, if our purpose is to travel, we can start small, by reading books about the countries we most want to

> "We can honour our purpose by finding possibilities in our existing lives for us to use our skills and enjoy whatever it is that lights us up."

Above: Volunteering for a community project can be a wonderful way to use character strengths of kindness and live purposefully, with intention.

visit, and then volunteer for a community project in one of those countries. If we want to coach people to get past whatever lies in their way, we could offer to mentor a colleague in our organization or a younger family member. If our purpose is to help people live more

harmoniously with their pets, we might provide dog-training classes for friends after work. By knowing what our strength is, we can endeavour to live more purposefully right away

In an ideal world we might all end up doing work that rewards us more than simply financially, and where the work is a positive end in itself. That kind of employment is a vocation more than a career or job. But what if our work doesn't affect us as positively as that? We can still work purposefully within any role, if we are able to connect our role and tasks to our values and our spark.

Perhaps we value kindness and love helping people. As such, our purpose might be to make life easier for vulnerable people. During our working day we could provide a list of resources to someone who needs them, or volunteer once a week after work in a homeless shelter. Finding ways to redesign our role to fit with our strengths, spark and values can be sufficient to give us a purposeful life.

> "The purpose of life is not to be happy. It is to be useful, to be honourable, to be compassionate, to have it make some difference that you have lived and lived well."

RALPH WALDO EMERSON, AMERICAN LECTURER, POET AND ESSAYIST

Your values

Our values are shaped by what matters most to us. They provide us with an inner compass to guide our day-to-day decisions and provide a lens through which we live our lives. This compass determines our direction, so it defines our purpose. We can evaluate our values, and figure out what matters most to us, by answering the following questions:

- **Which values are most important to you?** What do you/would you teach your children? What values do you want your life to reflect? Circle all those values that appeal most to you in this list, then prioritize five that are your absolutely non-negotiable values in life. Why are they so important to you? Consider whether you've chosen them based on your ingrained family or cultural teachings, or whether they are deeply truthful to you personally? The latter are the values that matter most in living a life that is most meaningful.

Opposite: Considering which values matter most to us can help us determine how we want to spend our working lives and how we can contribute to the world.

Which values matter most to you?

- [ ] Adventure
- [ ] Ambition
- [ ] Beauty
- [ ] Calm
- [ ] Cleanliness
- [ ] Community
- [ ] Compassion
- [ ] Cooperation
- [ ] Courage
- [ ] Creativity
- [ ] Decisiveness
- [ ] Democracy
- [ ] Discipline
- [ ] Diversity
- [ ] Encouragement
- [ ] Equality
- [ ] Excellence
- [ ] Faith
- [ ] Family
- [ ] Flexibility
- [ ] Freedom
- [ ] Friendship
- [ ] Fun
- [ ] Generosity
- [ ] Goodness
- [ ] Gratitude
- [ ] Growth
- [ ] Hard work
- [ ] Harmony
- [ ] Honesty
- [ ] Hope
- [ ] Humility
- [ ] Improvement
- [ ] Individuality
- [ ] Innovation
- [ ] Integrity
- [ ] Justice
- [ ] Kindness
- [ ] Knowledge
- [ ] Leadership
- [ ] Love
- [ ] Loyalty
- [ ] Meaning
- [ ] Mindfulness
- [ ] Peace
- [ ] Personal growth
- [ ] Play
- [ ] Pleasure
- [ ] Politeness/ manners
- [ ] Positivity
- [ ] Progress
- [ ] Quality
- [ ] Reliability
- [ ] Resilience
- [ ] Resourcefulness
- [ ] Respect
- [ ] Security
- [ ] Service
- [ ] Status
- [ ] Strength
- [ ] Success
- [ ] Teamwork
- [ ] Timeliness
- [ ] Tolerance
- [ ] Tradition
- [ ] Unity
- [ ] Wealth
- [ ] Wisdom
- [ ] Wonder

> "This is the true joy in life,
> the being used for a purpose
> recognized by yourself as a
> mighty one."
>
> GEORGE BERNARD SHAW, IRISH
> PLAYWRIGHT AND ACTIVIST

- **How do you wish to be remembered?**
What would you want your tombstone epitaph to say? What do you hope to be your biggest accomplishments? To have inspired others? To have provided a good life and stable foundations for your family? To have published a book? Done things your way? Left a legacy?

Does your life reflect these values? When our actions flow from our values, we can live a purposeful life. Yet sometimes, with so much going on, it can be easy to lose sight of our core values and to lose track of what matters.

Your answers to these questions will renew your insight into what matters most to you. Based on your findings, you can create your own personal inner compass, which can be used to guide your everyday actions. This will enable you to say "yes" or "no", depending on what matters most to you.

Your contribution

What constitutes nowadays a "life well lived" reaches beyond personal happiness, to other people's happiness and the pleasure that serving others can offer us. Such service provides us with a sense of contribution, a positive feeling that the way we've lived our lives has made a difference to other people. As the German philosopher Oswald Spengler suggested in *The Decline of the West*: "This is our purpose: to make as meaningful as possible this life that has been bestowed upon us; to live in such a way that we may be proud of ourselves; to act in such a way that some part of us lives on."[10]

Living a purposeful life that enables us to contribute to the wider world, and has a positive social impact, turns our "little-p purpose" of deploying our skills/spark/ strengths and staying true to our inner-compass values into a "big-P purpose", according to the career analyst and author Daniel Pink.[11] So consider:

Above: Speaking out about what matters to us and trying to make a difference to others can provide a huge sense of purpose and positively impact the world.

- **Which causes do you care most about?**
  What breaks your heart and/or makes you
  cross? If you had a magic wand, what
  would you change in society? Which one
  problem in the world would you fix? The
  glass ceiling? Fat-cat bosses? Human-
  rights injustices? Unrealized potential?
  Poverty? War? Gender equality?
  Education? The environment? List which
  causes you care most about. What do you
  care enough about that you'd be willing
  to give up your time to serve it?

- **Who or what do you feel most drawn to
  help/serve or be a voice for?** Why? This
  will probably tie in with your answer to
  the above question. It may be global or
  local. You may wish to serve your loved
  ones or your local community, and commit
  to spending more time caring for them;
  or you may wish to speak out for an entire
  generation, gender or group on a more
  global scale. Perhaps you feel compelled
  to be the voice for something that has no
  voice, such as the environment or wildlife.
  Whoever and whatever you feel most
  drawn to help will probably tie in with
  your prioritized values.

- **What kind of world do you want to live
  in?** What positive impact do you want to
  make on the world or on other people?

Right: Considering what we'd most like to fix if we
had a magic wand, we can discover what matters
most to us and how we might serve others.

Five ways to live more purposefully

When we link the values we hold most dear to the causes we have most empathy for, and bring our skills and spark along for the ride, we can live a purposeful life that matters to us, yet is significantly meaningful to many others, too.

1. Commit to curiosity. Each day for one week give yourself a word to get curious about. Take photos, collect objects, gather thoughts that relate to that word – in terms of natural phenomena that you notice or moments that you savour – then write in a journal about your findings. For example, you might choose the word "heart" or "love" and set about collecting and taking photos of objects that are heart-shaped or that represent love, before journalling about where you found these objects, and how the experience of seeking them made you notice your surroundings more and added a new level of vibrancy to your morning walk. This exercise gives you the opportunity to flex your curiosity muscles, with practice sessions for paying attention, noticing what captures your interest, finding meaning in exploring those things and capturing your findings.

2. Express your (best) self. Write in your journal for 15 minutes about your dream future in an ideal world, where everything is going as wonderfully well as it possibly can; where all is good in terms of your

Above: Journalling is a powerful activity, especially when we write about a vision of our best selves. This improves mood and helps bring clarity to living purposefully.

health, career, family and social life. Participants who did this exercise for two weeks in a 2006 study reported improved positive mood immediately afterward; and those who continued with the practice on a regular basis saw their mood improve up to a month later. This exercise also offers clarity around what your priorities are and where you hope to be in the future. It can therefore serve as a purposeful guide charting a directional course.

Above: Taking photographs is a great way to collect images of anything that sparks our curiosity or feels meaningful to us.

3. Imagine you have a chance to share with the world a message that will be beamed to many millions. It needs to be about something that matters deeply to you, which you have some knowledge of and that could positively impact on the world, and touch those who hear it sufficiently to compel them to do something for the greater good. Imagine yourself up on stage, feeling confident, relaxed and happy to be there. Smile at the audience and then tell them what you want to say. What is your message? What do you want the world to know? Imagine your message impacting upon people. This life-purpose visualization, whereby you consider your own future impact on others, was designed by researchers into life-coaching L Kelly and D F Curtis in 2012,[12] and provides incredible insight into what matters most to you and how you might contribute to the wider world.

Below: We all have something in us that is worth saying, which could positively impact the world. Figuring that out can guide us toward how we might contribute.

4. Reflect on what is meaningful to you.
Give yourself a project over the course of a week, by taking photographs of anything that feels meaningful to you. Seek out sources of meaning, including childhood memories and mementos, serene spaces that you love to visit, loved ones, books that have positively impacted on your life, and take lots of different photos of those meaningful things. At the end of the week reflect on the photos. Consider why each item is meaningful for you and write in your journal about this experience. Students who participated in this 2013 study felt a greater sense of meaning and life-satisfaction, and more positive emotions, as a result.

5. Consider your response, attitude and perspective in terms of experiences that you've had. How might you attribute more meaning to life events? What might be a different way of looking at challenges that you've faced or setbacks you've endured? How might you use that fresh perspective to shape your future? Who else might benefit from this reflection? How might you use the meaning that you've uncovered to help others? This exploration of attitude and perspective demonstrates that meaning is not only about purpose, but about response, too.

Indeed, as well as bringing more meaning into our lives by living purposefully, we can also endeavour to find space to respond well to each moment. For whether or not we have a purpose to drive us, we each experience moments that make up our lives. It is up to us how we respond to those moments and experiences to maximize their meaning. To do that, we need to give ourselves sufficient space in which to respond.

Below: Taking time to reflect on what matters most to us can give us a fresh perspective about how we choose to spend our days.

FINDING SPACE AND CALM IN THE NOW

"With the past, I have nothing to do; nor with the future. I live now."

RALPH WALDO EMERSON, AMERICAN ESSAYIST

Ignoring the precious present

Life flies by. We race around, too preoccupied, impatient and distracted to pay full attention to the present moment. That's just how *now* is, in our always-on, 24/7, point-and-click world.

With so much jostling for our attention in this overstimulated autopilot state, we get pulled out of the present, as we stress about the demands of the future and ruminate about the regrets of the past. Back and forth we go, toing and froing, as our attention shifts from judgements about what *has* happened to worries about what *might* happen. Yet this restlessness reduces our enjoyment of what is happening – right here, right now.

And therein lies the irony of the modern condition of life being lived at full speed. We have more to get done and yet, in our fast-paced state of overwhelm, we are less able to do well what needs to be done. Our minds are full, but we are not mindful; our lives are stretched, but we struggle to be flexible. We have so much demanding our attention, and yet we are not paying attention to the precious present, as it happens.

"Where did the time go?" we wonder. Yet time (and life) was right there, under our noses – if only we'd taken the time to notice it. So what is the solution, in order to gain control over our frantic lives and minds?

Opposite: Dandelion seeds remind us that life is short and we can be carried in all directions. But they also remind us to stop, make a wish and enjoy the moment.

Press "pause", find space and focus attention

Enter mindfulness: the art of cultivating calm awareness of the present moment, without concerning ourselves with the past or the future or being judgemental of our thoughts and feelings.

Mindfulness is the art of creating space between ourselves and our reactions; the art of pausing and paying attention to *right now*. For when we slow down and press "pause", we create stillness and sufficient space in which to think, breathe and respond. Space and stillness lead to awareness, which brings clarity. And with clarity comes ease – a sense of inner calm and an outer ability to cope and function well. Flourishing in life is about optimal human functioning, and mindfulness is a wonderful tool to help us to live our best lives.

As such, mindfulness gives us the chance to observe and absorb what is happening around and within us at any given moment, so that we can regain control of our fast-paced lives and of the choices we make. For when we stop to smell the roses, we can regain control.

The problem is that when we're busy, it seems counterintuitive to stop: we've got too much to do; we simply don't have the time. But as any mindfulness or meditation expert will tell you, pausing gives us:

- **Time** to regain control

- **Time** to think clearly

- **Time** to gain perspective

- **Time** to respond sensibly.

The best way to attend to our life, so that time works for us, is by being attentive.

Attention!

Paying attention to the present, and becoming aware of the moment, helps us to choose our response to whatever life presents us with. When we slow down, press "pause" and thereby discover the ability to notice our "now", we become better at handling future demands.

Here's why: according to studies by the University of Pittsburgh, practising mindfulness can lead to permanent changes in the brain, which impact upon our ability to gain perspective.

Flourishing fact

After an eight-week mindfulness course, MRI scans of 155 healthy adults carried out by neuroscientists at the University of Pittsburgh[1] revealed that the emotional region of the brain associated with fear, and responsible for the fight-or-flight stress response (the amygdala, see Chapter Five), appeared to shrink, while the logical part of the brain, responsible for concentration, awareness and decision-making (the pre-frontal cortex), thickened.

This means that rather than falling into the mind-traps that our amygdala often creates (such as jumping to conclusions, getting anxious about what might happen and generally freaking out), mindfulness gives us the space to let in our rational thoughts, enabling us to make more sensible decisions, get perspective and view life through a more accurate and flexible lens.

Left: Focusing on the present moment enhances our ability to watch our thoughts, concerns and judgements float past as we return our attention to right now.

An antidote to anxiety?

Mindfulness is a major enabler – a tool that can help us manage and cope better with life, as well as enjoy it more. The benefits of mindfulness include:

• **Increased enjoyment of life:** When we lose sight of what is happening now, our enjoyment of it diminishes. In this way, when we bring our attention back to the present and attend to our moment-to-moment experience, rather than ruminate on the past or worry about the future, mindfulness can help us live more fully (mindfully) in the present and enjoy *now* – and the moments that make up our lives – more.

• **Lower stress levels and reduced capacity to get stressed:** The University of Pittsburgh brain-imaging studies, and other research into brain greymatter density,[2] have discovered that mindfulness reduces our primal capacity to feel stressed. This is because the connection between the amygdala and the rest of the brain weakens, disconnecting us from our "stress centre". Notably, these tests were not done during meditation, while participants were in a calm state, but afterward, demonstrating that the positive changes to the brain are more permanent than might be expected.

• **Improved performance and optimized human functioning:** Studies into the benefits of mindfulness on children,[3] carried out collaboratively by psychologists at the University of Oregon and the Chinese Academy of Sciences, have also revealed that mindfulness strengthens our attention span and our concentration levels. Furthermore, when we attend to the current task as if it were the only thing to be done, we do it well. We do things better when we concentrate our attention on one activity at a time, rather than when we are multitasking or thinking about the next task while carrying out the current one.

• **Reduced anxiety:** Various trials of school children with ADHD (Attention Deficit Hyperactivity Disorder) who have practised meditation more than twice weekly have shown that silent reflection in education has led to an improved ability to cope with pressure, to improved concentration and reduced anxiety.[4]

Opposite: Concentrating on one activity and honing in on the present moment has many benefits.

- **Better emotional self-regulation:** When we learn stillness and how to develop that all-important pause "between stimulus and response", we can take better charge of our emotions and behaviour. This improved emotional control means that we are better able to "de-escalate" ourselves, when necessary. And in becoming more aware of our present thoughts and reactions, we are better able to recognize when we need to calm down. This also means that we are able to make more considered, and less impulsive, decisions.

- **Better perspective and fewer judgemental thoughts:** Numerous studies have proven that mindful meditation has some hugely beneficial effects on the brains of those who regularly practise it. Brain-imaging studies, such as those carried out in Pittsburgh, along with further studies at the Max Plank Institute for Human Cognitive and Brain Sciences in Germany,[5] have revealed that mindful meditation can profoundly – and permanently – alter how we think. It does this by shifting the way different brain regions communicate with each other and by enhancing our perspective, causing us to refrain from engaging in thought processes that don't serve us. As such, mindfulness allows us to choose our thoughts by attributing as much or as little meaning to them as we wish: the choice is ours. We can let go of any judgemental critical thoughts and assign value only to helpful ones. Indeed, "without judgement" is a cornerstone of mindfulness practice. And when we let go of judgement, we let go of our fear of failure and no longer need to grapple so much with our inner critic. And that is incredibly liberating.

Left: Mindful meditation helps us to ride the waves of our thoughts and responses so we can free ourselves of judgement and choose to focus on what best serves us.

Coming home to ourselves

Here's how to practise mindfulness and live our lives more mindfully. There are two steps to mindfulness: the pause, slowing down and stopping; and focused attention and connection, noticing *now* and coming home to ourselves, our surroundings and our experiences.

1. The Pause

Pausing before reacting prepares us to respond well. It prepares us to think with greater clarity and to act authentically and with integrity. This is especially true during moments of frustration or anger when, ordinarily, we might react without thinking. Given our automatic fight-or-flight tendencies (see Chapter Five), flying off the handle is the natural reaction. But when we pause long enough to breathe in and breathe out mindfully, we give ourselves the space to step back from the storm: to respond in a more measured way.

Here are some mindful strategies that may encourage you to pause:

- **Be still and listen.** Focus on what you can hear. What sounds are you noticing as you sit or stand quietly? First, listen closely to sounds nearby: tweeting birds, cars driving past, trees swaying in the wind, laughter. Did you notice those sounds a moment ago? Consider whether they are loud or soft, gentle, distracting, familiar or soothing, coming from nature or man-made. Next, focus on sounds that you can hear from far away. Then focus

"When we pause long enough to breathe in and breathe out mindfully, we give ourselves the space to step back from the storm."

your attention back on the sounds nearby. Are there any new sounds that you didn't hear before? Then listen to the sound of your own breathing, your stomach rumbling, your internal sounds.

- **Distract yourself from your internal critic,** or from concerns, by diverting your energy to counting backward from 100 in sevens, or by naming animals that start with A, B, C and so on.[6]

- **Trigger mindful moments** by setting regular alarms that remind you to pause. Notice your response as you hear the alarm.

Above: Stillness enables us to listen, notice and gain control, so we can think more clearly and accurately and respond more mindfully and thoughtfully.

Do you feel soothed? Annoyed? Joyful? Reluctant? Realize that none of these responses requires judgement, as you are simply feeling an emotion based on what you are doing when the alarm goes off. Close your eyes, take a big deep breath in and a slow breath out, and sense your feet connected to the floor. Notice what is happening in your mind and your body. Take two more slow breaths, then continue calmly with your day.

- **Use technology to trigger pauses:** each time your phone pings with a notification, focus on your breath before reaching for your phone. Decide in that moment whether you want to respond to this interruption now or later.

> "Mindful meditation isn't about emptying the brain of all thoughts, it's about the process of returning to our focused attention, returning to our breath, returning to ourselves."

2. Focused attention and connection

Focused attention – noticing *now* and coming home to ourselves – makes us function better in the following ways:

- **Paying attention to our thoughts,** with awareness and without judgement, enables us to better manage our thoughts, rather than be a victim of them.

- **Paying attention to our actions** improves our appreciation and concentration. It enables us to enjoy things more *and* perform better, so it offers a win–win situation, for we relish what we are doing far more when we focus our attention on it. Conversely, when we are thinking about what to do next, our enjoyment of our current activities is diluted.

- **Paying attention to our motivations** helps us to understand what really matters to us and why, so we may stay motivated in each moment, cherish whatever we are pursuing and truly savour our achievements once we reach them.

- **Paying attention to our surroundings** boosts our appreciation, as we are better able to savour and cherish whatever we are experiencing at the present moment. This helps us to be at one with what we are doing, and with whatever – and whoever – is around us.

Listening to ourselves

It is, of course, quite normal for our attention to wander. The act of bringing our wandering attention back, by focusing it on our breath, our surroundings, the sensations we feel in our bodies – that is the very essence of mindfulness. Indeed, mindful meditation isn't about emptying the brain of all thoughts, it's about the process of returning to our focused attention, returning to our breath, returning to ourselves.

Above: By fine-tuning the lens through which we see the world, we can see, hear and connect with more depth and clarity.

And when we strengthen the connection with ourselves we can listen more deeply to our intuition, to our ideas, to our thoughts, without limitation or judgement. We can get to know who we really are, and feel our bodies more fully. This improved self-awareness and deeper self-connection helps us respond better, decide better, create better, think better.

The best way to master this is to practise being still, by focusing our attention on our breathing, in order to anchor us to the present moment.

And breathe...

Practise mindful breathing regularly while you are in a calm state of mind. Doing so will make it easier to do this when you need it most – that is, when you feel anything but calm.

"The only way to regain control and become calm is to breathe, but when life feels stressful, it can be difficult to get mindful."

Our "pedal-to-the-metal" mentality of getting everything done can make us feel out of control and, ironically, less able to perform the tasks on our ever increasing "to-do" lists to the best of our ability. This level of stress leads to a state that psychologist Daniel Goleman calls "neural hijacking"[7] – when our rational brains become unavailable, replaced by a myriad of unhelpful thoughts and reactions, generated when our emotional brain assumes control. During this irrational state, we tend to react impulsively and to judge frequently. Our minds move from judgement to judgement, and from worry to worry.

The only way to regain control and become calm is to breathe, but when life feels stressful, it can be difficult to get mindful. This is why experts recommend practising mindful breathing when we are calm; it helps the body learn how to self-regulate, so that the next time we begin to feel overwhelmed, we're more likely to step off the hamster-wheel into a mindful breathing practice – to press "pause", focus our attention on the present moment and respond with grace.

When we anchor our attention to the breath, our nervous system steps down a gear from its high-alert status, and stops pumping adrenalin and cortisol. This slower and more relaxing state gives us the chance to be at peace with our thoughts, our emotions and our bodies.

Switching on to you

However, mindfulness meditation isn't about switching *off*, like pure relaxation is. Rather, it is about switching *on*: to you and what *you* experience in the present moment.

Mindful breathing involves focusing your attention on the gentle inhale and exhale of your breath. It is a type of meditation, although there are many ways to do this and many breathing methods you can use. You can do it sitting, standing or lying down; with a cushion or without; with your

Above: By using and controlling our breath, we become better at gaining control over our lives, thoughts and reactions to suit how we want to be.

eyes open or closed; counting as you breathe or choosing not to. You might opt to take an exaggerated deep breath first, or notice your natural breathing without adjusting it. Try a few different methods and positions to see which feels most comfortable to you, and which way helps you to maintain focus.

315

Mindful breathing step-by-step

Here's how to train yourself to pay attention:

1. Get comfortable: Find a stable position on a cushion or a chair, with your back upright or lying down. Rest your hands wherever they feel comfortable. Relax your body. Notice how it feels: the weight of your body connecting to the chair or floor and the sensations you feel, your body's shape. Tighten and release any areas where you feel tension. And relax.

2. Breathe: Inhale. Breathe in deeply through your nose, counting, if you wish. Hold for a couple of seconds and then exhale. Breathe out through your mouth, again counting if you wish to. Tune into your breath as it flows naturally in and out. There's no need to change your breathing to become longer or shorter, just breathe naturally in and out.

3. Focus: Notice how your breath feels, one breath at a time. Focus your attention on where you feel your breath within your body. Is it through your nostrils? Your abdomen? Your throat or chest? Follow that sensation. Notice the point where one breath ends and the next breath begins. Focus on how that feels.

4. Notice: You will find that your mind wanders as you become distracted by thoughts or bodily sensations. That's fine and completely natural. Simply notice this, without any judgement, and softly say, "Thinking". Notice any judgements, too. Take a mental note of them, then let them pass, along with any sensations they generate in your body.

5. Return: Gently bring your attention back to your breath. You may need to do this frequently during your mindful breathing practice, and that's okay. Consciously returning your attention back to the present moment, back to your breath, flexes your conscious-awareness muscles and, slowly but surely, cultivates a mindfulness practice. The more you can do this and return time and again to your breath, the more your ability to do so will increase, until it becomes second nature. That's when you will be able to deepen the sensation of being present, even when strong distractions arise.

6. Remain: Stay in this practice for several minutes. Continue to focus on your breath, notice your mind wandering and redirect it back to your breath. In a while, return your attention to your body as it sits or lies. Feel how your relaxed body feels, and feel grateful for taking this time to practise mindful breathing. Gently open your eyes.

That's it: that's how to practise mindful breathing. And the more you practise, the easier it will get, and the more able you'll be to pause and focus attention on your breath when you sense the need to calm down, find inner peace and come back to yourself.

Start by choosing a short period of time in which to practise meditation each day. The best way to build a practice is by doing it consistently every day, so commit to a manageable amount of time – whether that's five minutes or half an hour – and gradually add more minutes to it. Pay attention to your bodily sensations and movements, at intervals throughout the day. Notice your feet on the ground and how your legs feel. Pay attention to the position your limbs are in, your posture, and how your head, shoulders and neck feel.

Right: Sitting comfortably and tuning in to your body helps ground you before you start mindfully breathing.

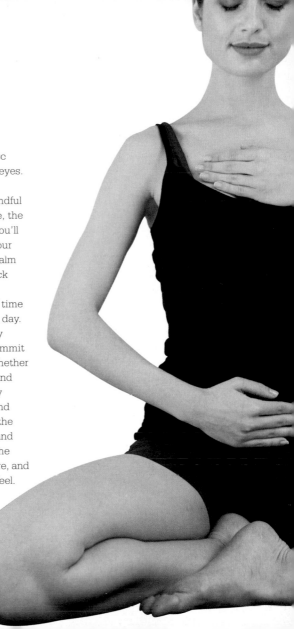

Variations

If you wish to practise different breathing strategies, to mix your practice up a little, try the following suggestions:

- **Act upon words,** to match your breathing. Say a different word with each breath. For example:

  One – UP. Stop, look up and take a big, deep breath. Looking up to the sky opens the chest, and the deep breath initiates your relaxation response and parasympathetic nervous system.

  Two – DOWN. Look down to your feet as you take a second breath.

  Three – BODY. Take your breath from your feet back up to your head and back again.

  Four – SMILE. Breathe deeply in and then, as you breathe out, turn up the corners of your mouth into a smile.

- **Inhale and exhale for different counts.** Instead of inhaling for five and exhaling for five, try distributing your breath equally between inhaling, holding and exhaling: breathe in for four, hold for four, exhale for four, hold for four, then repeat. If you need a burst of oxygen, try inhaling for twice as long as you exhale: inhale for eight, exhale for four, inhale for six, exhale for three. If you're feeling especially anxious, try exhaling for twice as long as you inhale: so inhale for four, exhale for eight, inhale for three, exhale for six.

- **Try deep, diaphragmatic breathing** to take fuller breaths. Place your hand on your stomach and imagine a balloon inside, which expands each time you breathe in and deflates when you breathe out.

- **Visualize releasing negative thoughts** as you breathe. Breathe in as if you are sucking up all the thoughts that are bothering you, then blow the thoughts out of your body as you exhale.

Above: Breath is an incredible leveller of emotions. Breathing practices can release tension and emotion, and calm us down so we may respond better.

319

Return to now: deepen the present

Mindful breathing isn't the only way to be mindful. Here are some other mindfulness practices that will further focus your attention and deepen your connection to your self and the present moment.

Walk mindfully

Walking mindfully is often described as "meditation in motion" and involves turning your full attention to the process of walking. Try this next time you walk to the car, your next meeting or wherever you need to get to.

1. Bring your attention to your feet. Notice how the ground feels underneath your feet, how hard it is (or soft and spongy, if you are walking on grass). Notice the touchpoint and how it feels to be grounded and stable; how sturdy the floor is.

2. Notice your steps and your stride. Is your stride rhythmic or not? How does it feel to shift your weight from one foot to the other?

3. Notice your arms. Are they hanging loosely or clasped behind your back? What sensations do you feel in your arms, and the rest of your body, as you walk?

4. Bring your attention back to your walk as your mind wanders, and let the feeling of stability move from the ground, as you touch it with each foot, right up your body. Add verbal cues to bring your focus back to your body, if you wish, such as "lifting" or "stepping".

5. Add a "gatha", if you wish to help support your focus. A "gatha" is a short verse that helps focus attention on the present action. For example, as you breathe in, say, "I am walking"; and as you breathe out, say, "in this moment".

• **Spend time alone with yourself.** Today we are hardly ever alone, even when there is nobody else around. All we have to do is pick up our phones and there is someone there to interact with. True solitude, without devices – with just ourselves – is a self-compassionate mindful practice. Schedule in time for self-care that involves nobody but you, and practise being mindful about the place you find yourself in. If you read a book, think about how the cover

Opposite: Noticing our feet on the ground is a grounding experience. It connects and stabilizes us so we may better focus on our surroundings.

feels, the touch of the paper as you turn a page; see the printed text as individual words chosen by an author, rather than as a story; notice the sensations in your body as you read. If you soak in a bath, close your eyes and focus on your breath, then open them and marvel at the light catching the bubbles, or how the water feels on your skin. If you take a shower, notice the droplets of water as they land on your skin; taste the water; feel the sensation as the water lands on and pours off your skin; notice the warmth and what your skin looks and feels like in this moment.

6. Focus on the movement of your foot and ankle as they lift off the ground and then step down in rhythm. Focus on that rhythm and how your body feels. Focus all of your attention on the parts of your body as you walk, and on the rhythm of your movement. As you shift your weight and place the heel and then the ball of your foot on the ground, notice how this feels on the ground, compared to when you lift your heel. Does walking in this way feel robotic or fluid? Notice whether this changes as you continue with this practice.

7. Focus on your surroundings and look in detail at one object and another. Look at how each object is positioned, and how its colours and textures contrast with other objects within the environment.

8. Focus on you, and on how you fit within this environment and how you impact on it. Focus on your breathing and its rhythm, and feel how you flow through this world, from one place to another, so freely.

> "Invite your child to join you in focusing attention on the breath."

- **Escape from sensory overload and renew your harmony with nature.** Feel the leaves underfoot, notice the raindrops on the leaves and find a place to pause – perhaps a tree to shelter underneath. Place your hand on the tree bark and notice how it feels to touch it, then look up the tree trunk and inhale. Look down toward the tree's roots, and exhale deep down into the earth. As you breathe in, look upward through the branches to the sky and then, as you breathe out, look downward to the forest floor. Each time notice how this feels and then start over again, deepening your connection with the tree, the sky above and the earth below.

- **If you are a parent, invite your child to join you in focusing attention on the breath.** Place a toy on the child's tummy and ask them to breathe slowly in and out, as if they are blowing up a balloon or blowing out candles on a birthday cake. It's their job to breathe gently and slowly enough not to wake the toy up. Whisper to them to focus on their breathing, and tap their hand any time their mind wanders toward a thought and away from their breath. Ask them to put each thought on a cloud and watch it float away, and return to keeping the toy asleep by focusing on their breathing.

Opposite: Children can join in with mindful breathing and take this tool with them through life. Suggest they smell the birthday cake (in) and blow out the candles (out).

- **Focus your attention on every note of a piece of music.** Listen intently to the melody, then hone in on each individual instrument.

- **Make, and eat, your lunch attentively.** Notice each item that you use to make your lunch, and slow the process down. Be aware of what you can see and touch: the textures of the food you are using. Pay attention to how it feels when you slice a knife through the soft bread. What does it smell like? Notice if your mind wanders, and where it wanders to. Notice the colours and textures of the finished lunch, before eating it mindfully. Keep your chewing action slow, so that you savour every moment of each mouthful. Notice the different tastes and textures. Consider how this experience compares to the way you might usually make and eat your lunch.

- **Water your garden mindfully.** Notice the bark of the trees, the flower petals and the pollen. Notice their texture and colour. Watch every drop of water soak into the soil and the droplets stick to the leaves. Watch the movement of the plants. Be aware of each plant and how it stands next to another one. Now close your eyes and listen to each noise you can hear; focus on the sounds nearby first, then notice the sounds far away.

Right: Stopping to smell the flowers, to notice every plant, petal, sound and colour helps us to appreciate everything more and ground ourselves in the present moment.

- **Choose a guided meditation.** Use an app such as Insight Timer or join a virtual-meditation group, such as *The Pause* via This Epic Life. You can select a gratitude meditation, a loving-kindness meditation (see below for an example), a mindfulness meditation or one to help you get to sleep or recharge. The Insight Timer app shows you who else is meditating nearby, which can make you feel supported by other people.

- **Relax your muscles as you inhale and exhale.** Squeeze and relax each muscle group throughout your body, to progressively relax each one. Breathe in and hold, then release the tension in the body part that you are focusing your attention on. Notice how heavy each body part feels. Start with the toes and repeat with each muscle group from your toes, feet, calves and knees to your thighs, up through your buttocks, to your stomach,

Above: A loving-kindness meditation enables us to connect more deeply with people, even those with whom we might be struggling to interact well with.

hands, arms and shoulders, through to your chest, neck, mouth, eyes and head. This can also be a helpful exercise to do as you lie in bed, to prepare you for a relaxing night's sleep.

Self-care for the mind

This connection between our mind, our body and conscious awareness is liberating. But it's not always easy. Some days living mindfully can be difficult, while on other days it feels simpler. That's why it's called a practice. Yet when we live mindfully and develop a consequential self-awareness and self-compassion, we can enjoy a sense of inner harmony.

In this way, mindfulness is self-care for the mind. Now all we need to do is to take care of our bodies, too. For the mind and the body are intrinsically linked.

Loving-kindness meditation

1. Get yourself into a relaxed and comfortable position.

2. Take a big deep breath in and count to five, then breathe out and count to five.

3. Bring to mind someone who makes you feel happy, and use that feeling of warmth and that vision of glowing light – that natural sense of loving-kindness – to wish yourself and others well. As you imagine your loved one in front of you, focus on that warm glow of loving-kindness, and where in your body you can feel it.

4. Now repeat the following mantra:

> "May you be safe and happy.
> May you be peaceful and calm.
> May you be healthy and strong,
> May you live with ease and wellbeing."

5. Extend those words to others, as you breathe slowly in and out, imagining the warm glow of loving-kindness as light extending outward and wrapping around more people, shifting your loving-kindness to reach out even further. Allow your loving-kindness to expand out in all directions to those you are experiencing issues with, people you may be struggling with and people you don't know – the wider world:

> "May all beings be well.
> May everyone experience great joy."

6. And from your loved one back to you, wishing you well. And may you feel well and safe and happy, peaceful and calm, healthy and strong, imagining your loved one saying this to you, before shifting that sense of loving-kindness back to yourself:

> "May I be safe and happy.
> May I be peaceful and calm.
> May I be healthy and strong,
> May I live with ease and wellbeing.
> May I accept myself just the way I am."

VITALITY IS VITAL TO LIVING WELL

"Energy is eternal delight."

WILLIAM BLAKE,
ENGLISH POET, PAINTER AND PRINTMAKER

Optimizing vitality

Can you remember running and dancing barefoot across the lawn? Climbing trees? Roller-skating? Cartwheeling? Riding your bike everywhere? When we were young we moved a lot. It's what children do. We moved from one activity to the next, full of energy, enthusiasm and vitality.

Our bodies are meant to move. They are designed for motion, and yet the human race is becoming increasingly sedentary. Back then, we looked up and danced. Now, we look down and sit. Indeed, according to the renowned speaker Nilofer Merchant, whose 2013 TED Talk, "Sitting is the Smoking of Our Generation", is in the top 10 per cent of TED's most viewed talks, we sit more and move less than we ever have, as we sit for an average of ten hours per day.

Yet, the more we move, the better our bodies and minds work. This is a scientific fact that we've known to be true since the first few centuries BCE. Indeed, the restorative qualities of physical activity are nothing new. Ayurveda – the ancient Indian philosophy of health – led to yoga, which was first codified in 600 BCE; Hippocrates referred to exercise and nutrition as "medicine" in the 4th century BCE; and Greek ideals of exercise led to the Olympic Games and the exercise system of Tai Chi, which first emphasized graceful movement as a route to health and vitality in 200 BCE.

Above: Hippocrates saw exercise and nutrition as medicine and today the field of mind-body medicine further demonstrates how moving our bodies can positively affect our minds.

Opposite: Movement is the route to good health and vitality, both of which are vital to our happiness too.

Nourishing leads to flourishing

Vitality – the state of being strong, active and alert, with optimal physical and mental energy – essentially puts the "being well" into "wellbeing". For we can only truly flourish when we are nourished. This may be why, in October 2015, Professor Martin Seligman acknowledged and accepted "Vitality" as a missing component of the PERMA model of wellbeing (see Chapter Four), which has since been tweaked by many leading positive psychologists to become the PERMA-V model.

Energy enables us to function well and to thrive. As such, to make the most of our lives, our energy reserves need to be regularly replenished. When we choose self-care, we pay a deposit into our personal energy banks and gain an energy boost. When we don't choose it, we make a withdrawal from our energy reserves and end up feeling depleted and low on energy. And everything feels more arduous when we lack energy.

Restorative activities, such as a good night's sleep and a strenuous physical workout, replenish our energy reserves and boost our vitality, which makes us better able to cope with life's inevitable challenges. To optimize our vitality then, experts suggest that we move more; and sleep, eat and breathe well.

Below: Topping up our energy reserves makes living easier. Moving more, eating, sleeping and breathing well are ways we can bolster our vitality.

Self-care is health-care

Both our mental and our physical health benefit from nourishment, so it's vital to take care of ourselves and to make our vitality a priority. For self-care is a nurturing and healing act.

Sometimes self-care is about the soothing and nurturing act of pampering: a massage, facial or haircut; a hot cup of frothy coffee or a long soak in a bubble-filled bath. Yet often self-care is about investing time in something that we might feel less motivated to do, such as jumping on the trampoline with the children, instead of putting our feet up with a cuppa; or going for a quick run round the block, instead of collapsing on the sofa. We owe it to ourselves to invest time in recharging ourselves. For running on empty – as a result of a lack of sleep, exercise and nutrients – can be incredibly bad for us.

Physical inactivity can lead to a number of diseases. Given that so many people spend all day sitting in front of a computer and then all evening sitting in front of the television, this is a problem that needs addressing. Such widespread inactivity, combined with insufficient nutrition and poor sleep, is a recipe for diminished energy levels, which have the knock-on effect of making it more difficult to manage our emotions, focus our attention and cope with life, let alone flourish.

So what can we do to boost our vitality and keep our energy banks in credit? We can:

1. **Move more:** The recommendations are physical activities that elevate the heart rate for 20–30 minutes three to five times per week, with children recommended to be active for an hour each day. However, even one hour per week lessens the health risks for adults.

2. **Sleep better:** Ideally ten hours per night for children, and at least seven to eight hours of sleep per night for adults.

3. **Eat well:** Eat nutritious, well-balanced meals and never skip breakfast or eat at your desk.

4. **Breathe better:** Master the breath, in order to aid relaxation and rejuvenation.

Opposite: A healthy balanced diet of nourishing good food helps our body and mind to function well so that we may flourish.

1. Move more

Exercise doesn't merely energize, for its benefits to our well-being are far more profound. As mind–body medicine reveals, movement has the power to lift mood, bolster brain power, remedy exhaustion and reduce depression. That's all thanks to the feel-good endorphins that are released when we exercise, which help us to think clearly and feel good.

Physical activity reduces anxiety and stress levels, lowers rates of mortality and disease and increases muscle strength. It improves bone and heart health and reduces cholesterol and blood-sugar levels. It can also help us to improve our quality of sleep and our quality of life, as regular exercise quietens the mind-chatter that can fill our brains before bedtime.

So why do so many of us struggle to fit exercise into our daily lives? Perhaps it's because of the way we view it – as a chore?

"Physical activity is effective in the treatment of clinical depression and can be as successful as psychotherapy or medication, particularly in the longer term."[1]

UK DEPARTMENT OF HEALTH

Below: Movement lifts our mood, improves our energy levels and enhances our mind. Habitually moving more needn't be seen as a chore.

Make it fun!

When we were children, moving was fun. All that tree-climbing, cartwheeling and roller-skating was so enjoyable that it didn't feel like exercise. And it needn't feel that way now. In fact that's the secret of maintaining an active lifestyle – finding a mode of exercise that engages and fulfils you, in the same way that scaling a tree or turning a cartwheel did when you were a child.

If we can invest time in the physical activities that we do best and enjoy most, then perhaps we can shift our perception of exercise overall to become a more positive experience. Just as the Dutch view cycling as a means of transport rather than as exercise, perhaps we should view exercise as something to enjoy rather than something to endure. You could also try the following approaches:

- **List all the physical activities you used to love doing as a child.** Tree-climbing? Skipping? Making up dance routines with friends? Roller-skating? Swimming? Think about how you might incorporate these activities into your week. Perhaps you were part of your school netball team? Look out for netball classes that welcome players of any age and skill level. Are there roller-discos operating in your area, which you could attend with friends? If you have fond memories of scaling a great tree, look out for tree-climbing events in your local area.

- **Involve your children and embrace your own "inner child".** If you have children,

Flourishing facts

A Psychosomatic Medicine study in 2000 of 156 adults with major depressive disorder proved that regular exercise minimizes the relapse rate of depression to 9 per cent, compared to 31–38 per cent for participants who combined exercise with medication or took medication alone.[2]

Meanwhile, a recent research study of more than 2,000 participants[3] has shown that physical activity is as good for our minds as it is for our bodies, as it helps us to improve the way we react to stressful events and process stressors in our daily life. Our reactivity to negative affect is enhanced by exercise.

join in their fun – offer to play football with them, have a trampolining championship, go on a family bike ride or play hopscotch.

- **Devote a month to finding your most fun form of exercise.** Try out different classes and types of exercise and compare how much fun each is. From cycling, running and swimming to group activities such as body combat, Zumba and netball, there is plenty to choose from. Once you've tried out a few different types, commit to attending the one class that you enjoy most, on a regular basis. Which activity makes you feel happiest and most energized? Block book that exercise activity for the next month/term.

Rejuvenating rituals

The more you can automate specific physical activities, the more they become habitual. To do this, you need to schedule certain rituals into your life.

- **Stretch.** Our bodies are designed to move, and we can stretch them wherever we are, even while sitting. Extending each part of your body on waking, before sleeping and a few times in between is what your body craves. Yoga enhances and optimizes the body's natural ability to function, so that it can perform at its best. By stretching each morning, even just for five minutes, you can give your body the chance to function at its best.

- **Recharge with regular energy breaks at 90–120-minute intervals throughout the day.** This taps into our physiological "ultradian rhythms", which are recurrent daily cycles based on the natural ebb and flow from high energy to low energy. After an "ultradian sprint" of 90 minutes, we tend to feel a lull of energy, as indicated by yawns, hunger and a restless lack

Right: Stretching is an important part of movement. So ritualizing stretching each morning, before we step out of bed, is a great way to start the day.

"The average person is most
alert and energized in the late
morning and mid-evening"

of concentration. A recovery period is
then required to restore our energy levels,
although people often ignore these signs
and work through them, burning out their
energy. Instead, by giving ourselves
intermittent renewal breaks, we can
give our body the period of recovery that
it craves toward the end of each cycle.
Doing so will result in improved
concentration and performance and
optimized energy levels. So set a timer
and move – whether it's walking over to
the water cooler, running up and down a
flight of stairs, dancing to a favourite piece
of music or doing 20 press-ups, regular
energy breaks will boost your vitality across
the day. You might decide that 90 minutes
is too long in between activities and set
an alarm at 45-minute intervals, allowing
you to do 15-minute bursts of physical
activity per hour. If a few of these micro-
breaks involve High Intensity Interval
Training (HIIT) – that is, cardiovascular

exercise that alternates short periods of
intense exercise with less intense recovery
periods – so much the better. However,
simply getting up from your chair to
move and stretch your body is enough
to make a difference to your vitality.

- **Cultivate a "movement mindset", by
building movement into your daily
routine.** Studies by clinical
endocrinologists[4] have found that NEAT
(Non-Exercise Activity Thermogenesis)
movements – that is, the energy that we
expend on activities other than sport-
based exercise – burn calories in a
cumulative way. This is often overlooked
when we consider how active we are.
Walking to the kitchen, putting dishes
away, even micro-movements such as
fidgeting from one foot to another while
standing in a queue – these all add up. So
consider ways in which you can up your
NEAT movements: for example, stretches,

lunges, squats, shoulder-rolls or arm-reaches, while standing around or waiting in a queue, sustain movement. Similarly you could do bicep curls as you hold a basket in a supermarket, or take the stairs rather than the lift at every opportunity.

Above: Our bodies have natural rhythms, so it makes sense to bear these in mind when we schedule movement into our days.

- **Use your body's natural circadian rhythms or BRAC (Basic Rest and Activity Cycle) to determine when best to exercise.** The average person is most alert and energized in the late morning and mid-evening, and at their lowest ebb mid-afternoon and in the early hours of the morning. To make the most of your body's natural cycle, aim to get physically active while at the bottom of your BRAC. So early in the morning and at 2.30pm go for a brisk walk, dance to music or partake in a quick burst of physical activity to boost your energy levels. Alternatively, if you benefit from short naps, this would be the best time to take one.

- **Dance.** Put on your favourite tune and dance. While dancing energetically gets your heart rate up, researchers from Northumbria University also found that classical music, such as Vivaldi's *Spring* concerto, enhanced alertness and memory and enabled participants to respond more quickly and more accurately to test tasks than those who completed tests in silence.[5]

- **Schedule regular periods of cardio and strength-training exercise into your week.** Experts recommend three periods of cardiovascular activity and one period of strength training per week, or a minimum of three exercise periods where you break into a sweat. Cardio strengthens the body's circulatory system (heart and blood vessels) and includes endurance exercise such as running, cycling, dancing and tennis. Strength training – such as Pilates, yoga, weight-training or bodyweight exercises like push-ups and sit-ups – uses resistance to improve aerobic endurance and strengthen muscles.

- **Learn to improve your posture and to sit, stand and walk better.** Pilates, yoga and the Alexander Technique can help to improve postural habits.

- **Stand on your head.** Doing so not only improves brain function, if you do it regularly, but MRI studies reveal that headstands can improve mood and release stress (unless you have a stress-headache of course).

Opposite: Standing on your head is a quick way to lift mood and decrease stress as well as giving you a fresh (albeit upside down) perspective on the world.

> "If you choose habits that provide physical energy restoration, you can experience the dual benefit of giving both your mental and your physical energy a boost."

- **Walk more.** Walking is a bone-strengthening, mood-lifting, ailment-avoiding wonder of a physical activity. It can help prevent (or manage) a variety of conditions and improve coordination. Get a pedometer to track your steps and to encourage you to do the recommended 10,000 steps per day. Just 30 minutes of walking each day is enough to dramatically reduce the risk of heart disease, some cancers and dementia. If that's not possible, break it down into more manageable mini-walks of ten minutes each.

- **Take your meetings on the move and/or set up a treadmill workstation.** Speaker Nilofer Merchant says that walking meetings are more productive than others and now account for 70 per cent of her weekly exercise. Workstations that enable you to stand and move while you type are becoming more prevalent, due to the negative impact of sitting on health and energy.

- **Get on your bike!** In Copenhagen there are five times as many bikes as there are cars, with Danes cycling an average of 1.5km (1 mile) every single day. Given the good-mood endorphins that are released when we exercise, this may be partially why Danes top the happiness ratings (see Chapter Three) with such frequency.

Energetic abundance

Vitality is about both mental and physical energy repletion, so if you can ritualize activities that serve both of these, then even better.

Create physical energy-boosting habits and replenish your mental energy as a bonus. Making habits freshens our cognitive resources, as it frees us from using our self-control to decide whether or not to make

healthy choices. As such, making habits actually saves energy by conserving willpower and removing the mental effort involved in decision-making. For example, if you arrange to cycle to work with a friend on specific days, you're no longer faced with the decision of whether or not to drag yourself out of bed to exercise each morning – the decision is already made. Similarly, the ritual of taking a nap or eating a protein

Above: Exercising is restorative but doesn't require a trip to the gym. There are many ways we can habitually move more, especially if we create a routine.

snack every day at 3pm, when you might ordinarily experience an energy-lull, simultaneously saves and gives energy. So if you choose habits that provide physical energy restoration, you can experience the dual benefit of giving both your mental and your physical energy a boost.

2. Sleep better

Sleep is essential to our wellbeing, but there's a secret about sleep that most people don't realize. Sleep is not merely a peaceful period of rest where our inactive brains switch off. On the contrary, our heart rate and breathing may slow down, but our brains are incredibly active while we sleep. It is our bodily muscles that rest, not our brains. As such, sleep is restorative rather than restful.

"A good night's sleep makes it easier for us to recall pleasant memories, whereas a lack of sleep can cause us to forget positive memories and remember primarily negative ones."

As we slumber, we drift through consistent cycles of light sleep, deep sleep and dreaming:

• **During the light-sleep cycle** we seal off our memories.

• **During deep sleep** we renew and restore ourselves, as the body produces growth hormones to stimulate tissue growth and muscle repair, and interleukin (naturally occurring proteins that mediate communication between cells) to support immune functioning. We spend 20 per cent of our sleep in this stage.

• **During the REM (Rapid Eye Movement) dream cycle,** which we drift into every 90 minutes, our brains race and our heart rate rises, as we spend 25 per cent of our sleep working through our worries and concerns. Neuroscientists have discovered that dreams facilitate both learning and memory. In this way, dreaming restores our mind, while deep sleep restores our body.

A good night's sleep makes it easier for us to recall pleasant memories, whereas a lack of sleep can cause us to forget positive memories and remember the primarily negative ones. This is due to the effect of sleep deprivation on the memory-storing hippocampus (the part of the brain involved in processing memory).

When we get sufficient sleep, we prime ourselves to flourish. When we don't, we prime ourselves to languish. Sleep boosts our vitality, as our alertness and energy increase and our concentration, creativity, memory and performance are improved. This is why sleep can have such an impact on our waking mood, which tends to affect how we feel during the day and has been proven to positively or negatively affect our performance.

What's more, we are – according to a British Psychological Society *Research Digest* study[6] – more sensitive to negative emotions such as fear and anger, the more tired we are. This negative emotional reactivity can be reversed by a short afternoon nap or a good night's sleep.

Below: Sleep is an essential ingredient in our happiness recipe. We need sufficient sleep to restore our minds and bodies so we can feel good.

The effects of sleep deprivation

Getting less than four hours' sleep a night is especially bad for us and is related to the onset of a number of diseases, with less than six hours' sleep linked to a greater risk of high blood pressure. This is especially true when we are deprived of REM sleep, as our bodies tend to enter this stage sooner and stay there longer, at the expense of the bodily-repair stage of sleep.

Lack of sleep causes tiredness, but continued lack of sleep causes sleep debt and deprivation, which causes exhaustion and can adversely affect health, career and happiness. In fact, a study carried out in 1999 by the researchers Williamson and Feyer,[9] which kept participants awake for 28 hours, showed that they performed as poorly as participants who were given 10–15 grams of alcohol at 30-minute intervals until their blood-alcohol content (BAC) was over the limit. Sleep deprivation also influences weight, and a 2004 Stanford University study[10] revealed that we crave and eat more food than usual after a lack of sleep. This is because our appetite is stimulated (by higher levels of the "hunger hormone" ghrelin) and we don't feel as full after eating (due to lower levels of the hormone leptin).

How to facilitate better sleep

The way to facilitate better sleep is to create optimal sleeping conditions by fostering habitual sleep rituals and getting to know your own sleep system and related cues:

- **Get to know your own sleep system.**
  Your biological clock (circadian rhythm) regulates your sleep–wake routine, makes sleep most desirable during the mid-afternoon "nap zone" and between midnight and dawn, and governs the release of hormones such as melatonin, which help you sleep. Certain external cues, called "zeitgebers" – such as dimmed lights and a tendency to look at the clock around

"bedtime" – support your biological clock, so look out for them.

- **Control your pre-sleep behaviour to support your body's natural sleep routine.** This improves your "sleep hygiene". For example:

1. Aim to go to bed each night and awake each morning at the same time. And try to keep consistent schedules for eating, exercising and socializing.

2. Wrap up your day and stop working at least an hour before bedtime. Write your

Above: There is much we can do to improve our sleep hygiene – from setting consistent sleep times to establishing pre-sleep rituals.

"to-do list" for the following day/week, so that your mind is relieved of tasks.

3. Wind down by having a bath or shower, reading a book, writing in a journal, meditating, doing gentle yoga stretches or listening to music – anything that doesn't involve a screen. Get into your pyjamas and brush your teeth during that wind-down time, rather than immediately before you get into bed, so that doing so doesn't diminish your drowsiness.

VITALITY IS VITAL TO LIVING WELL

- **Create a sacred sleep space.** Ensure the bedroom is dark, quiet, uncluttered and cool enough, with sufficient fresh air; and use a pillow that supports your neck. House plants make good additions to any bedroom, to improve the air quality, and bedside lamps should offer a warm glow rather than bright light.

- **Switch off the TV, computer, phone and LED lighting two hours before bed.** It's important to log off from your computer devices before you nod off to sleep, because the blue light suppresses the production of the sleep-inducing hormone melatonin, so it keeps you awake – 91 per cent of 18–24-year-olds who were surveyed don't do this.[11] Alternatively, use an app to dim or redden the screen light after dark, decrease the brightness levels yourself or invest in some amber-tinted glasses to block the light.

- **Dim the bedroom lights and only have night-lamps on, if you read in bed.** The amount and type of light can either encourage or suppress melatonin production, which makes you drowsy.

- **Limit caffeine, and avoid caffeinated drinks and foods that cause heartburn, after lunchtime.** While caffeine has neurological benefits in moderation, the earlier in the day we drink it, the better. This is due to its ability to block the sleep-promoting hormone adenosine.

- **Use progressive muscle relaxation or a guided sleep meditation to help you drift off to sleep.** This involves tensing each muscle group in your body, from your toes to your head, as you slowly inhale and exhale.

- **Count your blessings rather than counting sheep.** Visualize what you are grateful for, in pictures rather than words. Doing so can help you drift off to sleep in a positive mindset.

- **Take a short nap of 15–20 minutes if you feel drowsy in the mid-afternoon.** But only do so if it doesn't adversely affect your main sleep, and not if you suffer from insomnia (because naps can perpetuate an unhealthy sleep cycle). Brief naps can, according to a study of 1,000 participants conducted for the Edinburgh International Science Festival,[12] make you more focused, creative and productive, and can soak up sleep debt from previous sleeps when you may not have slept well. It's important to keep them brief, to avoid slipping into REM sleep.

Opposite: Naps can be especially nourishing and help us to be better at what we do.

3. Eat well

What we eat can have a major impact on our mental well-being, because food affects how we feel, as well as impacting on our physical health. In this way, healthy eating enables the win–win situation of boosting physical energy levels and enhancing our mood, by positively altering metabolism and brain chemistry. Good food also helps us to sleep better and gives us the energy we need to move more, thus impacting on three of the "core pillars of wellbeing" (see Chapter Four).

According to research by Cornell University in which 139 people took part, the average participant made an estimated 226.7 daily decisions about food.[13] No wonder that, having faced decisions down in every supermarket aisle about whether to opt for wholemeal or seeded bread and whether to base our choices on price or taste, by the time we reach the checkout we have little willpower left to resist the bar of chocolate that is cleverly positioned in front of us.

However, eating healthily isn't about eating less or eating "clean"; it's about eating well-balanced, nourishing food and not about restricting and limiting our diet. With that in mind, in order to eat well, for optimal wellness:

- **Focus on what you can eat, rather than on what you can't.** When you make food choices from a position of self-care rather than one of self-control, with the goal being good health and wellbeing rather

than to lose weight, you foster healthier eating habits. Conversely, when you restrict certain foods, such as sugar or carbohydrates, and partake in diets that restrict our intake, you often end up eating more, whenever you have the chance to. A 1999 clinical nutrition study of 3–5-year-old children attending daycare at the Pennsylvania State University Child Development Laboratory[14] found this to be especially true for children when they've been pressurized into restricting their food intake or eating less of certain foods – they eat more of it. Aim to teach yourself moderation rather than prevention. By focusing on choosing nourishing foods, rather than on limiting "bad" foods, you can create a healthier relationship with what you put into your body.

- **Learn to listen to your body.** Teach yourself about intuitive eating. This involves trusting your body and listening

to your hunger cues, so that you can better self-regulate how much to eat before you are full, and discover that foods should be eaten in moderation. The goal is to finish meals feeling physically and emotionally satisfied rather than angry or ashamed, so listen to your body. This is a happy alternative to turning dinnertime into a battlefield.

- **Enjoy food as a topic of conversation.** Talk about fullness and hunger, and what you are eating and why. Have conversations during meals about where the food comes from, how food is grown and why it is good (or less good) for your body.

Above: We can nourish ourselves by giving our bodies the correct portions of fruit, vegetables, calcium, protein, wholegrains and carbohydrates.

- **Plan balanced small meals and light snacks.** Each day should include two to three portions of calcium-containing foods, at least five portions of fruit and vegetables, along with nutritious protein sources, wholegrains, balanced snacks and small portions of carbohydrates at each meal. Carbohydrates are energy-giving, but are easy to overeat in large portions. A small fistful of pasta, potatoes or bread is enough to provide energy.

- **Choose good mood foods.** Blueberries, almonds, spinach, tuna, oranges, bananas, sweet potatoes, brown rice, avocado, Brazil nuts, sardines, oats, lentils, chicken and turkey, yoghurt, dark chocolate and oysters have all been shown to enhance mood.

- **Drink more water.** Our brains operate so much better when our bodies are well hydrated. Use an app or an alarm to remind you to drink water every hour, or use cues. For example, drink water every time you send an email or finish talking on the phone.

- **Eat (and drink) more fruit and vegetables.** Drink green smoothies and juices on a regular basis. Aim for antioxidant-rich berries and vegetables, and eat more apples. Smoothies are a wonderful way to consume more leafy greens, as spinach and kale make a good base for other fruit and vegetables.

- **Eat mindfully.** Use your senses of smell, touch, hearing and sight, just as much as taste, to fully enjoy each mouthful. How does the food sound as you chew? How does it smell? What does it feel and look like? What colours are on your plate? Mindful eating helps you to focus on the process of eating and become aware of when you are full, which is less easy when you are shovelling food into your mouth on autopilot or when you're distracted.

Right: Water hydrates us, which enables us to function and think better. Using a reminder to drink more water on a regular basis can be helpful.

Children and nutrition

Just as it's important to teach yourself about healthy eating, it's equally vital to instil that same awareness in children. So teach them about eating intuitively and in moderation, rather than forbidding certain foods, which can backfire as an approach. Get them to listen to their bodies, and talk to them about food. This provides the opportunity to teach nutrition without a restrictive mindset, which can cause a heightened fear of – or desire for – the restricted foods.

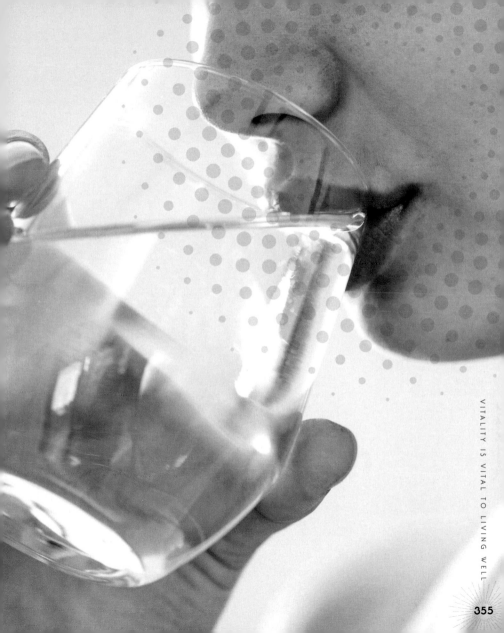

4. Breathe better

Mastery of the breath has a number of benefits for our vitality. From the emotional energy and diffusion of negative emotions that deep abdominal breathing affords us with, to the ability to either invigorate or calm the body, breathing well can help us remove fear and anger from our lives and feel more alert or at ease.

Breath-mastery makes us less weary, because gaining control over our breathing gives us the chance to gain greater control of our lives. When we learn to breathe better, we can prevent ourselves from expending energy on emotional black holes. In this way, breath-mastery is energy-enhancing rather than energy-draining.

Our breath is a direct link to our own nervous system. Inhaling activates our sympathetic nervous system, while exhaling activates our parasympathetic nervous system. As such, by mastering our breath we can gain more control over how we respond to external stimuli, because breathing affects both our fight-or-flight and freeze response and our rest-and-digest response.

- **Breathe in through your nostrils.** Doing so provides you with the opportunity to clean and warm the air you breathe in before it reaches your lungs. As such, it is better for your health than mouth-breathing.

"Energy and persistence conquer all things."
BENJAMIN FRANKLIN,
AMERICAN STATESMAN

- **Practise belly-breathing (diaphragmatic breathing).** Place your hands on your diaphragm and feel your lung capacity rise and fall, as you take three deep breaths in, to the count of three, and out to the count of six. Then switch to breathing in for six and out for three. This enables you to deepen your breath, strengthen the muscles involved and stimulate the vagus nerve, which runs from the brain to the abdomen and aids relaxation and rejuvenation.

- **Focus attention on your breath, to bring you into the present moment.** For more breathing techniques, see page 316.

Opposite: Moving our bodies keeps us fit and energized, but moving our diaphragms helps us to build muscles which aid relaxation and rejuvenation.

Invigoration exploration

It makes sense to take an individual approach to how we best care for ourselves, given that what nourishes one person may feel less nourishing to another. So we should listen to our bodies and minds, to determine whether low energy requires rejuvenation or relaxation as its tonic.

While a walk in nature is medicine for the soul and can lift even the darkest mood, sometimes a feeling of tiredness can only be rectified by a short nap. A bespoke self-care response is often required, depending on your individual needs. But we are better able to determine the type of vitality-boosting care if we have a solid understanding of what works best for us. So consider what invigorates and replenishes you. Is it a hot shower, a quick run, a leisurely walk? And try the following:

- **Create a list of energizing activities that you can undertake during low-ebb times at the bottom of your BRAC (see page 341).** Try them out to see which one works best for you. Jot down your findings.

- **Commit to taking a tiny step (or a series of small steps) to improve your vitality.** Perhaps you could set an alarm that reminds you to be active for ten minutes of each hour? Or walk for 15 minutes every morning? Perhaps you could

commit to drinking a nutritious green smoothie three times a week? Or to going to bed earlier? Try one small step for 21 days, and then another step.

A single tiny step has the knock-on effect of leading to the next step, and the next. Before you know it, your ten-minute walk has become a 30-minute stroll or a 20-minute run; your daily smoothie habit has led you to eat more nutritious breakfasts; your breath-mastery has enabled you to focus your emotional energy on what matters most to you.

Little by little you shift your lifestyle to one where you move more, sleep better and eat well. And you'll feel good – not just from the achievement of doing so, but because shifts in these areas will allow your body and mind to function better, with optimum vitality.

Right: Listing actions which replenish us, such as drinking a green smoothie or going for a run, can provide a useful aid to our self-care.

A HAPPY LIFE
is a compassionate, curious
and considered life

"Accepting ourselves is the first
step on the path to happiness."

ANTHONY SELDON, CONTEMPORARY HISTORIAN

Accept, know and love yourself

Life is a journey of self-discovery, on which we can either be our own best ally or our own worst enemy. It depends on whether we see ourselves through a critical or a compassionate lens; from a position of judgement and incessant striving or one of acceptance and gentle growth. It depends on whether we choose to accept and believe the stories we tell ourselves or recognize and question them with gentle curiosity.

It depends on whether we waste time concerning ourselves with external stimuli outside our control, or invest time in making informed choices around internal stimuli that are within our control. Only the latter can lead to sustainable happiness and growth. Only the latter can enable flourishing.

When we're compassionate, curious and considered, we get to live well-balanced and satisfying lives. When we accept, know and love ourselves, we get to be happy and at peace.

Right: The stories we tell ourselves can be intriguing works of fiction. Recognizing them as such, then questioning them, helps us rewrite them into more factual tales.

"Learning to love ourselves as we are is a critical first step, and can only come from cultivating self-compassion."

Be compassionate

Personal growth can give our lives meaning. Yet in a world of perpetual pressure to strive and constantly improve, it can be difficult to strike a healthy balance between growth and gratitude, between self-improvement and self-acceptance, between betterment and contentment.

In response to the status quo of striving, we tend to give ourselves a tough time as we yearn restlessly to become our best selves. Consequently a sense of personal deficiency, based on a feeling that we don't – or can't – measure up to societal and self-made expectations, has given rise to an epidemic of unworthiness.

A healthy acceptance of who we are, and what we have, seems to have been replaced by a low hum of dissatisfaction with ourselves. Yet even when we achieve our goals and reach our desired potential, we are still ourselves. We may be fitter or wealthier or calmer, but we are still us.

Given the bewildering and complicated nature of being human, shouldn't we give ourselves a break and balance the need to improve what we've got, and who we hope to become, with the need to appreciate what we already have and who we are *now*? Life can be tough enough, without being so hard on ourselves. And self-criticism only serves to decrease our capacity for happiness.

In response to this world of unworthiness, self-acceptance has become an integral part of our happiness journey. Learning to love ourselves as we are is a critical first step, and can only come from cultivating self-compassion.

A lens of acceptance

We know we need to take care of ourselves – and the one body we have – to take us through this life of ours. We need sufficient sleep, exercise and nutrition, but we also need to be kind to our minds. With so much outside our control, by showing ourselves some compassion and giving ourselves a break, we have the capacity to create an internal sanctuary. Yet in reality we may often find ourselves turning our safe haven into a place of harm, as our inner critic turfs us out and leaves us nowhere to find refuge.

Opposite: Being decent to ourselves is good practice for being the decent people we strive to be. Showing our beautifully flawed selves compassion is an enabling act.

"Gold cannot be pure, and people cannot be perfect."

CHINESE PROVERB

So we end up seeking compassion from others before we give it to ourselves.

Self-criticism is a prevalent human tendency, and yet what we are generally critical of is our humanity. We share flaws, imperfections, emotions and failures with every other person on the planet – even the seemingly "perfect" ones that we compare ourselves with on social media. Each of us has insecurities and weaknesses; we each hold resentment and judgements, to varying degrees; and we've all experienced anger, jealousy and fear. All of us have our fantastically flawed humanity in common, along with the shared desire, by the majority of us, to be decent humans.

Perhaps then, if we are so keen to be good people, we should practise by being good to ourselves – without waiting until we never make another mistake, or never

think another negative thought, or never lose our temper again. If we wait until then to be kind to ourselves, we'll never do it. Because being perfect is not being human. Being flawed is.

In accepting the whole spectrum of our emotions, our strengths and our weaknesses, our successes and our failures, we can embrace the complexity of humanity and, rather than criticize it, celebrate it. When we live our lives through a lens of acceptance, tolerance and compassion – both for ourselves and for other humans – we become stronger and better equipped to cope with, and cherish, life in all its occasionally brutal glory.

Opposite: Taking care of ourselves requires a large dose of self-compassion, which helps us to balance self-acceptance with self-improvement.

Cultivating compassion

There are many ways in which we can cultivate greater compassion for ourselves:

1. Accept discomfort. We need to experience difficult emotions in order to cope with life as it is, rather than as we hope it could be. Coping is as integral to living a good life as hoping. If we are to live meaningful lives of contribution and service, where we make a difference and achieve goals, then discomfort and difficulty are par for the course. We don't get to live a meaningful life without experiencing the full spectrum of human emotion – that's the price we pay for doing so. With the pursuit of happiness being so desired, we can often be critical of ourselves when we feel negative emotions, yet they are an important part of the raw experience of what it means to be alive. So let's accept and even value discomfort, for it is an important part of our diverse life experience.

2. Comfort yourself as you would a best friend. Just as discomfort is part of life, so is our need for comfort. If your best friend was hurt and experiencing pain, you'd comfort them and they would deserve your comfort. They would deserve safety, affection and kindness; love, patience and care. Yet we often fail to give ourselves such comfort, even when we're struggling. We easily criticize, blame and punish ourselves without consideration for what we may have been through. We dismiss the disappointments, confusion and challenges we've faced; the way we may have been treated badly by others; the fact that we may have faced cruelty, heartbreak or tragedy. However much or little adversity we've endured, we deserve care – and we shouldn't expect that care to come only from others. We need to learn to be our own best friend; to accept discomfort, but also provide comfort. So the next time you notice your inner critic, try responding with curiosity and compassion. What comfort can you offer? Reassurance? Forgiveness? Acceptance? A nice cup of tea? A good long walk? Some stretchy yoga and a shower? Give yourself the comfort you need and deserve.

3. Accept your own flaws. As a result of our tribal tendencies and ingrained desire to belong, we are hardwired to care about what other people think of us, and to fear humiliation and isolation, as they used to threaten our survival. Therefore in order to belong, and to compare favourably with others and gain their approval, we feel the need to measure up to a range of expectations. When we don't, we beat ourselves up about it – just as the people comparing themselves to us beat themselves up about it, too. Yet self-criticism doesn't remove the flaws, it simply makes us feel terrible about them. Accepting and celebrating our differences and imperfections lessens the prevalent pressure of social comparison, and empowers us to get on with just being ourselves.

Above: We all deserve comfort, and, while we must all accept some element of discomfort along the way, finding ways to give ourselves comfort is crucial.

4. Forgive yourself. Mistakes, annoyances and bad decisions are important teachers. Without them, we wouldn't learn or grow. As such, failure is an immensely valuable learning tool. It's ironic that we so frequently wish to remove flaws, make fewer mistakes and perfect what we do, in our continuous striving for betterment. For those mistakes and imperfections help us learn faster and achieve betterment quicker than perfection ever could. When we give ourselves permission to be human and appreciate the lessons we gain even from adversity, we thrive.

"Accepting and celebrating our differences and imperfections lessens the prevalent pressure of social comparison, and empowers us to get on with just being ourselves."

Be curious

We are the central protagonists in the stories we tell ourselves.
Sometimes we are the hero; at other times we are the victim.
Either way, we become a product of those stories and base our
decisions, actions and reactions on their narratives – narratives
that are based on the lens through which we (and those we
have been brought up and influenced by) see the world.

Yet those stories, as we have learned, can be skewed and selectively adjusted to fit a favoured viewpoint and a certain way of looking at things, which are not necessarily reality.

The story of my life

Such a defective script doesn't even come from us, but from a range of expectations, suggestions and versions of events that other people – an external cast of directors – write into the story of who we are and why things happen. Our families, peers, teachers, classmates, religion and other ideologies, social media and news media (a whole range of external authors, scriptwriters and directors) can have great influence and can shape our thoughts and beliefs into a truth that we accept. Yet they are often based on inaccurate thoughts, which, over time have become beliefs and mental schemas and stories that we tell

Below: The narrative of our life stories is often written or edited by others, if we allow it to be. It's up to us to grab the pen back.

ourselves about who we are and who we ought to become.

These stories map out whether we – our life story's central character – think we can or can't do something, and why circumstances are happening to us: whether situations are always happening or only temporary; whether circumstances are all-encompassing or isolated; and whether we are likely to succeed or fail.

True story

Given that knowing who we are right now (who we truly are) is an integral part of living a happy life, and given the governance these stories have over our lives in terms of the decisions we make and the self-criticism we take, surely we should make a concerted effort to ensure that these mental biopics are true? But we rarely do.

Rather, these stories dictate fictitious plot lines and characteristics, and we mistake works of fiction (such as "I always / never / can't do this, because I am xyz") as fact. As we go through our lives we collect evidence to support these beliefs and the mental schemas they have constructed. And, thanks to our inbuilt "confirmation bias" – which confirms anything that has a bias toward supporting the story, rather than anything that detracts from it, even if the story is untrue – we pay more attention to that evidence and story than to anything that might contradict the narrative.

And so we live our lives, and behave and think and believe and react accordingly, in ways that correspond with our character notes, and which fit the preferred plot.

But handing over control to external directors doesn't end there. Given our tribal nature and inherent human need to belong, we have a tendency to build our lives, behaviours and lifestyles with others in mind – to impress other people, to seek approval and validation. Yet we can't control what people think of us. What's more, our comparisons with others are often inaccurate, based on our preconceived judgements of our own inadequacies, which we compare to a plethora of edited and unreal realities and to Photoshopped images that filter out the flaws.

Life can be hard. Why make it harder on ourselves by paying so much attention to things outside our control? We give so much consideration to what others might think, and how they might respond, despite it being beyond our control. But we owe it to ourselves to give more of our consideration to ourselves: to what *we* think and how *we* respond, to that which lies *within* our control.

It is through shifting our consideration and curiosity inward that we can build our own self-awareness and, in doing so, seize control of the stories we tell ourselves, so that we can think and respond more accurately, and live happier and more authentic lives. Because curiosity trumps judgement, fear and criticism every time. It does so by increasing our self-knowledge, which helps us to regain control and become the authors – rather than the actors – of our true-life stories.

Be an authentic author

Our capacity for self-knowledge can be the catalyst for an optimally happy life. Ramping up our self-awareness gives us the opportunity to look inside ourselves and better grasp how we work, how we feel, what makes us tick and what we value; to explore who we are, what we think and believe and how we behave, with gentle curiosity and flexibility. Only then can we reframe and rewire our preconditioned thoughts and beliefs, based on our own inner consciousness.

Mastering our mind in this way, with gentle curiosity, equips us with the ability to tell ourselves more accurate stories and have greater control over our actions and reactions. Indeed, the more we get to know, understand and connect with ourselves, the more control we have over how we respond to the circumstances of our story, to those within our control and even to the scenes over which we have no control.

What happens to us often lies beyond our control, and yet we *do* have control over our attitude to living. We cannot control what other people think, say or do, but we can control what we think, say and do. We can control how we treat others and how we treat ourselves. And we can control how we react.

In other words, it is not life circumstances that cause our problems, but our reactions to them and the stories we tell ourselves about them. And the more we know ourselves, the better able we are to react and respond well to those circumstances that lie *beyond* our control, and to the thoughts, feelings and actions *within*

> "What upsets people is not things themselves, but their judgements about these things."
> EPICTETUS, GREEK STOIC PHILOSOPHER

our control. We have the luxury of making a conscious choice about the latter – that is the luxury of being human. When we exercise that choice and assume control of that which we are in charge of, we place ourselves firmly in the driving seat of our happiness journey.

This is how we can honour our authentic selves, assume authorship and rewrite a more accurate story of our lives. It takes just a little consideration, some gentle curiosity and a healthy dose of compassion.

Opposite: When we devote as much time to getting to know ourselves as to getting to know others, we can better understand what makes us tick and thrive.

Be considered

A considered life is one in which we explore and investigate and gently question our own thoughts, belief systems and reactions (rather than those of others). That's how we uncover the real stories, hidden truths and our own authentic character, so that we can unpick fact from fiction and become the author of a more accurate and flexible narrative, one in which we are neither the hero nor the victim, but the human.

As the founder of the Flourishing Center, Emiliya Zhivotovskaya, says: "self-awareness leads to self-compassion which leads to self-care". And, as we've explored in this book, each of these qualities is vital to improving our sense of wellbeing.

Based on the notion that a happy life is a compassionate, curious and considered one, and in summary of what we have explored in the pages of this book, we can enjoy a happier experience by giving consideration to the following:

- **What *is*, rather than "what *if*",** so that we can put our worries into perspective, designate worry-time and use breathing techniques to calm our emotional brain and allow our thinking brain to open up to more likely, and more healthy, possibilities.

- **How we judge ourselves and others,** so that we can first acknowledge, and then tame, our thoughts and cultivate more flexible and accurate thinking. When we notice our mind-chatter, our ANTs (Automatic Negative Thoughts, see Chapter Five) and our habitual thinking style, we can take our thoughts to court, dispute and reframe them, based on the accurate evidence we give ourselves, to prevent ourselves from falling into thinking traps that may restrict our happiness.

- **How we respond to what life gives us:** Do we respond with gratitude and positivity, so that we boost our cognitive capabilities and resilience? With acceptance and grace, by labelling and accepting our negative emotions, before letting them go? Noticing our response gives us the knowledge we need to proceed in a way that best serves our wellbeing.

- **How (and how often) we take in the good:** Considering how we seek out, express, record and savour that which we are grateful for helps us to cultivate an attitude of gratitude, maximize the joy that we gain from positive experiences and counter our "negativity bias" (see Chapter Two).

- **What sparks joy in us:** This means being aware of our character strengths, so that

we use them more; and considering what our most engaging activities are, so that we do them more.

Above: Regular reflection helps us to get to know ourselves better. Self-awareness leads to self-compassion, which leads to self-care.

- **What matters most to us and why:** Having clarity over our hopes for the future, our values and our purpose enables us to set aligned goals, contribute to the world authentically and reward ourselves as we go.

- **How much time we spend in nature:** Given the restorative wonders of the natural environment, and what it does for our wellbeing, this is an important consideration.

- **How much time we devote to the present moment by cultivating mindfulness and meditating regularly:** Ordinarily our thoughts, emotions, memories, regrets, hopes and fears about the past or future flood our existence. But by living in the present moment we can tune out the noise of our internal mind-chatter and see the honest truth of ourselves. Such awareness brings peace, acceptance and clarity, and enables us to find the space to respond well.

- **Which activities enable us to recharge and rest, so that we can boost our vitality and energy levels,** so that we commit to taking better care of the bodies that take us through this life.

- **Who we surround ourselves with and how we treat them,** so that we can ensure they are people who understand, encourage and love us, just as we are. And so that we can devote time to nurturing those connections with kindness, compassion and constructive listening.

- **What we have handled so far:** Understanding what we've been through, coped with and survived, and what we have learned from those adversities, boosts our confidence in our own coping abilities and reduces our future-based fears.

- **How we treat ourselves,** so that we can be our own best ally, rather than our own worst enemy, and can provide ourselves with the sanctuary and comfort we deserve as we navigate the complexities of life.

When we live with compassion, curiosity and consideration, we can live a more authentic life that is in tune with our true selves. We can find peace with our past, become optimistic about our future and content with our present. In this way we can tick the boxes of all three dimensions of happiness (hedonic, eudaemonic and cognitive, see Chapter One) by living a life with frequent good moods, which is as meaningful as it is satisfying.

Essentially, a considered life enables us to be happier with what we have, and with what we hope to have; to cope better and to hope better. Such balance is the epitome of long-lasting happiness.

May you be as happy as you can be.

Opposite: As we swing through the ups and downs of life, it's useful to understand what we need to live joyfully and cope sufficiently, whichever way life swings.

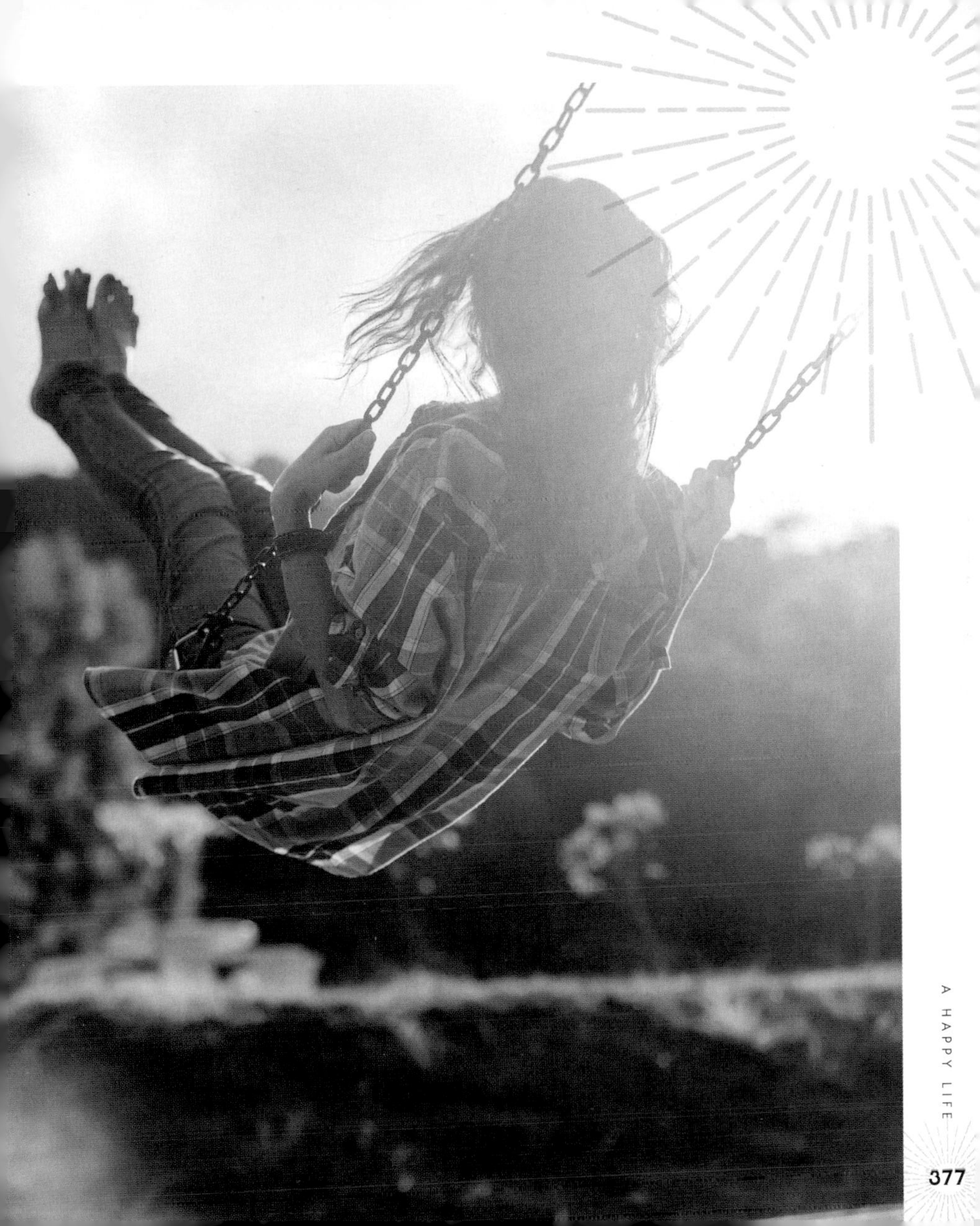

Endnotes

Chapter One: A history of happiness and why it matters

1 *The How of Happiness* by Sonya Lyubomirsky, 2010 (Little, Brown Book Group Ltd)

2 *Happiness: A Guide to Developing Life's Most Important Skill* by Matthieu Ricard, 2015 (Atlantic Books)

3 *The How of Happiness* by Sonya Lyubomirsky, 2010 (Little, Brown Book Group Ltd)

4 *The Little Book of Lykke* by Meik Wiking

5 http://worldhappiness.report/wp-content/uploads/sites/2/2012/04/World_Happiness_Report_2012.pdf

6 *Positivity: Groundbreaking Research to Release Your Inner Optimist and Thrive* by Barbara Fredrickson, January 2011

7 *Happiness and Productivity* by Andrew J Oswald, Eugenio Proto and Daniel Sgroi; https://warwick.ac.uk/fac/soc/economics/staff/eproto/workingpapers/happinessproductivity.pdf

8 https://peerj.com/articles/289/

9 "Why happiness is contagious": https://www.weforum.org/agenda/2015/10/why-happiness-is-contagious/

Chapter Two: The paradox of positivity

1 "Perceiving social pressure not to feel negative predicts depressive symptoms in daily life" by Egon Dejonckheere, Brock Bastian, Eiko I Fried, Sean C Murphy and, Peter Kuppens; http://onlinelibrary.wiley.com

2 Ibid.

3 www.mindful.org/what-is-happiness-anyway/

4 *Positivity* by Barbara Fredrickson

5 *How to Live a Good Life* by Jonathan Fields

6 Fiske, S T (1980). "Attention and Weight in Person Perception: The impact of negative and extreme information" *Journal of Personality and Social Psychology*, 38, 889–906. Fogarty, F A, Lu, L M, Sollers III, J J, Krivoschekov, S G, Booth

7 *Emodiversity and the Emotional Ecosystem* by Jordi Quoidbach (Universitat Pompeu Fabra) and June Gruber (Yale University)

8 *Beyond Happiness* by Anthony Seldon

9 https://greatergood.berkeley.edu/article/item/a_healthier_kind_of_happiness

10 *Flourish* by Martin Seligman, 2011

11 "A wonderful life: experiential consumption and the pursuit of happiness", Thomas Gilovich, Amit Kumar, Lily Jampol, August 2014, *Cornell University, Journal of Consumer Psychology*, Elsevier.

Chapter Three: Global glee

1 Helliwell, J., Layard, R., & Sachs, J. (2017). *World Happiness Report 2017*, New York: Sustainable Development Solutions Network

2 https://www.washingtonpost.com/world/obamas-speech-at-mandela-memorial-mandela-taught-us-the-power-of-action-but-also-ideas/2013/12/10/a22c8a92-618c 11e3-bf45-61f69f54fc5f_story.html?utm_term=.04c33ef2dc23

3 *The Little Book of Hygge* by Meik Wiking

4 The Happy Research Institute's Happy Danes report, which surveyed 10,000 Danish citizens; http://denmark.dk/en/~/media/Denmark/Documents/Meet%20the%20danes/TheHappyDanes%20Webedition.pdf

5 "Why is Norway the happiest place on Earth?" by Eric Dregni, *The Star Tribune*

6 Exam Factories Report, https://www.teachers.org.uk/files/exam-factories.pdf

7 *The World Happiness Report*, 2012

8 The Happy Danes Report, http://denmark.dk/en/~/media/Denmark/Documents/Meet%20the%20danes/TheHappyDanes%20Webedition.pdf

9 J F K Presidential Library and Museum; www.jfklibrary.org/Research/Research-Aids/Ready-Reference/RFK-Speeches/Remarks-of-Robert-F-Kennedy-at-the-University-of-Kansas-March-18-1968.aspx

10 "Gross national happiness in Bhutan: the big idea from a tiny state that could change the world" by Annie Kelly, The Guardian, 2012; https://www.theguardian.com/world/2012/dec/01/bhutan-wealth-happiness-counts

11 Ibid.

12 "PM speech on wellbeing", 2010; https://www.gov.uk/government/speeches/pm-speech-on-wellbeing

13 *Beyond Happiness* by Sir Anthony Seldon

14 Helliwell, J., Layard, R., & Sachs, J. (2017). *World Happiness Report 2017*, New York: Sustainable Development Solutions Network

Chapter Four: Positive psychology: the science of flourishing

1 *Flourish* by Professor Martin Seligman, 2011

2 Ibid.

3 *The How of Happiness* by Sonya Lyubomirsky, 2010 (Little, Brown Book Group Ltd)

4 *Flourish* by Professor Martin Seligman, 2011

5 *The How of Happiness* by Sonya Lyubomirsky, 2010 (Little, Brown Book Group Ltd)

Chapter Five: Thieves of happiness and barriers to wellbeing

1 *A Scientific Guide to Flourishing* by Emiliya Zhivotovskaya

2 *Hardwiring happiness: The practical science of reshaping your brain – and your life* by Rick Hanson

3 Ibid.

4 Ibid.

5 "Anxiety and cognitive performance: Attentional control theory" by M W Eysenck, N Derakshan, R Santos and M G Calvo, *Emotion® Journal* (2007), 7 (2): 336–53

6 "Imagery neurons in the human brain" by G Krelman, C Koch and I Fried, Nature, 2000

7 *The Resilience Factor: 7 Keys to Finding your Inner Strength and Overcoming Life's Hurdles* by K. Reivich and A. Shatté, 2002

8 *Learned Optimism* by Martin Seligman

Chapter Six: Mind-mastery: breaking down the barriers to wellbeing

1 *Man's Search for Meaning* by Viktor E Frankl

2 'The Simplest Way to be Happy' by Helen Keller, *Home Magazine* (February, 1933), courtesy of the American Foundation for the Blind, Helen Keller Archive

3 *Notes from the Universe* by Mike Dooley ©Mike Dooley, www.tut.com

Chapter Seven: Other people matter: connection, community and communication

1 *Barking Up the Wrong Tree* by Eric Barker; http://www.bakadesuyo.com/2012/01/what-are-your-relationships-worth-in-dollars/

2 *Loneliness: Human Nature and the Need for Social Connection* by John Cacioppo

3 https://www.psychologytoday.com/blog/the-good-life/201006/gratitude-letting-other-people-know-they-matter-benefits-us

4 Adult Development Study; http://www.adultdevelopmentstudy.org/

5 National Institute of Health Record; https://nihrecord.nih.gov/newsletters/2013/05_10_2013/story3.htm

6 Ibid.

7 Ibid.

8 "Will this man make you happy?" by Stuart Jeffries, the *Guardian*, June 2008

9 "Volunteering predicts happiness among older Maori and non-Maori in the New Zealand health, work, and retirement longitudinal study" by P L Dulin, J Gavala, C Stephens, M Kostick and J McDonald, *Aging & mental health* (2012), 16 (5): 617–24

10 "It's good to do good and receive good: The impact of a 'pay it forward' style kindness intervention on giver and receiver wellbeing" by

S D Pressman, T L Kraft and M P Cross, *The Journal of Positive Psychology* (2015), 10 (4): 293–302

11 L B Aknin, E W Dunn, and M I Norton, "Happiness Runs in a Circular Motion: Evidence for a Positive Feedback Loop between Prosocial Spending and Happiness." *Journal of Happiness Studies 13*, no. 2 (April 2012): 347–355.

12 *Flourish: A Visionary New Understanding of Happiness and Wellbeing* by Martin Seligman, from E Diener and M E P Seligman, "Very happy people", *Psychological Science* (2002), 13: 80–3

13 *The Longevity Project: Surprising Discoveries for Health and Long Life from the Landmark Eight-Decade Study* by Howard S Friedman and Leslie R Martin, 2012

14 "Neural Responses to Taxation and Voluntary Giving Reveal Motives for Charitable Donations" by William T Harbaugh et al., *Science* (2007), 316: 1622

15 "A Neural Basis for Social Cooperation", *Neuron* (2002), 35: 395–405

16 "Pursuing sustained happiness through random acts of kindness and counting one's blessings: Tests of two six-week interventions" by S Lyubomirsky, C Tkach and J Yelverton, unpublished data, University of California, 2004

17 Danish Institute for Voluntary Effort

18 *Connected: The Surprising Power of Our Social Networks and How They Shape Our Lives* by Nicholas A Christakis and James H Fowler, 2009

19 OECD report, Skills for Social Progress: The Power of Social and Emotional Skills

20 "Will You Be There for Me When Things Go Right?" by Shelly L Gable, Gian C Gonzaga, Amy Strachman, University of California, *Journal of Personality and Social Psychology*, 2006 by the *American Psychological Association* 2006, Vol. 91, No. 5, 904 –917

21 Marshall B Rosenberg of the Centre for Nonviolent Communication; www.CNVC.org

Chapter Eight: Happy thinking: finding the good and navigating the negative

1 *Positivity: Groundbreaking Research to Release Your Inner Optimist and Thrive* by Barbara Fredrickson, 2011

2 http://positivepsychologynews com/news/seph-fontane-pennock/2015012030937 (January 2015)

3 Ibid.

4 "The joyful, yet balanced, amygdala: moderated responses to positive but not negative stimuli in trait happiness" by William A Cunningham and Tabitha Kirkland, *Social Cognitive and Affective Neuroscience* (1 June 2014), 9 (6): 760–6; https://doi.org/10.1093/scan/nst045

5 Ibid.

6 Ibid.

7 "Putting Feelings into Words: Affect Labeling Disrupts Amygdala Activity in Response to Affective Stimuli" by Matthew D Lieberman, Naomi I Eisenberger, Molly J Crockett, Sabrina M Tom, Jennifer H Pfeifer and Baldwin M Way, University of California, Los Angeles, 1 May 2007

8 *Hardwiring Happiness: The New Brain Science of Contentment, Calm, and Confidence* by Rick Hanson, 2013

9 *The Grateful Heart: The Psychophysiology of Appreciation* by Rollin McCraty, PhD, and Doc Childre

10 *Spirituality in Clinical Practice*® edited by Lisa Miller and Len Sperry, *American Psychological Association*; http://www.apa.org/news/press/releases/2015/04/grateful-heart.aspx

11 *Hardwiring Happiness: The New Brain Science of Contentment, Calm, and Confidence* by Rick Hanson, 2013

12 *The How of Happiness* by Sonya Lyubomirsky, 2010 (Little, Brown Book Group Ltd)

13 *Three Good Things Intervention* by M E Seligman, T A Steen, N Park & C Peterson

14 *Flourish: A Visionary New Understanding of Happiness and Wellbeing* by Martin E P Seligman, 2012

15 https://positivepsychologyprogram.com/barbara-fredrickson/

16 "It's a Wonderful Life: Mentally Subtracting Positive Events Improves People's Affective States, Contrary to Their Affective Forecasts" by Minkyung Koo, Sara B Algoe, Timothy D Wilson and Daniel T Gilbert, *Journal of Personal Social Psychology* (2008)

17 *The Luck Factor* by Richard Wiseman, 2003

18 https://www.ted.com/talks/ron_gutman_the_hidden_power_of_smiling

19 "One smile can make you feel a million dollars", March 2005; https://www.scotsman.com/news/one-smile-can-make-you-feel-a-million-dollars-1-738272

20 https://www.ted.com/talks/ron_gutman_the_hidden_power_of_smiling

21 "The Voluntary Facial Action Technique: A Method to Test the Facial Feedback Hypothesis" by Ulf Dimberg and Sven Söderkvist, *Journal of Nonverbal Behavior* (March 2011), 35: 1, 17–33

22 "Feasibility and utility of positive psychology exercises for suicidal inpatients" by Huffman J C, DuBois C M, Healy BC, Boehm J K, Kashdan T B, Celano C M, Denninger J W, Lyubomirsky S, *General Hospital Psychiatry* (Jan–Feb 2014), 36 (1): 88–94

Chapter Nine: Goals and growth

1 Bronnie Ware, *The Top Five Regrets of the Dying*, 2012 (Hay House)

2 *How to Live a Good Life* by Jonathan Fields, 2016

3 "Setting Goals for Life and Happiness" by E A Locke, in C R Snyder and S J Lopez (eds), *Handbook of Positive Psychology*, 2002

4 http://nickgrantham.com/

5 Wegge, J, & Haslam, S A (2005). Improving work motivation and performance in brainstorming groups. The effects of three group goal-setting strategies" *European Journal of Work and Organizational Psychology*, 14(4), 400-430.

6 *Creating Your Best Life: The Ultimate Life List Guide* by Caroline Adams Miller and Michael B Frisch, 2009

7 Ibid.

8 Ibid.

9 "Implementation intentions: Strong effects of simple plans" by P M Gollwitzer, *American Psychologist* (1999), 54 (7): 493–503

10 "The triangle model of responsibility" by B R Schlenker, T W Britt, J Pennington, R Murphy and K Doherty, *Psychological Review* (1994), 101: 632–52

11 "Vacationers Happier, but Most not Happier After a Holiday" by Jeroen Nawijn, Miquelle A Marchand, Ruut Veenhoven, *Applied Research in Quality of Life*, 2010, Volume 5, Number 1, Page 35

12 *Mental imagery during daily life: Psychometric evaluation of the Spontaneous Use of Imagery Scale* by Sabine Nelis, Emily A Holmes, James W Griffith and Filip Raes, 2012

13 "Perspectives on prediction: Does third-person imagery improve task completion estimates?" by R Buehler, D Griffin, K C Lam and J Deslauriers, *Organizational Behavior and Human Decision Processes* (2012), 117 (1): 138–49

14 "The health benefits of writing about life goals" by L A King, *Personality and Social Psychology Bulletin* (2001), 27: 798–807

15 "How and why do positive activities work to boost wellbeing? An experimental longitudinal investigation of regularly practicing optimism and gratitude" by S Lyubomirsky, R Dickerhoof, J K Boehm and K M Sheldon (Manuscript under review) (2008)

Chapter Ten: Nourished by nature

1 "The influence of urban green environments on stress relief measures: A field experiment" by Liisa Tyrväinen, Ann Ojala, Kalevi Korpela, Timo Lanki, Yuko Tsunetsugu and Takahide Kagawad, *Journal of Environmental Psychology* (June 2014), 38: 1–9

2 "The physiological effects of Shinrin-yoku (taking in the forest atmosphere or forest bathing): evidence from field experiments in 24 forests across Japan" by B J Park, Y Tsunetsugu, T Kasetani, T Kagawa and Y Miyazaki, *Environmental Health and Preventive Medicine* (2010)

3 Act for Nature: The campaign for a Nature & Wellbeing Act; http://www.wildlifetrusts.org/naturewellbeingact

4 "Effect of phytoncide from trees on human natural killer cell function" by Q Li, M Kobayashi, Y Wakayama, H Inagaki, M Katsumata, Y Hirata, K Hirata, T Shimizu, T Kawada, B J Park, T Ohira, T Kagawa and Y Miyazaki, *International Journal of Immunopathology and Pharmacology* (Oct–Dec 2009), 22 (4): 9519

5 "Vitalizing effects of being outdoors and in nature" by Richard M. Ryan, Netta Weinstein, Jessey Bernstein, Kirk Warren Brown, Louis Mistretta and Marylene Gagne, *Journal of Environmental Psychology* , 2009

6 Ecotherapy – the green agenda for mental health report; https://www.mind.org.uk/media/273470/ecotherapy.pdf

7 "Alone or with a friend: A social context for psychological restoration and environmental preferences" by Henk Staats and Terry Hartig, *Journal of Environmental Psychology* 24 (2), 199-211, (June 2004)

8 *Vitamin N* by Richard Louv, (2017)

9 UC Berkeley psychologist Dacher Keltner; http://news.berkeley.edu/2015/02/02/anti-inflammatory/

10 http://www.wordcentral.com/cgi-bin/thesaurus?book= Thesaurus&va=wonderment

11 "The role of transcendent nature and awe experiences on positive environmental engagement" by Davis, Nora, Ph.D., University of California, Irvine, 2016

12 "An occasion for unselfing: Beautiful nature leads to prosociality" by Jia WeiZhanga, K. Piffa Paul, Iyer Ravi, Koleva Spassena and Keltner Dacher, *Journal of Environmental Psychology* (2014)

13 "Awe, the small self, and prosocial behavior" by K. Piff Paul, Pia Dietze, Matthew Feinberg, Daniel Stancato and Dacher M Keltner, *Journal of Personal Social Psychology*, American Psychological Association, (2015 Jun)

14 Ibid.

15 "NHS prescribed record number of antidepressants last year" by Denis Campbell, health-policy editor, the *Guardian*, June 2017; https://www.theguardian.com/society/2017/jun/29/nhs-prescribed-record-number-of-antidepressants-last-year

16 Ibid.

17 World Health Report; http://www.who.int/whr/2001/media_centre/press_release/en/

18 "Influence of Forest Therapy on Cardiovascular Relaxation in Young Adults" by Juyoung Lee, Yuko Tsunetsugu, Norimasa Takayama, Bum-Jin Park, Qing Li, Chorong Song, Misako Komatsu, Harumi Ikei, Liisa Tyrväinen, Takahide Kagawa and Yoshifumi Miyazaki, *Evidence-Based Complementary and Alternative Medicine*, Vol 2014. (2014)

19 "Forest Research – Benefits of green infrastructure" by Terry Hartig, Institute for Housing and Urban Research and Department of Psychology, Uppsala University, Sweden;

https://www.forestry.gov.uk/pdf/urgp_evidence_note_008_Psychological_health_and_mental_well_being.pdf/$file/urgp_evidence_note_008_Psychological_health_and_mental_well_being.pdf

20 "Ecotherapy – the green agenda for mental health report"; https://www.mind.org.uk/media/273470/ecotherapy.pdf 2014()

21 "Examining group walks in nature and multiple aspects of wellbeing: A large-scale study" by M R Marselle, K N Irvine and S L Warber, *Ecopsychology* (2014), 6 (3): 134–47

22 "The mental and physical health outcomes of green exercise" by J I Pretty, J Peacock, M Sellens and M Griffin, *International Journal of Environmental Health Research* (2005)

23 "Ecotherapy – the green agenda for mental health report"; https://www.mind.org.uk/media/273470/ecotherapy.pdf

24 "Green space as a buffer between stressful life events and health" by A E van den Berg, J Maas, R. A Verheij and P P Groenewegen, *Social Science and Medicine* (April 2010)

25 Ibid.

26 "View through a window may influence recovery from surgery" by Roger S. Ulrich, *Science* (27 April 1984), New Series, 224: 4647

27 "A prison environment's effect on health care service demands" by E O Moore, *Journal of Environmental Systems* (1981), 11: 17–34

28 *Handbook of Virtual Environments: Design, Implementation, and Applications*, edited by Kelly S Hale and Kay M Stanney

29 "Stress recovery during exposure to natural and urban environments" by Roger S Ulrich, Robert F Simons, Barbara D Losito, Evelyn Fiorito, Mark A Miles and Michael Zelson, *Journal of Environmental Psychology* (Sept 1991), 11 (3): 201–30

30 "Sowing the seeds or failing to blossom? A feasibility study of a simple ecotherapy-based intervention in women affected by breast cancer" by Ceri Phelps, Carole Butler, Alecia Cousins and Carol Hughes, *Ecancermedicalscience* (Dec 1 2015)

31 "Coping with ADD: The surprising connection to green play settings" by A Faber Taylor, F E Kuo and W C Sullivan, *Environment & Behavior* (2001), 33: 54–77

32 "A critical exploration of the role of the learning disposition "resilience" in the learning and development of young children" by Rowena Kenny; http://www.academia.edu/541952/A_critical_exploration_of_the_role_of_the_learning_disposition_resilience_in_the_learning_and_development_of_young_children

33 http://www.independent.co.uk/life-style/health-and-families/features/when-we-stop-children-taking-risks-do-we-stunt-their-emotional-growth-9422057.html

34 *Vitamin N: The Essential Guide to a Nature-Rich Life* by Richard Louv, 2017 www.dirtisgood.com/uk/truth-about-dirt.html

35 "Dirt Is Good" survey by Persil, 2016 www.dirtisgood.com/uk/truth-about-dirt.html

36 "The urban brain: Analysing outdoor physical activity with mobile EEG" by P Aspinall, Panagiotis Mavros, Richard Coyne and Jenny Roe, *British Journal of Sports Medicine*, Vol 49, issue 4, Feb 2015

37 "Stanford study finds walking improves creativity", April 2014; https://news.stanford.edu/2014/04/24/walking-vs-sitting-042414/

Chapter Eleven: Find your forte and go with the flow

1 *Practicing Positive Psychology Coaching: Assessment, activities and strategies for success* by Richard Biswas-Diener, 2010

2 "Which character strengths are most predictive of wellbeing?" by S B Kaufman, S Greenberg and S Cain, *Scientific American* (2 August 2015)

3 "Strengths deployment as a mood-repair mechanism: Evidence from a diary study with a relationship exercise group" by Shiri Lavy, Hadassah Littman-Ovadia and Yariv Bareli, *The Journal of Positive Psychology* (2014): 547–58

4 "The relationships between character strengths and life fulfillment in the view of lay-people in Argentina" by A Castro Solano and A C Cosentino, *Interdisciplinaria Revista de Psicología y Ciencias Afines* (2016), 33 (1): 65–80

5 "Positive psychology progress: Empirical validation of interventions" by M E P Seligman, T A Steen, N Park and C Peterson, *American Psychologist* (2005), 60: 410–21

6 "Using personal and psychological strengths leads to increases in wellbeing over time: A longitudinal study and the development of the strengths use questionnaire" by Alex M Wood, P Alex Linley, Todd B Kashdan and Robert Hurling (2011) *Personality and Individual Differences*, Volume 50 (issue 1), pp. 15-19.

7 "My strengths count: Effects of a strengths-based psychological climate on positive affect and job performance" by M Van Woerkom and M Meyers, *Human Resource Management* (2014)

8 "Character Strength-Based Intervention to Promote Satisfaction with Life in the Chinese University" by Wenjie Duan, Samuel M Y HoXiaoqing Tang, Tingting Li and Yonghong Zhang, *Journal of Happiness Studies* (December 2014), 15 (6): 1347–61

9 *Finding Flow* by M Csikszentmihalyi, 1997

10 *Everyday creative activity as a path to flourishing* by Tamlin S Conner, Colin G DeYoung & Paul J Silvia, Pages 181-189, 17 Nov 2016, *The Journal of Positive Psychology*, Volume 13, (2018) Issue 2

Chapter Twelve: Meaning and purpose: what matters most and why?

1 "Purpose in life as a system that creates and sustains health and wellbeing: An integrative, testable theory" by P E McKnight and T B Kashdan, *Review of General Psychology* (2009), 13 (3): 242–51

2 "Factor structure of mental health measures" by W C Compton, M L Smith, K A Cornish and D L Qualls, *Journal of Personality and Social Psychology* (August 1996), 71 (2): 406–13

3 *Meaning in Life* by Michael F Steger, *The Oxford Handbook of Positive Psychology* (2nd edn), ed. Shane J Lopez and C R Snyder, 2009

4 "Purpose, Mood, and Pleasure in Predicting Satisfaction Judgments" by Ed Diener, Frank Fujita, Louis Tay and Robert Biswas-Diener, *Social Indicators Research* (February 2012), 105 (3): 333–41

5 "Origins of purpose in life: Refining our understanding of a life well lived" by T B Kashdan and P E McKnight, Psychological *Topics* (2009), 18: 303–16

6 "Living On Purpose: Why Purpose Matters and How to Find It: A Framework for Gen X Women to Thrive" by C L Rockind (2011), Masters thesis

7 *Man's Search for Meaning* by V E Frankl, London: Hodder & Stoughton, 1963

8 "When is the search for meaning related to life satisfaction?" by N Park, M Park and C Peterson, *Applied Psychology: Health and Wellbeing* (2010), 2 (1): 1–13

9 "Living On Purpose: Why Purpose Matters and How to Find It: A Framework for Gen X Women to Thrive" by C L Rockind (2011), Masters thesis

10 *The Decline of the West* by Oswald Spengler, 1918/1922

11 *Drive – The Surprising Truth About What Motivates Us* by Daniel H Pink, 2011

12 "Effect of a quality of life coaching intervention on psychological courage and self-determination" by D F Curtis and L Kelly, *International Journal of Evidence Based Coaching and Mentoring* (2013), 11 (1): 20–38

Chapter Thirteen: Finding space and calm in the now

1 "Dispositional Mindfulness Co-Varies with Smaller Amygdala and Caudate Volumes in Community Adults" by A A Taren, J D Creswell and P J Gianaros, *PLoS ONE* (2013), 8 (5): e64574; https://doi.org/10.1371/journal.pone.0064574

2 "Mindfulness practice leads to increases in regional brain gray matter density" by Britta K Hölzel, James Carmody, Mark Vangel, Christina Congleton, Sita M Yerramsetti, Tim Gard and Sara W Lazara, *Psychiatry Research* (30 January 2011), 191 (1): 36–43

3 "Short-term meditation training improves attention and self-regulation" by Yi-Yuan Tang, Yinghua Ma, Junhong Wang, Yaxin Fan, Shigang Feng, Qilin Lu, Qingbao Yu, Danni Sui, Mary

K Rothbart, Ming Fan and Michael I Posner, *Proceedings of the National Academy of Sciences* (2007); http://www.pnas.org/content/104/43/17152.short

4 "A Randomized Trial of Mindfulness-Based Cognitive Therapy for Children: Promoting Mindful Attention to Enhance Social-Emotional Resiliency in Children", *Journal of Child and Family Studies* (April 2010), 19 (2): 218–29

5 https://blogs.scientificamerican.com/guest-blog/what-does-mindfulness-meditation-do-to-your-brain/

6 *CAPP Training Manual*, The Flourishing Centre

7 *Emotional Intelligence: Why it Can Matter More Than IQ* by Daniel Goleman, Bloomsbury Publishing, 1996 edn

Chapter Fourteen: Vitality is vital to living well

1 "Exercise therapy and the treatment of mild or moderate depression in primary care"; https://www.org.uk/sites/default/files/up_running_report.pdf

2 "Exercise treatment for major depression: maintenance of therapeutic benefit at 10 months" by Babyak M Blumenthal JA, Herman S Khatri P, Doraiswamy M, Moore K, Craighead WE, Baldewicz TT, Krishnan KR, *Psychosomatic Medicine* (September–October 2000), 62 (5): 633–8

3 "Physical activity and negative affective reactivity in daily life" by Puterman E, Weiss J, Beauchamp MR, Mogle J, Almeida DM, *Journal of Health Psychology* (December 2017), 36 (12): 1186–94; doi: 10.1037/hea0000532. Epub 2017 Oct 9

4 "Non-exercise activity thermogenesis (NEAT)" by A. Levine, *Best Practice & Research Clinical Endocrinology & Metabolism* (December 2002), 16 (4): 679–702

5 Experimental Psychology; https://www.sciencedaily.com/releases/2013/03/130318104950.htm

6 *Research Digest*, British Psychological Society; https://digest.bps.org.uk/2011/03/21/an-afternoon-nap-tunes-out-negative-emotions-tunes-in-positive-ones/

7 *Night School: The Life-Changing Science of Sleep* by Richard Wiseman, 2015

8 Sleep Disorders and Sleep Deprivation: An Unmet Public Health Problem by H R Colten and B M Altevogt (eds), Washington, DC: *National Academies Press*, 2006

9 "Moderate Sleep Deprivation Produces Impairments in Cognitive and Motor Performance Equivalent to Legally Prescribed Levels of Alcohol Intoxication" by A Williamson and A Feyer, *Occupational and Environmental Medicine* (October 2000), 57 (10): 649–55

10 https://news.stanford.edu/news/2004/december8/med-sleep-1208.html

11 *Night School: The Life-Changing Science of Sleep* by Richard Wiseman, 2015

12 http://www.independent.co.uk/life-style/short-naps-happier-happiness-napiness-university-of-hertfordshire-reveals-study-a7659746.html

13 http://cvidencebasedliving.human.cornell.edu/2010/03/02/so-many-decisions-so-little-time/

14 "Restricting access to palatable foods affects children's behavioral response, food selection, and intake" by Jennifer Orlet Fisher and Leann Lipps Birch, *American Journal of Clinical Nutrition*, 1999

Index

Picture Credits

Alamy Stock Photo Andor Bujdoso 209; Art Collection 2 12; Blend Images 265; Ghislain & Marie David de Lossy/Cultura Creative (RF) 105; GL Archive 14; Gregg Vignal 112; Hero Images Inc. 55, 142; Hongqi Zhang 186; Image Source 317; Pictorial Press Ltd. 330; pmgimaging 250; Radius Images 204; Randy Plett/Blend Images 49; Zave Smith/Image Source 9al. **Cheryl Rickman** 139. **Dreamstime.com** Candy1812 234; David Cabrera Navarro 311; Johncarnemolla 85; Katarzyna Bialasiewicz 53; Maiju Annika 240; Oksana Kiian 51; Ponqmoji 96; Tatyana Kalmatsuy 70; Vladislav Gajic 203; Warrengoldswain 226. **GAP Photos** Elke Borkowski 195. **Getty Images** Ariel Skelley 88; Becky Scrivens/EyeEm 43; Christoph Hetzmannseder 16; Dan Bannister 59; Fancy/Veer/Corbis 335; J. Countess 62; Mike Pont/WireImage 11; Mikey Schaefer 118; Portra Images 54; Victor Estevez 34; xijian 277; Dan Brownsword 400. **iStock** AlekZotoff 178; amenic181 63; AMilkin 242; Andreka 249; anyaberkut 298; Asia Images 172; Bayram Gürzoğlu 158; bee32 50, 219; blanaru 263; bluejayphoto 197; brazzo 296; Brzozowska 320; CatEyePerspective 225; CatLane 135, clu 281; danielobrienphotography 365; den-belitsky 223; diego_cervo 91; DimaBerkut 257; eclipse_images 177; emholk 323; EpicStockMedia 159; Everste 98; franckreporter 212; freemixer 160; Geber86 261; GeorgeRudy 138; gipi23 156; gpointstudio 351; GrapeImages 331; graphixel 253; hadynyah 292; hyunah Kang 367; Jacob Ammentorp Lund 224; jacoblund 149; Jan-Otto 342; john shepherd 108; Juanmonino 221; LeoPatrizi 74; Lisa5201 216; lolostock 163; loops7 31; luckyraccoon 94; maodesign 167; Martin Dimitrov 2; martin-dm 357; mikkelwilliam 200; moisseyev 27; MommoM_ns 313; monkeybusinessimages 128, 228; nd3000 140;

Ncustockimages 295; Oinegue 290; Oleh_Slobodeniuk 56; PeopleImages 72, 150, 244, 338, 349, 375; PeskyMonkey 315; seb_ra 354; SIphotography 103; skynesher 373; SolStock 269, 358; Steve Debenport 286; sturti 289; svetikd 345; swissmediavision 47, 332; Tamarabegucheva 67; timsa 145; Tinpixels 270; vgajic 255; victorass88 120; xavierarnau 65; XiXinXing 92, 190; Zerbor 127. **Science Photo Library** Sciepro 87; Evan Oto 82. **Shutterstock** Africa Studio 275; Alex Staroseltsev 136; Andrei Mayatnik 9ar; asife 206; Billion Photos 107; Bizi00 39; Brian A Jackson 302; ch_ch 318; Chantal de Bruijne 17; cosma 282; De Repente 369; Dean Drobot 111; DGLimages 133; Dietmar Temps 131; Eric Gevaert 32; Evgeny Atamanenko 36; Filipe Frazao 9bl; Giantrabbit 273; giovanni boscherino 115; g-stockstudio 125; Hrecheniuk Oleksii 76; Iakov Filimonov 9cl; iko 308; IM_photo 258; Jacob Lund 15; Jeanne Provost 9cr; JeremyRichards 90; jesadaphorn 307; KeongDaGreat 157; Kichigin 29; KonstantinChristian 324; Lisovskaya Natalia 353; Luna Vandoorne 182; Mainlake 102; Maksym Povozniuk 294; Matej Kastelic 193; Michael Chamberlin 279; mimagephotography 9br; Monkey Business Images 20, 147, 155; Nataliya Olar 181; OndroM 170; Osadchaya Olga 174; Patiwat Sariya 231; Repina Valeriya 19; Rido 164; Robert Kneschke 169; Seasontime 347; SFIO CRACHO 341; Skylines 370; Sunny Forest 304; SunnyGraph 362; Suti Stock Photo 41; Syda Productions 336; Tetiana Iatsenko 151; Thomas Andreas 284; Toa55 247; tomcrtu 190; tommaso79 81; Viktor Gladkov 377; wavebreakmedia 13, 69; wk1003mike 326; Yulia Mayorova 25; Zai Aragon 116; ziviani 189. **Unsplash** Annie Spratt 237; Vincent van Zalinge 233.

Acknowledgements

For my own ray of sunshine, Brooke Denise.

And for my late parents, Denise and Roger, from whom I learned the importance of making the most of every moment of this one precious life.